WE WENT TO WAR

We Went to War

New Hampshire Remembers

Meg Heckman and Mike Pride

Illustrations by Charlotte Thibault
Portraits by Ken Williams

MONITOR PUBLISHING CO.
Concord, New Hampshire

Designed and composed in Warnock Pro with Cronos Pro display at Hobblebush Books, Brookline, New Hampshire (www.hobblebush.com)

Printed in the United States of America

Publisher's Cataloging-In-Publication Data
(Prepared by The Donohue Group, Inc.)

Heckman, Meg.
    We went to war : New Hampshire remembers / Meg Heckman and Mike Pride ; illustrations by Charlotte Thibault ; portraits by Ken Williams.

    p. : ill., maps ; cm.

    Includes index.
    ISBN: 978-0-9818215-0-4

1. World War, 1939-1945—Personal narratives, American. 2. World War, 1939–1945—United States—History. 3. Soldiers—New Hampshire. 4. Soldiers—New Hampshire—Biography. I. Pride, Mike, 1946- II. Thibault, Charlotte. III. Williams, Ken (Ken L.), 1935– IV. Title.

D811.A2 H42 2008
940.5481/742   2008936002

Published by:
MONITOR PUBLISHING CO.
P.O. Box 1177
Concord, New Hampshire 03302-1177

www.concordmonitor.com

*To Mom for making me sound out the words,
to Dad for making me watch* Memphis Belle,
and to Jimmy, just for being you.
— M.H.

To Monique and our new life together.
— M.P.

Contents

Introduction

On a brilliant day halfway through September 1939, hundreds of men assembled on the fields near the Concord airport. They were newly federalized members of the New Hampshire National Guard, preparing to serve what they believed would be a one-year hitch with the regular Army. With sporadic training and outdated equipment, they had come from posts all over the state. During maneuvers, weapons were so scarce in one unit that the men used sticks. They spent the night in pup tents, ate biscuits for breakfast, and caught a train bound for Texas at the downtown station. For many, it would be nearly six years before they returned.

Among the soldiers who left Concord that day was Harlond Perry, a nineteen-year-old from Keene who would endure a brutal tour in the Pacific. Sixty-eight years after his train ride, Perry responded to another call: He answered our invitation in the *Concord Monitor* for members of the World War II generation to contact us. We wanted to help them tell their stories in the newspaper, where we worked as reporters.

Although this generation is rapidly dying, the response was overwhelming. More than a hundred people called, e-mailed, or wrote us. During the next nine months, we interviewed roughly half of them. Oral histories of their wartime experiences appeared in the *Monitor* from September 2007 through April 2008.

We Went to War: New Hampshire Remembers compiles most of

the stories we told in the paper and adds several others. These stories recount the experiences of thirty-eight people who were of age (or nearly so) during World War II, who lived in New Hampshire more than sixty years later, and who were willing to share their recollections with us and our readers. During the run of the newspaper project, we also published wartime letters and diary excerpts. *We Went to War* includes two diary accounts, one describing a determined effort to celebrate Christmas, the other chronicling the closing days of the war in Europe. One further piece presented here is a poem written by a deceased infantryman who described his wartime exploits in verse.

Although no single book could possibly cover the full spectrum of Americans' experiences during the war, the stories we collected after the newspaper series add fascinating dimensions to *We Went to War*: submarine and frogman duty, the horrors of being a prisoner of war in the Pacific, chance encounters with Generals Dwight D. Eisenhower, George Patton, and Douglas MacArthur, and one man's decision to become a conscientious objector. In an appendix, we have also recognized people whose stories appeared in the *Monitor* but, for space reasons, are not told in full in these pages.

Our subjects cover a lot of ground. In *We Went to War*, you will hear from a man who landed on Omaha Beach on D-Day and a man who slept with rats on the island of Biak. You will read about New Hampshire-trained nurses who brought care and comfort to wounded and dying men. You will meet men who jumped out of airplanes over hostile territory and others who landed airplanes in fields and on carrier decks. You will salute a proud female Marine. With two sailors, you will witness the destruction of the USS Franklin with great loss of life. And you'll hear from grunts, including a man who left one leg in France and one in England and a soldier who killed his buddy out of compassion.

For many of these men and women, the war lasted long after 1945. A dime-size bullet hole through an old mortar-man's breastbone is still calcifying, causing him new pain. A young girl who lost her father in France spent years trying to overcome the burden of being not only fatherless but also different from her friends. A survivor of the Bataan Death March took decades to recover from his hatred of the Japanese. Harlond Perry's nightmares still wake his wife more than sixty years later.

The people we interviewed taught us a great deal about their time. They taught us how gender, race, and homosexuality were viewed in their day. They taught us about family. Nearly all of them exhibited a humility that seems foreign in this age of callow self-promotion and empty celebrity. Most referred to their wartime experience as just a job they had to do. "There's nothing special about my story," they said, even when there was.

We came to admire the national unity of the war years. Even in a time when communication was far less immediate than it is today and regional differences remained sharper than they are now, monumental events galvanized the nation. Pearl Harbor stunned people into shared sacrifice for the common good. Americans all awaited the invasion of Europe with anxiety and hope. When Franklin D. Roosevelt died in the war's waning days, they felt the loss of a leader and the unfairness of his not having lived to see the surrender.

In these pages, readers will note a stronger hatred for the Japanese than for the Germans. The reasons are complex. For some people, no doubt, it was easier to hate an enemy who looked different from most of them. But what Americans knew, and when they knew it, also influenced their attitudes. The Japanese carried out a sneak attack on Pearl Harbor, treated prisoners with extreme cruelty, and fought to the death rather than surrender. By contrast, the Germans treated American prisoners of war relatively well, and German soldiers surrendered by the thousands, confident that they would be safe in Allied hands. Although the Nazi concentration-camp atrocities horrified Americans, they became widely known only late in the war. These factors may not fully explain the difference in attitudes toward the two enemies, but as we interviewed veterans, it often seemed to us that America had fought two separate wars at the same time.

For readers today, a primary lesson from the nineteen-forties is in geography: World War II was indeed a world war. The names of farflung places still convey instant meaning to the war generation.

The Hump, Saint-Lô, Monte Cassino, Tinian, Camp Lucky Strike, the Red Ball Express, Mindanao, Camp Miles Standish, Stalag Luft 3, Grenier Field—many people over the age of eighty nod at the mere mention of these names.

The human lessons we learned from our subjects are timeless, lessons about battlefield conduct, love, and a desire for peace. You will read the stories of prisoners of the Germans, who abided by the Geneva Conventions, and of the Japanese, who did not. In many accounts you will see how completely the reality of war dashed any enthusiasm for war. And you'll learn that, sometimes, love really does triumph over chaos, carnage, and fear.

A word about methodology: Once we had identified a subject, we interviewed him or her and recorded the interview. We transcribed the recording. While being true to the words spoken during the interview, we cut some episodes and moved others around to create a chronological narrative. We checked and double-checked place names, dates, and other facts. Where things were unclear or vital elements seemed absent, we made note of it in the copy. Then we sent the transcript to the subject, asking him or her to read it carefully, correct it, and suggest changes and additions. After making the subject's changes, we edited the transcript again, taking out extraneous words and repetition. We published the completed oral histories in the *Monitor* with the logo "My War."

We received extraordinary support during this project from several quarters. Charlotte Thibault, the *Monitor's* artist, translated the experiences of our subjects into maps and graphics. She shared the geography of the "My War" episodes with readers while also showing them what the USS Franklin or a B-17 looked like. Charlotte also came up with the book's title and designed its cover. Ken Williams, the *Monitor's* veteran photographer, took portraits of our subjects. When they still fit in their World War II uniforms, he sometimes persuaded them to pose in those. He also helped us collect wartime photos so that, when possible, we could show our subjects then and now. We have used much of Charlotte and Ken's work in this book.

The editor of the project, Ari Richter, was busy, too. In addition to editing the oral histories, he provided direction and moral support to us for months on end. He also helped us turn the project into a multimedia experiment on our website, concordmonitor. com. There you will still find supplementary material—video and sound of interviews along with diaries, letters, and photographs not published in these pages. In addition, the website contains the full stories we had to omit here for space reasons.

We are grateful to Charlotte, Ken, and Ari for their work on the project, to Mark Travis, Felice Belman, and Monique Pride for reading early versions of our manuscript, to columnist Ray Duckler for contributing two stories to the series, and to other colleagues at the *Monitor* for supporting our work.

We also thank a team of teachers and their students at John Stark Regional High School in Weare, New Hampshire, who responded to our invitation to participate in the project. About sixty teenagers interviewed veterans during the fall of 2007. Their participation illuminated another dimension of this project, one that transcends geography and time. Many of the stories in these pages are about coming of age in the midst of a global conflict. One young woman saw similarities between a plane crash witnessed by an Air Corps veteran and her own memories of watching the Twin Towers burn on TV. The enemy, the battlefields, and the technology have changed, but the human experience endures.

The students are too numerous to name, but their work can be viewed at concordmonitor.com/mywar. Their teachers, Matt Colby, Carol Brown, and Phil Matzke, displayed enthusiasm, leadership, and flexibility in guiding them through the project. We hope other schools will take up this cause. History isn't just in books. It is also in your community, where people in their eighties and nineties, and even younger, have stories to tell. Oral history is real history. It is also grist for further scholarship. As an appendix to this book, we've prepared a brief how-to guide on interviewing veterans and others in your community.

Our greatest debt of gratitude is to our subjects. They were patient, open, and gracious. They welcomed us into their homes and shared stories that were often intimate and painful. They understood our desire to show the war in human terms with no sugar-coating. They were perhaps more aware than we were that time is running out on them and their stories. Because more than a year has passed since we began interviewing, the ages we give in introducing chapters have advanced a year or two. At least three of our subjects, Bill Snow, Gertrude Hankins, and Harold Jaques, died this past summer.

We regret that we could not interview everyone who contacted us, but we were pleased to bring so many stories to the attention of *Concord Monitor* readers. And we're glad now to have them preserved in this more permanent form for generations to come.

Meg Heckman, Mike Pride
Concord, New Hampshire
September 2008

WE WENT TO WAR

"I was real lucky," Roland LaFleur says today.

Roland LaFleur

"The Pain, It Was Severe"

Omaha Beach was strewn with bodies when Roland LaFleur landed two weeks after D-Day as a replacement rifleman for the Third Army, 28th Division. His outfit captured towns, dodged German tanks, and suffered heavy losses. One morning in July, LaFleur marched down a dirt road, unaware that his time on the front lines was about to end.

When I got hit, I had two hundred rounds of ammunition on my shoulders, armor-piercing bullets, a fragmentation grenade in one pocket, and a phosphorous grenade in the other. I was loaded for battle that day.

It was about eleven o'clock. We'd just packed up and left the little field where we'd spent the night. We were walking along in a staggered formation, waiting to catch up with the Germans.

I don't think we had gotten two hundred, three hundred feet down the road when, all of a sudden, the shells came over. It was an antitank grenade. It lit up right by my left foot and exploded. Blew a hole in the ground a few feet deep. That was the end of it. Knocked me right down. The pain, it was severe.

I went down, but I was real lucky—I don't think the medics were more than three or four hundred feet behind us. They rushed right in and just ripped my pants off. The blood was flowing because both legs were blown to hell. They put a tourniquet on this leg and a tourniquet on this leg, put on some powder, and just wrapped me right up. They gave me a blanket and loaded me on the side of a jeep.

They gave me a shot in the arm. It must have been morphine because a little while later, I went out. I don't remember anything until I woke up in the field hospital in France.

They had already amputated my right leg just below the knee, but they were trying to save my left leg. They had a transport plane to carry us to England, but the runways were just dirt and it was so muddy they couldn't take off. It was three or four days that we had to stay in France. A German boy came in and said he was a prisoner. He had been a medic and had volunteered to help me.

What could I say? I had to agree. I needed help. I was almost like an infant. I couldn't do anything. I couldn't pick myself up. I was weak. I took fifteen quarts of blood and plasma.

I don't recall any of the procedures. All I know is they took me from the tent and put me in a C-54, a prop plane. They laid us right there on the floor, on stretchers. There were a lot of other guys besides me. There was a nurse on there, and attendants.

I landed in the 112th General Hospital in southern England. A little nurse from Nebraska had been assigned to take care of me. I told her my ankle hurt and asked if she could relieve the pain. She got the doctor and he cut the cast a little bit. Puss rolled right out. Then I started going into convulsions. All I heard was the nurse say, "For Christ's sake, hurry up. You've got to get that guy some oxygen before he dies."

Gangrene had set in so they had to amputate. I've got one leg in France and another in England.

You don't know what to think then. You're a double amputee. You don't have legs to walk on. You're down. You did know that they make artificial limbs, but you don't know what's going to happen to you. I was pretty alone. I went downhill wicked.

I was twenty-three years old. I didn't know how my mother, my father, my wife were going to take it. Back then, when you lost your legs, you were crippled. You couldn't do anything. You just had to sit there and look out the window.

LaFleur was a rifleman with the 28th Division.

I had been married in 1938. My wife didn't know I'd lost my legs until I got back to the States. I couldn't write to her while I was in the hospital. I was supposed to have been on the front lines. She got a telegram saying I was in a hospital in England. All it said was that I was injured in battle.

I came back on the Queen Mary and landed in New York City. They took us off the boat and put us on the pier. There were two or three hundred servicemen, everybody wounded. An officer asked you what hospital you wanted to go to. I said I wanted to get as near Boston as I could. They sent me to Atlantic City, New Jersey. The government had just taken over a big hotel on the boardwalk to make into a hospital.

When I got there, I telephoned my wife. It was around Thanksgiving. She was working in a beauty shop in Boston. I told her. It was real heartbreaking, because I didn't know what was going to happen or how we were going to make it together.

She came down immediately by train. Her mother came down, too. They felt real sorry for me. I told them they didn't have to feel sorry, because it's just one of those things and there's nothing you can do about it. I made arrangements for my wife to come down and stay. She got an apartment and worked in a beauty shop there.

They gave me an operation to trim it all up. What I had over there was what they called a guillotine operation. The bone was sticking out. It was just real quick.

I had to learn to walk all over again. It was tough getting going. The legs were pretty crude then, but they made me a pair and I started walking right around the first of February, 1945. I said, "You give me the damn things and I'll make them go." I got oh, real sore, because your body's not designed to walk like that.

A lot of servicemen never could wear artificial legs. I was lucky. I never had any trouble with my legs. I've worn out about fifteen legs in my lifetime. This set I've got on now, these cost the government ten thousand dollars. When they first made them, they cost about three hundred dollars.

I came home on a thirty-day furlough in April 1945 and stayed here in Epsom with my wife. It was beautiful to be home in New

Hampshire, but everybody told me I couldn't do this and I couldn't do that. I told them not to worry, I'd overcome it.

You've got to hold your mind to a future of doing things that you did before, but you have to do it in a different way.

Roland LaFleur was discharged on June 20, 1945. In Epsom he worked as a building contractor and heavy equipment repairman, managed his farm, and raised at least thirty foster children. He and his first wife, Louise, had one son, who is now in his sixties. Thirteen years ago, LaFleur and his second wife, Beverly, adopted a little boy. Now twice a widower, LaFleur is teaching his younger son to rebuild engines.

Currier with her best friend, Nell Ross.

Olga Currier

Proud Marine

As a member of a military family, Olga Currier learned to present arms while she was still in grade school. When war came, Currier couldn't wait to turn twenty, the minimum age to become a Marine. In late 1944, she dropped out of college and asked her mother to drive her to Boston to enlist.

Everybody knew the Marine Corps was the best, and that's what I wanted to become a part of. I went in in December. It stands out in my mind because that was my first Christmas away from home. You'd hear people crying at night. We were all in one big squad room. Boot camp was very challenging, physically and mentally. I'd had a sheltered existence. I thought I was pretty special until I got into the Marine Corps. They set me straight in a hurry.

We wanted to enlist to "Free a Marine to Fight." That was the slogan then. Many of the people were older than me, but we were all young—teachers, college students, secretaries, from all parts of the United States. Some of the women had husbands who were also Marines, and they joined the war effort. They needed Marines to

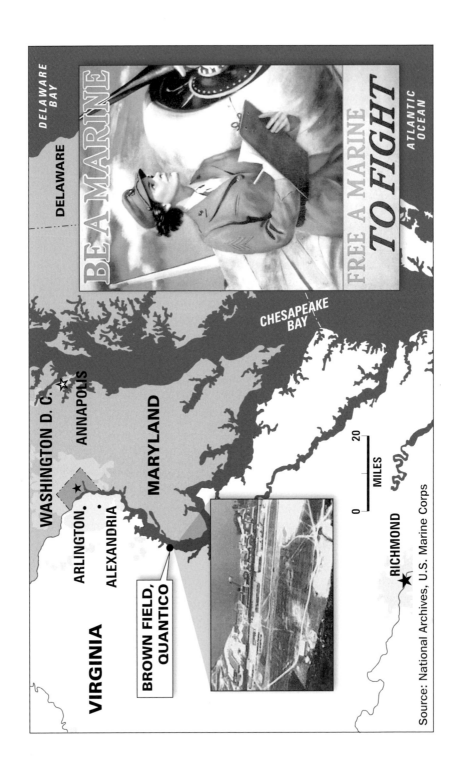

DELAWARE BAY

DELAWARE

BE A MARINE

FREE A MARINE *TO FIGHT*

ATLANTIC OCEAN

CHESAPEAKE BAY

WASHINGTON D. C.

ANNAPOLIS

MARYLAND

ARLINGTON.

ALEXANDRIA

VIRGINIA

BROWN FIELD, QUANTICO

20

MILES

0

RICHMOND

Source: National Archives, U.S. Marine Corps

fight in the South Pacific. The death toll was horrific, children fighting children, really. Some of the Marines wanted to go over, some didn't.

You were working for a good cause, working for people you cared about, not thinking that there's a darker side to freeing a Marine to fight. We were freeing a Marine to die, but at eighteen or twenty, everyone felt immortal.

They weren't used to women being in the Corps. We had an old gunny—a gunnery sergeant. He was devastated that women were in the Corps. He said, "First the dogs, then the niggers, then the women. What the hell is the Marine Corps coming to?" About a month later, I was going out, probably on a date, and there was the gunny showing three women Marines how to spit-polish your shoes. They came around. They were our brothers, friends, and protectors. To this day, there is a special bond among the Marines, and there always will be.

Our drill instructors and teachers at boot camp were South Pacific veterans, and they were tough. We went to class every day and every afternoon. We learned everything that the male Marines learned. The history of the Corps, all the different battles, administrative—everything you could cram into your brain in six weeks. We scaled the walls with rope ladders, went over the logs, and jumped from a tower. We went through a tent filled with tear gas to learn how to use the gas mask. We never learned how to use an M-1 rifle, but everything else, we did what the men did.

They called on us to do more than I ever thought I could physically do. I'd never done laundry. I'd never ironed shirts. Somebody had always cleaned my room. I was just spoiled, I guess, and it was a rude awakening. You got head duty. The head is the bathroom. You have to clean a toilet. Oh my God! Totally different. It was good for me. We had two ironing boards for a squad room of a hundred women. When they'd see me go to the ironing board, everybody would groan.

Fortunately, I was chosen to go with the Marine Air Wing Squadron 21 at Quantico, Virginia, the nerve center of the Marine Corps. The officer candidate school was there. There's all kind of rugged terrain where they could train right on the Potomac River. I was

Olga Currier wanted to join the best.

at Brown Field, on the edge of Quantico, which was a sleepy little Southern town until the Marines got there.

First I went into Navy supply with a big burly Marine named Sam and a little skinny dark-haired fellow. They were both First Division Marines who had landed on Guadalcanal. They were both yellow from malaria and Atabrine. One of them had mu-mu, which is elephantitis—a horrible disease you get in the tropics. The legs swell out and other parts of the body. Very painful.

We had to keep track of aeronautical supplies on a huge Cardex file system. It really makes you appreciate computers today. Every little bolt, screw, and aeronautical part had to be entered and kept track of. Terribly boring. My next job was for a lieutenant commander in aeronautics and repair. I was in charge of civilian payroll. Our offices were on the side of the airstrip where our beautiful and deadly F4U Corsair fighter planes and J-3 reconnaissance planes were parked.

A lot of the Marines and Marine women worked there, but they had to have civilians work there also, mostly people from Quantico. It was an intensely secret place because they had one of the first radars there. You had to have a purpose for going on the base or you were not allowed in.

We were letter writers in those days. We had a huge beautiful lounge in our barracks, and people would be there listening to music and writing letters home or to their husbands or their boyfriends overseas.

We did a lot of dancing. Name bands would come: Stan Kenton and Glenn Miller. We had good times. We were thirty miles from Washington, D.C., so we would go up there. Once we stayed at the Shoreham hotel and crashed a dance in the ballroom filled with uniformed men and women in beautiful ball gowns. My friend and I were the only women in uniform. Of course, we were immensely popular and everyone was dancing with us. I danced with Gene Kelly! Can you imagine? He was in the Navy, a boatswain's mate. He was shorter than me and had a blue mole on his cheek.

We were a pretty positive lot, until you saw those Marines return from battle and saw how radically they had changed. It

*Female Marines like Currier served
stateside, allowing the men to fight.*

was something about the eyes. They called it the thousand-yard stare. They'd be focused on something else. A lot of them would be wounded, but everything was gung-ho. We're going to win, it's going to be all right.

My friend Paul Sampson was from Boston. He died on Iwo Jima. I remember a woman getting news that her husband had died on Iwo. I remember her screams. It was awful. She found out by telegram. We were in the same squad room. Double-decker bunks all the way down, probably sixty bunks. Nothing was private. She just broke down completely, screamed and screamed. Just horrible, but her friends were there for her. She stayed in the Corps. Never looked the same.

On April 12, 1945, President Roosevelt died. Most of us never knew another president, and it was a terrible blow. He had been secretary of the Navy and always loved the Marines. He referred to himself and the Marines as "we." The base emptied as we went to D.C. and joined the somber crowds, silent except for the sobs of the people lining the streets.

On V-J Day the barracks emptied again. Everybody wanted to go up to Washington. It was wild. Everyone was just delirious with happiness. The war was over, and nineteen thousand women Marines could return home.

After the war, Olga Currier married a fellow Marine and eventually settled in New Hampshire. She worked for GTE Sylvania before retiring. She is eighty-three years old, lives in Weare, and still fits in her white dress uniform.

Hollon "Bob" Avery was unprepared for the order "Abandon ship!"

A Bump in the Night

Hollon "Bob" Avery graduated from Concord High School in 1942 and joined the Navy that September. After radio school, he wound up in New Guinea. There he joined the crew of the USS Perkins, a destroyer commissioned in 1936 and named after Commodore George H. Perkins, the Civil War hero from Hopkinton, New Hampshire. The ship was designated DD-377. It was a number Avery has good reason to remember.

We were sent up to Buna, New Guinea. That's where Amelia Earhart took off—where they started the search for her. Our job was to shell the beach with five-inch guns. We went in within a couple of miles of the beach. We could see the shells bouncing around under the palm trees.

I was assigned to load a gun. I didn't know much. I just thought we were having a lot of fun. All of a sudden I saw this huge thing coming toward us. It looked like a fifty-gallon drum, glowing red. I said, "What the heck is that?" and someone said, "They're shooting back, of course."

That was the summer I turned nineteen. We spent that summer and early fall shelling all up and down the coast. Milne Bay was our base. There were no buildings there, but that's where the Perkins always hid—in the same place, under the palm trees.

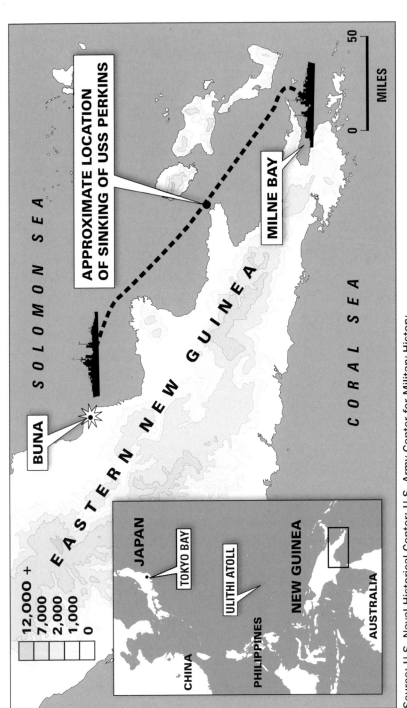

SOLOMON SEA

CORAL SEA

EASTERN NEW GUINEA

BUNA

APPROXIMATE LOCATION
OF SINKING OF USS PERKINS

MILNE BAY

12,000 +
7,000
2,000
1,000
0

50

MILES

0

JAPAN

TOKYO BAY

ULITHI ATOLL

NEW GUINEA

CHINA

PHILIPPINES

AUSTRALIA

Source: U.S. Naval Historical Center; U.S. Army Center for Military History

The Japanese still had control of the skies. One night when we were out on a mission, we had so many of them dropping bombs on us that we were sure we were going to be sunk. As the planes were thinning out, a bomb exploded right above us. It killed several people. We were covered with shrapnel, and the ship was full of holes. That's why they called it a tin can—there was nothing but a thin layer of stainless steel above the hull, and the hull was probably only half-inch steel.

We had our lifejackets inflated because we thought we were going to be sunk. When dawn finally came, I looked down and mine was deflated. There was a hole where a piece of shell went in and came out the other side. Boy, was I lucky. A guy right below me had his arm cut off at the elbow.

Bettys—that's what we called their night bombers. They liked to send them after destroyers. A Betty came in to throw "fish" at us, we'd say, meaning long-lance torpedoes.

They'd fly low along the water to avoid shells, but they're out there within the range of the five-inch guns, and we'd start punking shells down in front of them to send up a big geyser. If they hit that, it was like hitting a concrete bridge. If they got through that, we'd pepper them with forties. They'd eventually get within range of the twenty-millimeters. They'd drop their fish and fly right over us. And then we'd shoot at them on the other side. Then they'd come around and try to hit us with a second fish. None of them ever made it twice.

The Japanese were much better equipped than we were at this point. When their torpedoes hit something, it was destroyed. Sometimes ours wouldn't explode. It was discouraging. It was a year or two before our torpedoes worked.

We weren't afraid of Japanese submarines. That's what destroyers are for—to destroy submarines. We could drop a whole pattern of depth charges and keep them down all night if need be. They stayed away from us.

On October 28, 1943, we left Milne Bay. We started out late in the evening and steamed up the coast. I was in my sack asleep. All of a sudden, there was a heck of a racket. We were hit by something—I didn't know what. I put on the dark blue work shirt we always wore and made my way up. It was pitch black. When my eyes got accustomed, I saw the bow of a big ship pulling away from us. It was like looking up at the corner of a skyscraper.

Then I looked out, and I could see a ship number out there. My first thought was that it was the ship that had hit us. And I looked and the number was 377. And I said, "What the heck? That's our fantail!"

What had hit us was a big Australian troop ship, the Duntroon, an ex-passenger liner. It had hit us right between the smokestacks, and it broke the keel. I could hear somebody hollering, "Abandon ship!" Jeez, I had my shirt on, no pants. I ran back down one deck and put on my pants—dungarees. I don't know why I did that. I shouldn't have.

The Duntroon had been running at high speed. The big ships didn't have to worry about submarines because they ran so fast the submarines couldn't maneuver to torpedo them. They didn't go with escorts, but they didn't have radar either.

We had radar, and we saw them—we were trying to keep out of their damn way. But they made a turn at the same time we did, and they were still headed right at us. We were stopped dead in the water when they hit us—the worst possible situation.

It was no more than three or four feet into the water from where I jumped off the deck. It wasn't cold, but the water was full of oil. At least there was no fire. By the time I got off the ship, there were quite a few guys there. I didn't have a lifejacket or anything, but I saw a raft, and I swam to it right away. There were three or four of us on the raft, all of us covered with oil. We got as far as we could from the ship. It had broken in two, and we watched both pieces go down.

Then we started to worry. We didn't know where we were or how far from shore, but there were sharks in the water and cannibals in New Guinea. There were Japanese on an island over next to us. We didn't know how we were going to get out of that mess.

But the radio guys on the ship apparently got off an SOS. Being a radioman myself, I was sure proud of them. They sent the Duntroon back after us, and were we glad to see it. We'd been in the water maybe three, four hours. They came right up next to us. They had a big net for us to crawl up. Boy, was that a bugger to get up.

The USS Perkins

The Duntroon took us to port in New Guinea, and from there they took us to the States on the SS America, a liner that had just been built. This thing was brand new—it hadn't even been serviced yet. But the government had the option of taking it over as a troop transport. My bunk was in the ballroom—can you imagine? Bunks, three high, spiked to the floor in the ballroom.

We were on thirty days' survivors' leave. I came back to Concord, and then I was sent to Boston and put on a new destroyer, the DeHaven, which had just come from Bath, Maine. We were the first of the new 2,250-ton destroyers. I was a radioman, one of three combat veterans responsible for a flagship's communications. We joined Admiral Halsey's fleet at Ulithi atoll—that was the Third Fleet's headquarters—just as the second battle of the Philippines was about to begin.

We were all over the place from the northern coast of Japan down through the China Sea and eventually to Iwo Jima and Okinawa. In December of 1944, we were in the big typhoon off Luzon where three destroyers rolled upside-down. Nearly eight hundred men were lost. We didn't lose a damn thing.

You couldn't see the typhoon coming. It just started raining and kept raining, and the waves got so dang high you couldn't see out of the ships. The waves would be thirty, forty feet high. You'd be down in a trough and couldn't see anything. It lasted two or three days.

In July of 1945, the DeHaven and her destroyer squadron went right into Tokyo Bay. We fired everything we had on board, even torpedoes. Every gun was firing right into the beach. There was a convoy of Japanese ships heading out. We sank them all. There was no resistance—they didn't think anybody would be in their harbor. I was working in the radio shack, but I got out to watch. All I could see everywhere I looked was flashing guns. Every time I hear or sing "The Star-Spangled Banner," I think of that night.

The closer we got to Japan, the more kamikazes we saw. It felt to us like things were getting worse and worse. The atom bomb saved my life. We were right off the coast of Japan when we heard about the surrender. I still have copies of the radio messages:

Avery saved the radio messages at war's end.

"Aug. 11: Take all precautions. Avoid any false sense of security as a result of Japanese newspaper announcements of a peace proposal. Remember Pearl Harbor. The Japanese were talking peace to our president at the very moment of that infamous attack. An all-out suicide attack is more than probable. Keep your eyes open and your powder dry."

"Aug. 12: The United States agreed today to accept the Japanese surrender offer provided the supreme commander of the Allied powers rules Japan through the authority of the emperor. This was officially announced a few minutes ago by Secretary of State James Byrnes. Byrnes made this offer on behalf of all the four Allied powers, the U.S., Soviet Russia, Great Britain and China."

My brother's ship, the Southerland, led the procession into Tokyo Bay for the surrender on September 2. As the flagship, we were the first ship in Tokyo Bay during the war, and he was on the first ship into Tokyo Bay for the surrender ceremony.

We were there for the surrender, too. It was a beautiful day, calm, of course, because we were in the harbor. We anchored right off the Missouri. You could see what was going on, and we could listen to it by radio.

We were so relieved. We never thought we would survive the war.

I would never trust the Japanese again, no matter how peace-like they might seem to be. They were a cruel people. They were almost like these people we're fighting now. They would give up their own life just to get rid of two of you.

As a boy growing up in Concord, Bob Avery learned a great deal about automobiles and things mechanical from his father, a freight-car repairman on the Boston & Maine Railroad. After the war, he returned to school and was hired by General Electric. As a dynamics engineer for GE and Raytheon, he solved vibration and balancing problems on radar and submarine equipment and other machines. His career also included stints in manufacturing and in R&D for medical equipment.

Robert Graves with the tool that operated the B-17's radar.

Robert Graves

The Pathfinder

Robert Graves, ninety-two, lives in Laconia, New Hampshire. He was
working for a carpet service company in Boston when the Japanese
bombed Pearl Harbor. He had just passed the entrance exams for Yale,
but he postponed college, enlisted in the Army Air Corps, and began
two years of training. After eleven missions as a B-17 navigator, he
was chosen as a radar man for the Pathfinders, which led bombing
missions over France and Germany. He flew with Squadron 333
of the Eighth Air Force, completing thirty-two missions in all.

Nineteen forty-three was a bad year for the U.S. Air Force in
England. We lost a lot of crews, and the bombing was very
poor. The generals decided they were relying too heavily on
young volunteers. They formed a cadre of officers, and they went
around to the bases of the Eighth Air Force and cherry-picked a
pilot here, a navigator there, a bombardier over there. I had finished
eleven missions, and one day they came along to my base in Great
Ashfield and lifted me right out of my crew.

I was sent off to a special base, Alconbury, which had been made
into a Pathfinder school. They picked me because I had good navigation experience plus I was approaching twenty-nine. These kids
of eighteen were so terrified once they hit major flak that the first

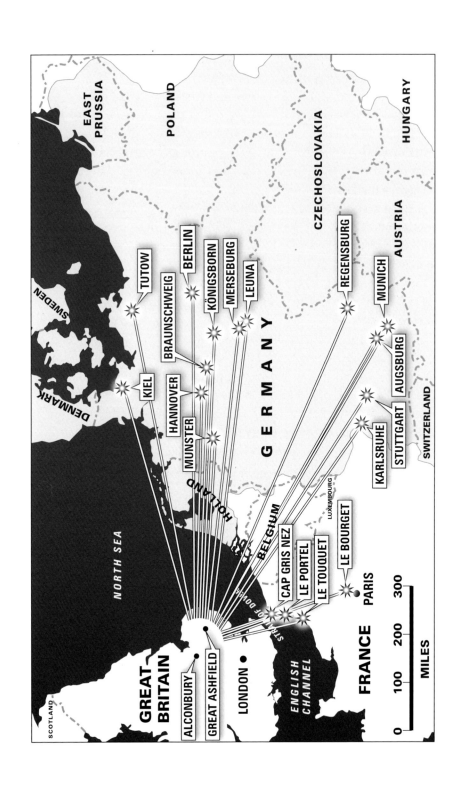

thing was, "Dump the bombs and let's get out of here!" They plowed up more fields than they ever hit targets.

I spent a concentrated two months—April and May of 1944—learning two new things. I had to learn to operate the Norden bomb sight, and I had to learn this new thing called radar. The British had huge radar installations pointing toward Germany to warn them when the German bombers approached, but there was no such thing as airborne radar.

I have a souvenir. [He produces a stubby screwdriver with a wooden handle.] This is what you used to operate a new radar. There were no dials. You had little holes and you poked the screwdriver in and you turned it a little bit. The reason the handle is made of wood is that, up where we flew, it starts at about twenty-five below zero, but normally it runs thirty or forty below. So you can't touch metal. You would stick to it.

My nickname as the radar guy was "Mickeyman." I was a navigator using my navigation technique with radar. I was also a backup for the bombardier. If anything happened to him, I was to crawl through the bomb bay, dive under the pilots, work my way up to the front, and do what he was supposed to do. Thank God that never happened because it's nice for them to say that's what you do, but to actually do it would be damn near impossible. You had heavy clothing on and you were attached to oxygen. Above ten thousand feet you always go on oxygen.

We were in a B-17 Flying Fortress. The normal crew was ten men, but we had eleven—I was the eleventh. In the front was the bombardier, behind him the navigator, behind him the flight engineer and two pilots. Then you come to the bomb bay, which normally contained twelve five-hundred-pound bombs, and on the other side of the bomb bay were the radio operator and the radar—me. Behind us were two waist gunners, and underneath them was the ball-turret gunner, which is an unenviable position. To be a ball-turret gunner you had to be no bigger that five-foot-five. You had to squeeze in that ball. Way in the back was the tailgunner.

The radar sends out an ultrasonic signal which hits something and bounces back. The radar measures the time it takes for the signal to go out and return to the set. It can measure with extreme accuracy how far you are from what that signal hit. That's what my main job was when we got to fly. I navigated the ship and all the ships behind me so we didn't inadvertently fly over a flak area. You couldn't see a flak area because you're flying over clouds all the time. You never see the ground. The thing that sees the ground is the radar.

German towns are encircled with artillery. I had to keep the pilot informed where we were. We're flying straight ahead, but there's always a strong north wind pushing us, and if you allow it to push us long enough, it's going to push us right over a flak area. I have to steer between flak areas, so we're equally distant from the two. My major job is to keep my pilot and all the pilots flying behind us safe in between these danger zones.

On the ground all these guys can hear us coming. They know we're up there. They can't see us, but they have ground radar. And they're just waiting for us to get close enough so they can get a good shot at us. Berlin had four hundred heavy guns. Imagine—four hundred antiaircraft guns surrounding that one city—to protect Adolf.

Once we get to the target, it gets pretty obvious. The sky fills with black puffs. When we turn to the target, I have to turn my attention strictly to the bombardier because with radar, even though it's cloudy, I can give the bombardier a general idea of where his target is.

The big one that I got so much credit for was an enormous synthetic oil refinery in Leuna, south of Merseburg, on July 29, 1944. The Germans were such clever chemists. Once the Mediterranean was sealed by the British and they couldn't get oil from the Mideast, they set to work to make their own. This was one of their attempts to make their own oil—this refinery—a prime target for us.

Before you go out after such a target, you get thoroughly briefed. They have aerial photographs. We knew what we were going to bomb. Whether we could see it or not was another matter. The minute the bombardier could see it, he could lock onto it with his bomb sight, and the bomb sight controlled the plane. The pilot could just sit back. Whatever way he turned the bomb sight, that's where the plane turned.

On the way to the target, you're diving into a wall of flak—black puffs all around you—and I'm trying to keep a bead on the essential target, in this case the iron work in a synthetic oil refinery. I'm hoping there'll be a little hole somewhere in the clouds where the bombardier can see it because he can lock the bomb sight onto that one place, and that's where the bombs will hit.

At the proper moment the bomb sight will release the bombs. Our plane and the deputy lead plane were the only ones with bomb sights—the deputy had one in case we were hit. But in back of us are all bombardiers in their planes with a toggle switch. We had twin marker bombs in our plane. And when we dropped the bombs, two smoke bombs would come out of the plane. The minute the planes in the back saw these smoke bombs, they would pull the toggle switch and release their bombs. That way we got a better concentration. They knew that when our bombs went away, the bombardier had actually seen the target.

The Germans were always aiming at us, but if they missed by just a little, they would hit the one next to us—the deputy lead. More than once we saw him blown apart, and we figured, "Oh boy, the whole thing is on us now."

On the mission to the oil refinery, we had about six hundred or eight hundred planes behind us—the whole Eighth Air Force. We were just one squadron, leading a group, and that group was part of a wing, and that wing was part of a division, and there were three divisions that made up the Eighth Air Force. We had all those behind us.

I would get very busy once we hit the IP—the initial point from which you turn and start your bomb run. I would be coaching the bombardier that he should be turning a little bit this way or that way, according to what radar was telling me, and praying that he would be able to see something. On that one day he finally did get to see the Leuna synthetic oil plant. All of us dumped the bombs, and apparently we hit the target. They were all so overjoyed—they gave us all Distinguished Flying Crosses.

My first two missions, before I became a Pathfinder, were top secret. The Germans were doing real damage in London with V-1 and V-2 rockets, and we were sent to try to knock out their launching platforms on the coast of northern Europe. The bomb crews had had no success at twenty-five thousand feet, so they told us to go in at thirteen thousand. They figured we'd be able to hit the targets better, but in fact it made it easier for the Germans to hit us. They shot us right out of the sky.

I made it back, but most of us didn't. I lost many comrades. I remember coming back to the barracks and seeing people packing up all the foot lockers of the men who were lost to send them home. In the typing room, they were writing letters of condolence. There was no way of knowing how many were killed and how many captured, but it was a bad introduction to flying missions.

You'd be surprised how many people ended up the war in a German prison. If you could see a couple of people exit a stricken plane, you'd say, well, they might make it. But you never knew.

I don't think I ever met any of the men in the other planes. There was no real fraternization, no buddy-buddy stuff. Each one had a job to do and he concentrated on that particular job. So if I lost the guy on the other side, well, that's too bad because that imposes a burden on me and my crew. If you got too close to people, then you'd start to worry about them—not a good thing.

I received what was called a Lucky Bastard certificate. This was given in all earnestness. It's laughable now, but it's signed by colonels. If you could live through twenty-five missions, you were unusual. At the time this was designed, very few people ever made it through twenty-five. You were dead by mission eighteen or nineteen or something. If you survived twenty-five missions, automatically you beat the odds and you were known as a Lucky Bastard.

I didn't think about my own death. You steel yourself against that. Nobody wants to die—you sort of put that out of your head. You're most worried about being seriously wounded, where you lost an arm or you went blind.

At one point I thought I had lost my right foot. We got a big burst of flak and it tore my radar set apart and I was covered with splinters from the table I was working on. I felt this pain in my ankle. All of a sudden you don't dare to look. But since I didn't feel any blood, I finally got the courage to look. I slowly went down to see what it was. Sure enough, it had blown the boot off my foot practically, and pieces of the zipper were stuck in my flesh. What a relief.

In my first eleven missions I had a double-barreled .50-caliber

*As a Pathfinder, Graves led bombing
missions over Germany.*

machine gun, and I would shoot back at the Messerschmitts. One
time I shot until I had spent shells all around my ankles. The bombardier had special machine guns that were semi-controlled. He
could lock on to somebody. You've got to have a little calculator
that figures out how fast he's going and how fast you're going and
somehow the bullet is going to get in the middle of all that and do
some damage. My gun didn't have a calculator. If you're an old duck
hunter, maybe you've got an advantage, but for a city kid like me, I'm
out there just shooting away with a .50-caliber machine gun.

One time on a ten-hour flight we were trying to climb over a
weather front. We got up to thirty-two, thirty-three thousand feet. It
was fifty-five below zero. Our breath condensed and the area where
I was sitting was covered with frost. The pilot decided the engines
couldn't breathe properly at that altitude and decided we'd abandon
the mission, so we turned around and flew back again. It was too
dangerous to land with our bombs. You'd put the bombardier to

work, tell him to pick out a target from a list of alternates, and we'd just dump the bombs.

I never thought about the people on the ground. They were the enemy. They were those dirty Nazis down there, and the more we killed the better.

The British flew at night, we flew in the daytime. Usually we were in the air for eight hours. On a typical mission day, you're jostled out of your bunk at about three o'clock in the morning. You'd clean up and shave and get dressed. Then you are summoned to the mess hall and fed a carefully designed breakfast. You can't eat anything that would cause gas. Baked beans would be a real no-no because when you get up at altitude, everything expands. You'd be in excruciating pain at twenty-five thousand feet. Anything you ate that caused gas would be pressing against all the organs.

After breakfast you'd be summoned to the briefing room. The commanding officer would say this is the mission for today. He would show you a map, and with the map would be aerial photos of what we were going to aim at. He would give you the big picture. The meteorologist would tell you what the weather was going to be like over there. The pilots would get a special briefing telling them what frequencies were going to be used to direct them and what the altitude and air speed would be.

Then we would break down into separate groups. The bombardiers would all get the fine details of what they were going to try to bomb. And the navigators and radio men would be apprised as to what direction they're going to get by radio.

After the briefing, at about seven in the morning, we would go out to our planes. The weather was generally deplorable, but once you got up, you were above all that in the clear air with clouds underneath.

The most dangerous time was during takeoff and the climb through layers of clouds to achieve the planned formation of the mission. Each plane had to fit into a certain part of a squadron. And the squadrons all had to fit together into a group. We lost a lot of planes during the assembly where you had to get these people all in line and nicely spaced and separated from each other. If you're not quite sure of your plane's place—if you think you're going to fly high and you're supposed to fly low, you're going to run into somebody. And that means two planes down. I saw this happen.

The most feared mission was that first one to Berlin. The night before my first one, everybody was writing that final letter home. All over, men were writing their folks, and their girlfriends and their wives, "This may be my last letter, but I want to tell you how much I love you," and all that business. As it turned out, we hit a lot of flak, and I don't think we did much good.

My last mission was August 6, 1944, and it was my sixth mission to Berlin. The flak was still heavy, and I lost my radar. It was blown off. So I crawled ahead and stood by the bombardier. That was a big treat for me—my first chance to see anything. And there was nothing to see. I'm standing behind the bombardier looking over his shoulder, and I said, "What the hell can you find to hit?" It was a wasteland down there. There were no buildings standing—just rubble. And he shrugged and said, "We'll drop a few bombs on the local aerodrome outside." And that's what we did.

One reason it was total devastation was that the British did such a job on Berlin. That was retribution, a vendetta. The Germans had bombed London, and they were going to pay them back. The British obliterated Berlin.

I didn't know the Berlin mission would be my last until it was over, but they let you know when you're finished. You're summoned to put on your full dress uniform. You line up with other people. If you have a Distinguished Flying Cross, it's pinned on you with the proper decorum. It's a formal ceremony saying goodbye.

I had a great sense of relief that day because every next mission is probably your last. You always had that feeling: This could be my last one.

After the war, Robert Graves went to Yale. He became a technical market researcher whose work entailed the placement of manufacturing plants. He was called back to the service during the Korean conflict and flew as a radar-man on a B-29 Superfortress in North Africa. The mission, he said, was to let the Russians know the United States was not so preoccupied with Korea that it couldn't defend its interests in the Middle East, the Mediterranean, and North Africa.

Walter Holden was one of the few in his company to escape capture.

Walter Holden

Foot Soldier

Walter Holden of Franklin, New Hampshire, was a high school senior in New Jersey when Pearl Harbor was bombed. He tried to enlist, but first his mother and then the Army's eye test stopped him. That didn't keep him from being drafted in April 1943—or from close encounters with the Germans as an infantryman in Europe.

First, they put me in ASTP—the Army Specialized Training Program. They were going to make us engineers and second lieutenants. I ended up at the University of Delaware for about nine months.

After a while we were kind of ashamed that we were going to college while others were being killed overseas. We'd go to New York City. We wore this patch which was the Lamp of Knowledge—we called it "the flaming pisspot." We'd kind of crawl along the side of buildings so nobody could see our patch.

They broke the ASTP up in March of 1944. I went to Camp Carson, Colorado, and joined the 104th Infantry Division. Our general was Terry Allen, who had commanded the First Division in Africa. He and his assistant commander, Teddy Roosevelt Jr., were fired in Sicily. Terry was our commander—good for us, good for him.

From D-Day into August, we got ready to go to Europe. It took

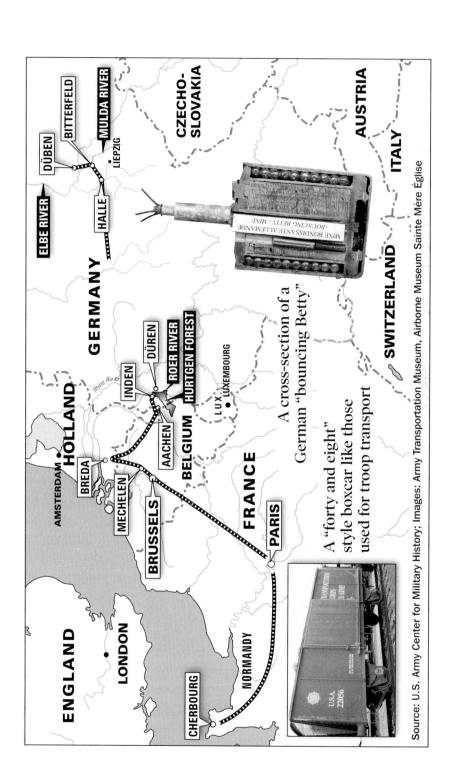

ELBE RIVER

DÜBEN

BITTERFELD

MULDA RIVER

HALLE

LIEPZIG

CZECHO-SLOVAKIA

AUSTRIA

ITALY

GERMANY

DÜREN

INDEN

ROER RIVER

HÜRTGEN FOREST

AACHEN

Rhine River

HOLLAND

AMSTERDAM

BREDA

MECHELEN

BRUSSELS

BELGIUM

LUXEMBOURG

LUX •

SWITZERLAND

A cross-section of a German "bouncing Betty"

MINE BONDISSANTE ALLEMANDE
"BOUNCING BETTY" MINE

A "forty and eight" style boxcar like those used for troop transport

FRANCE

PARIS

ENGLAND

LONDON •

NORMANDY

CHERBOURG

TRANSPORTATION CORPS U.S. ARMY

U.S.A. 22056

Source: U.S. Army Center for Military History; Images: Army Transportation Museum, Airborne Museum Sainte Mère Église

us seven days to cross the Atlantic, which was pretty safe by then. We landed at Cherbourg, the first division to do so.

In Normandy, we stayed in an apple orchard till October because our truck drivers were taken to drive the Red Ball Express, the highway for supplying the advancing armies. The French people had seen a lot of Americans by that time. They weren't as friendly as we thought they should be. We didn't come to save them because they were already saved.

They were sharp traders. They had a product called Calvados—like apple cider, only stronger. And we found that the married men in the ranks seemed to need a certain kind of trade more than some other people did. I guess they missed it.

Finally, they loaded us on train cars called "forty and eights," for forty men and eight horses. But the ones we got on had had sheep on them, not horses, and they didn't have time to clean them afterward.

We went through Paris and Brussels and ended up at Mechelen, Belgium. We were under Bernard Montgomery, in the British army. We had a Polish division on one side of us and a Canadian division on the other. We crossed into Holland. Our objective was to clear the way to Amsterdam. Our attack was on Breda, a good-sized city.

The first night everybody was scared. There was a lot of getting up to go to the latrine. Men got sick to their stomachs. There wasn't really any danger that night, but we didn't know that.

The next day we moved, and I saw my first dead German, lying in a ditch. The first action we had was a sniper trying to slow us down at the edge of a village. We stopped. You're not supposed to do that. A major came up and got us moving again. The sniper ran out of ammunition and surrendered. He was an older man. The Germans had a lot of old and young guys in that area. Our lieutenant pushed the sniper into a canal. He took out his .45 and shot close to him, trying to get information. We didn't get much out of him.

That night, we were next to a minefield and didn't know it. One of the men went out and stepped on a mine and yelled for a medic. The medic stepped on a mine. So the lieutenant went out and stepped on a mine. The lieutenant got it the worst. He was lying in the field all night yelling, "Kill me! Help me! Kill me! Kill me!" But nobody did. The next morning, another medic went out and got them. They were all alive.

We called those mines the bouncing Betty. When you stepped on it, it would knock your foot off. If it did it a certain way, it bounced up and hit you in the testicles. That's what happened to the lieutenant. One of our officers later saw the lieutenant in a British hospital. Both his legs were gone, and the man who saw him said he was shaped like an egg and couldn't do anything but eat.

Our next fight was a night fight across the Maas River. I had a good buddy killed by machine gun fire there. He was at Delaware with us. His name was George Hart, and he had a great sense of humor. When he went to tell the college chaplain he was going to get married, the chaplain asked if he was going to have a military wedding, with crossed swords. "No," he said, "just crossed textbooks."

This was a scary operation. We had little boats to cross the Maas. The Germans were on the other side in the village, and they didn't want us to cross. George and a lot of other guys got killed crossing.

That was the first time I fired in combat, but I didn't see anything. Usually you don't see anything. The idea is to keep up a steady fire— keep the other guy's head down. Of course, that doesn't help you see him, but it prevents him from firing at you.

We didn't carry much. If the march was too difficult, guys would throw away their overcoats. Then at night, they'd wish they had them. We carried a raincoat in the back. We had bandoliers for ammunition—just a strip of cloth really. We had cartridge belts. We had a little pack where we were supposed to carry more bullets, but usually that's where your cigarettes went. And we had a canteen, and some guys carried two canteens—one for water. We had a small first-aid kit.

In winter we carried half a pound of dynamite. That was to blow a hole in the ground if you needed to, to break the ground if your fold-up shovel wouldn't do it. The first time I tried the entrenching tool was in Holland, and we got to water at about two feet, but you kept digging because you wanted cover.

One time in Holland, maybe the last night there, a fellow named John Tolman and I were in a foxhole. The D Company machine gun

Holden learned a lesson about why men fight.

moved in right next to us. We said, "Gee, this is great. We've got all this protection."

Well, we were a little green. We were facing a town. We could see the lights. We thought A Company was there, but the next morning, whoever was in the town started firing at us. We were out in plain flat open space. Tolman and I realized that that machine gun wasn't a very good thing because they could see it and they were firing on it. The mortars were coming right in on us—twelve holes within ten feet. They finally knocked out the machine gun. This is one of the things you feel bad about: We felt good because the Germans stopped firing mortars.

That was the same day a British Spitfire came in and started firing on us. He was off course. The air force and the army really didn't cooperate well. So our antiaircraft guns shot the Spitfire down, and we were glad about that, too. Those things happened.

When we finished the Holland campaign, a lot of guys had trench foot. We had been in water the whole time and couldn't dry our feet off. You could get gangrene and lose a foot.

We relieved the First Division and finished taking Aachen. We were north of the Hurtgen Forest, but we crossed from Aachen into the dragon's teeth—the Siegfried Line. The First had been there before us, too. One place where we spent a couple of nights, they had left cans of C-rations lined up all along a wall. There were three kinds of C-rations—hash, stew, and beans. Well, at first we thought, "Gee, we don't want the beans." It turned out we didn't want the hash or the stew either.

In November, we fought at Inden, on the Inde River. We got to Inden at night. As we were moving in behind a covering barrage of our own artillery, a mortar shell went off near me. I think it was one of our own. I felt a blow to the back of my neck, and it knocked me down. Like many of the other men, I had a towel around my neck. A piece of the mortar had chewed a hole in the towel, but it didn't reach my neck. Probably the towel saved my life.

Our company, Charlie Company, was the first into Inden that night. We got in a factory building—a long building with a railroad track running through it. We weren't there long before the Germans started firing in on us. We were in the middle of the building, and they came in the front and the back. We could see the Germans—they were maybe twenty yards from us. We were swamped—no chance at all. The men closest to the Germans were quickly captured, so our guys couldn't defend themselves without risking shooting our men.

We thought we were going to be captured. It was a helpless feeling. But we had a man with our squad named Cliff Johnson who had been a scout. He said, "I think I can get us out." It was a choice of being killed or being captured or getting out. Our squad, maybe ten men, went out the side window. I was the last one out. There was a canal out there with a board across it, and Cliff led us across it.

As far as I know, we were the only ones who got out. At least sixty men in our company were captured. The captain was calling for help on his walkie-talkie. A lieutenant from I Company could hear him, but he couldn't answer. Eventually the walkie-talkie gave out and the captain gave up.

After we crossed the canal, we got into a building with some men from A Company. There was a BAR man (Browning Automatic Rifle) firing down the street. A Tiger tank was trying to come up. When it started up, he'd shoot at the infantrymen who were with it. Tanks are practically helpless at night, and the tank wouldn't move up without infantry. That guy held off the tank all night.

Two months later, we got up to the Roer River not far from Duren. The Germans had let loose the dams and flooded it so we couldn't cross. Finally, at the end of the Bulge, we got ready to cross. On February 23, 1945, at 2 a.m., we started. We had wooden boats. They were supposedly propelled by engineers. There were two engineers and ten infantrymen to a boat.

Our boat got hit by a mortar shell before we even got it in the water. We were carrying it on our shoulders, twelve guys. Six of the guys were wounded. One of them, a friend of mine named Benny Cohen—Benny's Achilles' tendon was clipped. We took him in. Stocky Stockwell and I were not hit, but the boat was done, so we crawled into a shell hole. A lieutenant came up and said, "We're going to try another crossing." And we did, and we got across.

The next day, we were searching buildings in Duren. Two guys and I were in a building. We heard a "Plunk!" Grenade. We were in a hallway. I pushed these guys back, and I got them into a room. I almost got in myself, but I got a piece of grenade in my leg.

We got out of the building, and I could see blood pouring out of my left boot. I couldn't feel it. The lieutenant sent me back to the medics, and I wound up in a hospital in Paris. On the side of my leg you could see where the piece of the grenade was, but it wasn't doing any damage. It had been a big river crossing with many wounded, a lot of them badly, so it was three or four days before they got around to taking care of me.

The first night I was there, a French nurse said to me, "You're lucky to be here. You're almost done." I had been in combat long enough that I was almost worthless, and she could see it. We both liked Tarzan, and we talked about that, but I never saw her again.

They took the fragment out. It was smaller than a penny. I carried it around for a while, but then I was really ashamed because it was so small. So I threw it away—I wasn't going to show anybody that.

Joe Hill and I went into Paris. He didn't have a thumb on his right hand. He said, "You know, I thought that would keep me out of the infantry, but it didn't because I can fire a machine gun." That day in Paris was the day I learned to hate red wine.

On my way back to the front, I heard President Roosevelt had died. We knew we were at the end of the war. Everybody thought it was terrible that he didn't live to see it. Truman, we didn't know. Most people probably didn't know that he was the vice president.

I got back to the outfit, and I felt good to be back with my friends. It's a funny thing about the Army. The thing you'll fight for is so you'll look good in the eyes of your friends. You fight for your friends, you don't fight for your country or whatever.

This was a great campaign because from there on, we rode tanks. We were tied with the Third Armored Division. We'd go into a town and we'd say, "Where's the burgomeister? Pile up all your weapons—old deer rifles and everything else—cameras and watches, too." There was very little fighting.

Halle was a beautiful old city. The defender of Halle was Count von Lucknow, a famous submariner in the First World War. Terry Allen, the general, somehow got in touch with von Lucknow and said we didn't want to destroy the city. It became an open city and we walked right in.

Winston Churchill said, "The Hun is either at your throat or at your feet." The Germans were submissive in this period. They knew they were beaten—had known it for months.

We went from Halle to Bitterfeld, and then we went across the Mulde River to Duben. We weren't supposed to do that. That was the agreed-upon dividing line between our forces and the Russians. That's when we started to get Germans saying to us, "I live in Aachen, you've got to let me through." They were afraid of the Russians.

Cliff Johnson, the scout in our company, and I were on a road-block, and a German came up on a horse. He had a sidearm. He said, "I got a battalion out here, and I want to surrender them." So I looked at Cliff and he looked at me. Here we were, a sergeant and a private. We said, "Bring 'em in." So he did. We made him give us his sidearm first—a P38 Walther pistol.

It was a Hungarian battalion, and they didn't want to fight anyway. They had six wagons loaded with rifles. We sent them into town, but by the time they got there, there were only five wagons. We never did find out what happened to the other wagon.

That was the last combat we had.

After returning to the States, Walter Holden was sent to Oakland with the 104th Infantry Division to prepare for the invasion of Japan. During his trip west, the atom bombs ended the war. Discharged, Holden came home to Weare, where his mother lived. He earned bachelor's and master's degrees from the University of New Hampshire, where he met his wife, Barbara. He became a teacher, textbook editor, and Civil War historian and writer. Now eighty-three years old, he lives with Barbara in Franklin.

George Hollis faced hard fighting as a scout with "Jungle Platoon."

George Hollis

No Glamour, No Glory

*George Hollis, who lived in Weare, New Hampshire, joined
the Army shortly after the bombing of Pearl Harbor.*

I enlisted in Manchester. They told me I could pick more or less
what I wanted to do in the Army. Now that was a lot of bull. They
just shipped me where they wanted me, which happened to be
Camp Boyd, Texas, and right into the 31st Infantry Division. That's
where I did my training—there, and then Fort Sill, Oklahoma, and
Camp Shelby, Mississippi.

They shipped us to Camp Pickett in Virginia and said they were
going to send us overseas. We figured we were going to Europe, but
no, we didn't. We went through the Panama Canal and landed in
New Guinea.

When we went overseas, four of us more or less swore that if
somebody picked me for patrol work, the others would volunteer
to go with me. Or I would volunteer with them. We'd watch each
other's backs. We lost two of the four.

On New Guinea, they came up with a special platoon. We called
it Jungle Platoon. When a company wanted someone to scout an
area, they'd call us. When we made the landing, we were all one
group, but once ashore, we did mostly scout work—find out where
the enemy is and what he's doing and all that baloney.

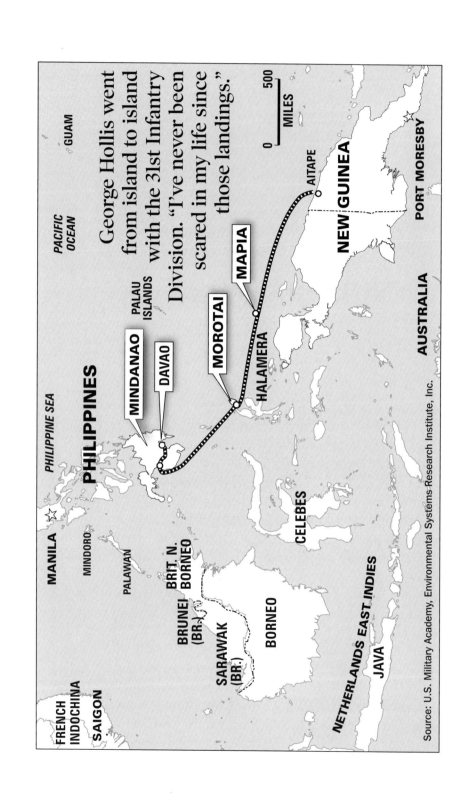

George Hollis went from island to island with the 31st Infantry Division. "I've never been scared in my life since those landings."

GUAM

PACIFIC OCEAN

PHILIPPINE SEA

PHILIPPINES

MANILA ☆

MINDORO

PALAWAN

PALAU ISLANDS

MINDANAO

DAVAO

MOROTAI

MAPIA

HALAMERA

AITAPE

NEW GUINEA

PORT MORESBY ☆

AUSTRALIA

CELEBES

NETHERLANDS EAST INDIES

JAVA

BORNEO

BRIT. N. BORNEO

BRUNEI (BR.)

SARAWAK (BR.)

FRENCH INDOCHINA

SAIGON

0   500
MILES

Source: U.S. Military Academy, Environmental Systems Research Institute, Inc.

Part of New Guinea was in U.S. hands, part in Japanese. We went up above on the point and landed on the beach and drove the Japs off.

I took mostly ammunition when we got ready to go in. I had an M-1, and I was carrying a loaded .45 automatic in a shoulder holster. On the M-1 you have a clip of eight, and you have a bandolier with six or eight clips in it, and I usually had three bandoliers. In my backpack I had something to eat, but mainly it was filled with shells for the .45.

I'll tell you something: I've never been scared in my life since those landings. The Navy shells the beach and rakes the land. When your landing craft hits the water, they're not firing anymore. Two of my three landings, we went in on track vehicles that we called alligators. They go off into the water and right up on the land. You don't have to go in the water. They sound like tanks, a squeaking, roaring noise. When you're in the landing craft, you're thinking, "What the hell am I doing here?" There's not much talking. It's quiet.

My main motivation was always that I wanted to get home, I wanted to live. Why wasn't I killed? When you first went into combat, you had the idea that it couldn't happen to you. It could happen to the other guy, yes, but not to you. But after a while, you began to realize it can happen to you, too.

Each landing made you feel that way. Here you're coming off a little boat, maybe landing in water up to your waist, as I did on my first landing. You've got to wade up to a shore, and then you've got beach—probably a hundred feet or more with nothing to hide behind. Men are dropping around you. There's a bunch of enemy up there. You can't see them because they're all dug in. You're wide open. You might as well walk up to the line and say, "Here I am—shoot me!"

On my first landing I looked back and saw bodies on the beach. Some men never even got out of the water. After that I never looked back at the beach again.

You can hear the gunshots from the beach, but there's too much going on to tell one from another—it's steady shooting. But if a bullet comes near you, it goes like that. [He snaps his fingers.] And you heard that pretty much all the way across the beach, a bunch of popping around you. The main thing coming across the beach or coming out of that boat is to find a place to hide. When you finally get up to the bank, you're safe for a few minutes maybe—of course, they toss grenades over. Then you have to go up and get them.

It was dangerous all the time. One time in New Guinea, we were back for a rest period. We were standing in line, and they were cooking breakfast for us. All of a sudden three men dropped. There were snipers up in the trees, and there were a lot of trees. We grabbed machine guns and raked every tree. There wasn't any firing after that, so we must have hit them.

I only saw one sniper in New Guinea, and I got him. I didn't actually see him, but it didn't look right up in the tree. I put three or four rounds up there just as fast as I could pull the trigger. He fell— he was tied up there. He came down on the end of a rope. Tying themselves up there—that was the end of the line for them. It was like those guys who would fly an airplane into a ship.

My rifle and my .45 never left my side for two years. They were part of me. But one time I lost my rifle briefly. We were on patrol, about ten men, and the Japanese came right at us out of the bush with bayonets. They had no ammunition left, but they came after us. Somehow one of them hooked my rifle strap with his bayonet and took my rifle out of my hands, slick as a whistle. I fell backward and pulled out my .45, and I shot three Japs with it.

The New Guinea landing was not real heavy. We made another landing at Morotai, which was called "a small landing," but I don't know what that means. When we landed, we could see the Japanese in their pillboxes covered with palm trees, and in the front there was a slit. And we had to get them out of there. So we charged them.

We had flamethrowers. I hated those things. You got close to a pillbox and opened up with a flamethrower. You squirted the flames and you hit the slit, and that would finish it off. I don't care who the man is, if he's an enemy or what he is, to see him come out of that pillbox, just one big flame, screaming his head off and running like mad—it's horrible.

We had three men go up to a pillbox, and all three were hit. One was killed and the other two were wounded. So like a dumb idiot, I said, "I'll go up and get the flamethrower and see if I can finish it off," which I did. The man came running out the back, all aflame. That's no way to die.

We lost the first of our group of four buddies at Mapia Island—damn island. It was so small, but there was a Japanese radio station there, and they were guiding their bombers, so we had to wipe them out. And we did.

Hollis proudly displays a captured Japanese flag.

The one that sticks with me happened on Mindanao. It was like a small mountain, but it was rough terrain. We couldn't seem to get the Japs off the top of it. So we radioed back for the planes to come over and drop firebombs on them. We told them we'd drop mortar shells—smoke shells—on them so they'd have something to line up on. But the Japanese were smart, too. They dropped smoke shells on us. So the first planes that came through saw the smoke and let the bombs go. They hit *us*—didn't hit the Japanese.

Somebody said, "There's a guy up there who's badly burned." I went up there, and I thought, "Who is it? I don't recognize him." I mean he was burned everywhere. I asked the two medics there, and they couldn't even touch him. He'd scream his head off.

So I said, "Who is this?" My friend spoke right up, and he said, "It's Smitty. Is that you, Hollis?" He was so badly burnt that the medics said, "He should be dead now. He shouldn't be talking." And when he said, "Is that you, Hollis?" I said yes, and he said, "Would you put a bullet in my head? I can't take it any longer."

To get back to an aid station would have been at least two or three miles over rough terrain, and you couldn't even touch him. You could reach down and take part of his jacket and you'd take flesh with it. His face—it was black and burned and his teeth were all sticking out. So I knew he wouldn't make it. I felt terrible. I didn't know what to do. But then I thought, if it was me, I would want the same thing, and he would do it for me. So I did as he asked me.

Here's another part. He was the type of friend that never said thank you. But he'd come up to you and take you by the shoulder and kind of nod his head. And after he died, I felt a pressure on my shoulder. And I said, "Okay, I got the message."

From there we had to march about thirty miles toward Davao, and they said we could rest after that. It was during the rainy season, so there was mud up almost to your knees in parts of the road. So we got up there, and it's raining like mad, and they say, okay, you can take it easy for a while. I put my poncho around me and I must have been asleep before I hit the ground.

It wasn't five minutes later that they come around kicking you and saying, "Get up! The Japs have broken through the line." My feet had blisters on 'em big as a half-dollar. But when the bullets started singing around your ears, you forgot your feet.

We were dug in, more or less, maybe a hundred feet from the Japanese when they moved in. Somebody shouted down the line, "The war is over!" You know what a reception that guy got. We're in battle and he's yelling that the war is over. But it was true—it was over—our guys were getting killed, probably after the war was over.

I shot maybe three men that day. When you shoot a man, you don't think too much about it because you're protecting yourself— he's shooting at you, too. Long after, I always said, why in hell do grown men have to kill each other—for nothing, really? If there were two men left on Earth, they'd be fighting each other.

Early the next morning—it must have been August 15—here came the Japanese with a white flag. Some of the guys were ready to shoot 'em down regardless of the white flag, but no, we let 'em in.

We were slated for the invasion of Japan, so when it sunk in that the war was over, our thought was we don't have to make that damn invasion.

We stayed just outside of Davao on Mindanao for probably two months, and then we got a boat home. We got off in San Francisco, and they shipped us right to Sacramento. They had a huge mess hall there. You could walk in and order anything you wanted. I asked one of the cooks what the men wanted most, and he said, "Milk!"

Over the years I've thought about the war a lot. I am proud of what I was—a soldier—but there is no glamour or glory in war. We were just kids in 1941, just out of high school, and suddenly we became men. It's too bad so many of us had to end their lives that way. They hadn't even begun life.

George Hollis worked a variety of jobs after the war. For many years he was a sign-maker and commercial artist. He still works, as a driver for the Concord School District. He is eighty-six years old and lives in Concord.

Gerry Smith was knocked unconscious when the German fighters struck.

Gerry Smith

In Enemy Hands

Gerry Smith wanted to finish his sophomore year at the University of New Hampshire, but the Army Air Corps had other plans. Smith, a member of the school's ROTC program, was ordered into pilot's training in the spring of 1943. By the following summer, he was a second lieutenant with the 12th Air Force in Sardinia, Italy. A co-pilot, he volunteered for as many missions as he could in hopes of fulfilling his quota and returning to school. It was only a matter of time before Smith's eagerness led to trouble.

W e were flying B-26s, the Martin Marauder. Two engines, Pratt and Whitney. The normal crew was six. Range was about five hundred miles. When I first got there in August, we were flying all our missions into southern France, getting prepared for a beach invasion, which happened on August 15, 1944. After the invasion, we did a few support missions and then turned our attention to the mainland in Italy. In late September we moved from Sardinia to Corsica to get closer to our targets.

I was on either my twenty-sixth or twenty-seventh mission when we were shot down. The night before the mission, the whole crew was on orders to go to rest camp in Rome. The CO (commanding officer) came in and said, "I can't ask you to fly, because you're on orders, but we need one more crew for tomorrow and it's supposed

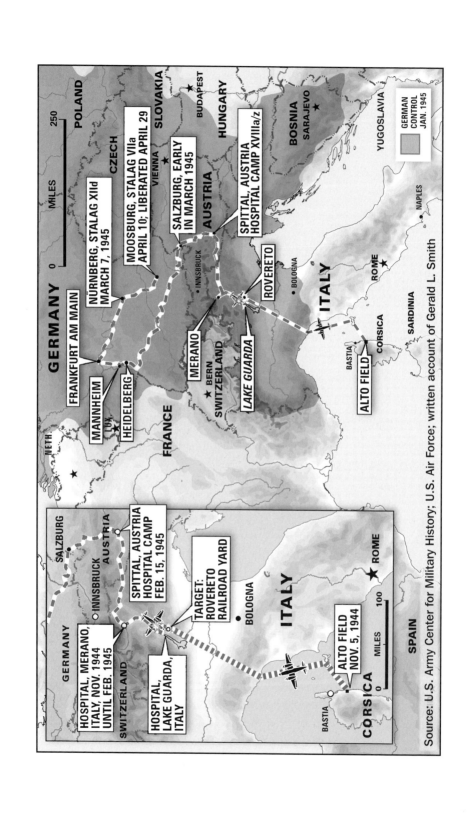

Source:: U.S. Army Center for Military History; U.S. Air Force; written account of Gerald L. Smith

to be a milk run." I said I'd just as soon fly. It would get us one mission closer to home. The pilot agreed. Didn't think anything of it. We'd be home in time to go to rest camp.

On the way to the target, we were picked up by an enemy fighter. We knew we were in trouble because we couldn't see our fighter cover. They were dive-bombing targets of opportunity down by Bologna. By the time they got up to us, we had been jumped by twelve to fifteen German fighters. It felt like thirty.

There were eighteen of us. One plane was shot down on the way in to the target. We dropped our bombs and got hit by a 20-millimeter cannon from a Messerschmidt-109. It shot out the pedestal between the pilot and the co-pilot. The co-pilot always rode with his hand on the pedestal, on the gas control mixtures, so if an engine got hit, you could cut the gas. The shrapnel hit me right in the wrist, just took everything out right down to the bone. The concussion of it knocked me unconscious. The bombardier slapped my face and brought me to. He got me down through the emergency hatch. He had to jump on my chute to get me through.

The pilot, the co-pilot, the bombardier, and the radioman all got out. The tailgunner and the engineer didn't make it. They were sitting in the waist window, so we don't understand why.

On the way down, it's a newsreel of your life. You hear people say it and it's true. I thought nobody could lose as much blood as I had and still be alive, so I must be dead. When I got a little more rational, I realized my flight suit was coated in hydraulic fluid, which is red. It looked like blood in my semiconscious state, I guess.

I landed almost in the center of a German antiaircraft outfit. They formed a circle around me and protected me from civilians. A lot of people have said the civilians wouldn't have hurt me, but would you want to write an insurance policy for someone who got shot down in Durham after he bombed Portsmouth? I don't think so.

They put me on a truck. A wood-burning truck, by the way. They took me to a military hospital at the edge of Lake Garda. They had me on the operating table within a half-hour of the time I landed. They cleaned up my arm and put me in a butterfly cast.

The target that day had been Rovereto, a railroad yard. We did a reasonably good job on it. That night the Germans were going to ship us out, but when we got to the railroad yard, the time-delayed bombs were still going off, so they brought us back. The first day we had good cloud cover, they sent us up to Merano. The city had a hundred hotels. All but one was a hospital.

I stayed there from roughly November 10 to February 15. Except for one pilot from Hartford, Connecticut, I was the only American there. I saw him for just a few minutes down in the toilet area. At night we had Catholic sisters taking care of us. They came in one night and told me to be in the toilets at a certain time in the morning and they'd have this other American down there so we could visit. We probably visited for ten or fifteen minutes before the Germans found us. They weren't happy.

We left Morano for Spittal, Austria, where there was a prison hospital run by the British. I was there maybe three weeks. The doctor was a POW. The dentist was a POW. I was in a room with British subjects taken at the first battle of El Alamein, in 1942. They were experienced prisoners and they taught me a lot. They had illegal water heaters. They're simple: two pieces of metal separated by a wooden slat and a metal can with water in it. They'd put the least little bit of salt in the water. Plug that in and it will heat up in no time. Of course, it does quite a job on the current. You get all the British heating water at the same time, the lights would go down. The Germans knew what was going on, but they couldn't find the heaters.

The Brits had a signal. As soon as the guards left the guard house, everybody in camp knew they were coming for an inspection. It gave everybody time to hide stuff. There was a loose board. We took it out, put the things underneath, and slid it back. Within fifteen minutes after the guards left, we were drinking tea.

They had a black market. You saved your cigarettes from the Red Cross parcels and traded them for black bread or other foodstuffs. They knew how to sabotage if they were out on work details. Sugar was scarce, but urine wasn't. And if you put urine in a gas tank, it serves the same purpose as sugar. Sometime down the road, the engine is going to freeze up.

When my arm had healed enough and there was no danger of an infection, they planned to send me to a camp outside of Frankfurt. They sent three German guards and four of us: two South Africans and two Americans. I was the highest-ranking person, so I was responsible. The German under-officer always communicated with me for any command.

We walked. We went by oxcart. We went by boat. We went by truck. We went by train. We went any way we could to get up there. Things were pretty well shot up. We eventually got up to Frankfurt, and they put us in the railroad station all day. That didn't make me happy because I knew what the American bombers could do. Around 3 p.m., the under-officer said the Americans were supposedly four days out, so we had to go back to Nuremberg.

We left on an early train the next morning. We'd been out maybe twenty minutes and I looked up and saw some P-47s overhead. I told the under-officer they were going to strafe the train. I'd seen those machine guns pointed the other way, and I didn't want to see them pointed at me. He wasn't going to let us off the train, but finally I told our boys to just leave. The German guards followed us, thank goodness. Fortunately, there was a ditch that all our fellows got into. You could see the P-47 pilot's face as he was strafing the train.

We got on another train and went probably half, three-quarters of an hour and realized that one was going to be strafed, too. We went out through the window. I still don't know how we got out. They destroyed that train. The under-officer came up to me and said, "Schmitty, we walk from now on. At night."

We were looking for a railroad tunnel to get in for protection and we were strafed by another plane. He was after a riverboat and we were walking along the river. You could see the bullets coming up the black-top road. As soon as we found a tunnel, we stayed in it during the day and just moved at night.

We came to a small town. The under-officer's family was there and he wanted to know if we'd object to staying two or three days. We said no. Anything was better than prison camp. They put us up with a farm family. He asked if we'd try to escape. I said no, we won't. My reasoning was there was safety in numbers. And we could see from being behind the lines that things were coming to an end sooner or later, hopefully sooner. As soon as the guards left, the family brought out jellies, bread, meat, potatoes. But when the guards were around, there was no food. They were playing the game.

For Smith, the Statue of Liberty was a welcome sight.

We went through Wuerzburg, which had been firebombed by the British. The ruins were still so hot you couldn't get too close to the foundations. It was devastated.

We got to Nuremberg. The first day we were there, I was going through the tents looking for someplace to make a bed and I heard my name. It was a fellow who was in training with me. Stood right beside me at Barksdale Field. His name was C.J. Smith. I'm G.L. Smith. I said, "Can I join your group?" The answer was yes.

We were in combines. You always worked through the group. One person from the combine collected rations. He got the provisions and he divided them five, six, seven ways. He always got the last portion so that it was fair. I stayed with him, and he gave me a wool sweater that I wore for years.

Every night they had radios that could listen to the BBC. You have a part, I have a part, he has a part. We meet at a certain time at a certain place and put the radio together. Somebody takes shorthand and takes the news down. The radio comes apart. Everybody disappears, so if they have a shakedown no one has a radio. Then other people would take the shorthand and transcribe it onto paper. Then other people would make copies so each barracks or tent would have a copy, so if the Germans heard you reading the news and took yours, others could fill in.

I was interrogated in Nuremberg in late March. They took my military watch away from me. They gave me a receipt for it so I could turn it in and prove they'd taken it and I hadn't sold it. Even in the chaos of war, they would write you a receipt for a watch. The interrogator asked me about the flight. I told him I'd been so sick I didn't remember anything. Then he went and got a folder and read me everything about the flight. The headings, the speed, the mission. They just asked what altitudes we flew at, what airspeed, what we were carrying for bombs.

On Easter Sunday, the first of April that year, they told us to be ready to leave on fifteen minutes' notice. We left around noon and I understand it took them two days to empty the prison camp. We were moving away from the American front and toward the Russian front.

That afternoon we saw a lot of flatbed railroad cars with jet engines on them. It took us a while to figure out what they were, but we had seen the ME-262 a lot. That was the first German jet.

The next day out, the big boys bombed Nuremberg. You know the ripple effect you see of a stone in the water? We saw the vapor trails and it looked just like that going out. Like waves in a pond.

A ten-day march put us down to Moosburg, and we stayed there until we were liberated. Food was always scarce, wood fuel to cook with, always scarce. I was shot down weighing a hundred and eighty pounds, and when I left the hospital in Merano I weighed a hundred and twenty.

We made fun of the soups we got. Green death. It looked like alfalfa cooked up. We used to have a little game to see who was going to get the most cockroaches. We ate them. If you're hungry enough, you eat most anything. The people who didn't make it were the ones who gave up.

We were liberated by Patton's Third Army on April 29, 1945, but I wasn't back in military control until May 5. Believe it or not, that was the leanest period there was. The Germans wouldn't feed us because they weren't there. The Americans couldn't feed us because they had extended their line so far. I think the whole prison population in that camp was forty thousand. We had hoarded some food. You heard the nightly news, so you knew what was going on. They wanted you to stay within the compounds after you were liberated. A lot of them didn't. Some of them went out on stealing sprees. I couldn't condemn them for it, but I wouldn't do it myself.

They took us to a field hospital just outside Landshut and put us on strict rations. If you ate too much, you'd be sick. It wasn't until we'd been in the hospital about a week that they'd finally let us eat what we wanted.

They had picked up a lot of the internees at Dachau—political prisoners, mostly French people. They were so far gone nutritionally that they couldn't even tolerate IVs. That first night in the field hospital, out of maybe sixteen or eighteen in our tent, we must have lost at least six or seven of them.

We flew out to Paris. The most seriously injured went home first. We left on May 30, 1945, and landed on Long Island the next day. The pilot was good. He said, "Don't get out of your seats. I will fly twice around the Statue of Liberty so that you all can see it." There wasn't a dry eye on the plane.

I never got into the Red Cross chain, so my family didn't know I was alive until they got a V-Mail letter from me. In fact, I got a letter to them quicker than the military could. They just had so many people repatriated. When we got into the hospital in Long Island, the first thing they made us do was call home.

Gerry Smith remained in the Army until 1947, spending most of his time at Cushing General Hospital in Framingham, Massachusetts. He underwent about a dozen surgeries on his injured arm. While recovering from one operation, Smith met an Army nurse cadet who eventually became his wife. He taught animal science and agriculture at the University of New Hampshire for many years. In 1979, he returned to Europe to retrace his route. Only then did he begin to talk about the one hundred and eighty-one days he spent as a POW.

*Mary McDonnell worked with mental
patients and German POW's.*

Mary McDonnell &
Edith Drake Beaurivage

Classmates

By 1943, Concord's three nursing schools had sent dozens of young women off to war. An undated newspaper story from the time mentions ninety service stars awarded at the city's three nursing schools: thirty-nine from the state hospital, thirty-one from Margaret Pillsbury, and twenty from Memorial Hospital. Among the nurses were Edith (Drake) Beaurivage, and Mary McDonnell, classmates at Memorial.

McDonnell joined the Army because it was the only branch that accepted married women. She was sent to Europe. Beaurivage, a member of the Air Corps, spent the war on an air evacuation crew taking wounded soldiers home from the Pacific.

Mary McDonnell

"IT WAS ALL TENTS AND IT WAS ALL MUD"

Mary McDonnell, who is eighty-eight years old, joined the Army in the spring of 1944. Her unit arrived in Normandy a few months after D-Day and spent the cold, damp winter tending to wounded troops, many from the Battle of the Bulge. Her patients included German

POWs. She remembers one prisoner in particular, a large boy named Draga who spoke fluent English.

We went into Fort Devens, twenty-seven of us inducted at the same time. They drilled us. They taught us about saluting. We had to hike, and we had to set up a pup tent. Mine collapsed. It was the first and last time I ever saw a pup tent.

We were going to go to the Pacific, but after D-Day the orders were changed. When the guy came to get our footlockers, I asked him what kind of a boat are we going on. He said, "The Queen Mary." I said, "Aw, get out of here." Well, we went up this big stairway, and there was a large oil painting of the Queen Mary.

It was a five-day trip and it was the most beautiful weather. There was no convoy with us. We were all alone. If you looked back, you could see the ship, about every three minutes, change its course. It was so the enemy couldn't get us in their sights long enough. Later, we got on an English ship and sailed across to Normandy.

Because we thought we were going to the Pacific, we had all summer clothing. It was getting cold, and it rained constantly. I had boots like galoshes. We didn't have any combat boots. I wrote to my mother and said: Please send me some long underwear.

It was all tents and it was all mud. There were six of us in the tent, and there was a potbelly stove. We got one helmet full of coal every twenty-four hours to keep the stove going. The tents for the patients had three potbelly stoves to keep them warm. We had a cot, but we slept in a sleeping bag and two army blankets. When you went in the truck, you took one of those blankets with you to wrap around you.

At night when you went down to the club, there was nothing to do. They'd give you a big handful of letters and you had to censor them. I got so tired of reading, I just looked for capital letters, and if it was the name of a town, I just crossed it out.

For a while in Normandy, I think it was five days, we got Brussels sprouts. I've never eaten another one. I never drank coffee until I went overseas. Once in a while they'd have a can of condensed milk. I only weighed ninety-eight pounds. And it rained. But going off duty, I used to whistle and swing my helmet. One of the other girls

Mary McDonnell cared for wounded soldiers, many from the Battle of the Bulge, at a tent hospital in Normandy. She later traveled inland, finishing the war in Germany.

Source: U.S. Army Center for Military History

said to me, "How can you be so happy?" I said, "We're here, we've got to make the most of it. What are you going to do?"

The ward held forty-five. On night duty, you had six wards. The Battle of the Bulge, that's where the patients came from. Those trucks kept going up night and day. I had GIs when we first got there. I had one fellow who had part of his leg off, a lot with shrapnel in their backs. I had one Russian. I don't know where he came from. They would have an envelope pinned to them that would tell who they were and what should be done. I took the dressing off his head and I could see his brain beating.

I lost only one patient. He came in and he had to go to the O.R.

McDonnell was an indifferent censor of soldiers' letters.

I took all the stuff out of his pockets. One of my tent-mates, she was in the O.R. She told me he'd died. He was from the Midwest. I brought all his stuff to the post office. He had the other half of a roundtrip ticket for home.

All of a sudden, they cleared out the GIs, and I had mental patients. They were depressed, couldn't talk. One of the boys had his leg off. He was very depressed. He said, "I don't know what's going to happen, Lieutenant, when I go home. I'm newly married, and my wife loved to dance." I said, "She didn't marry you because you danced."

The GIs, after they were discharged, they'd send things. I told one I'd like a German flag. A month after he left, I got a package with a letter in it and this German flag.

Then I got German POWs. They all came in and the Red Cross was waiting, writing up serial numbers. We got along very well. They liked to talk about what they knew about America. Some of them had read all about the girls on the beach in Miami and said they would like to go there. Then Draga said some of them would like to go to the King Ranch in Texas. They knew how big it was, how many head of cattle.

Day and night, the trucks were going for the Battle of the Bulge. There was a dirt road going out to the main road, and the Germans were out there in "USA" maroon corduroy bathrobes, waving to all the Americans going out. The guys are waving back and giving them the "V" for victory. They didn't even know they were Germans. Back in the tent, Draga said to me, "You know, Left-tenant, we've been there and we know what it is and we feel sorry for them. We're safe here now, but we wish them luck."

One morning there was a little tiny Christmas tree in my ward that the POWs had found. I said: "Draga, I'm not going to ask you where you got it." I took all my Life Savers and put them on a string and decorated it. At Christmas, we went down to a school. The children sang for us. They were orphaned. It was Christmastime and they didn't have a stocking on their feet. We had a lot of them come for Christmas dinner. Christmas Eve, the Germans started to sing "Silent Night." And then the Americans joined in. The Germans sang in German. The Americans sang in English. Beautiful.

You had to be adaptable. You didn't have any running water in the wards. I remember trying to make a breast binder to keep the dressing on a soldier's back. He was open on both sides. I had towels and then I used bandages for the straps. You had to mix penicillin. You'd put it in, shake it, and that bottle was ready to use.

I got transferred to Paris to start a new unit. Then we went into a town called Mourmelon, which was outside of Reims. That was permanent. That was real nice, instead of tents. We were there until '45, right after the Germans surrendered. I had signed up to go to the Pacific. Then the Japs surrendered. They flew a small outfit of nurses into Germany to start a small hospital for the army of occupation. We flew around the Alps. We couldn't fly over because they were neutral.

I was there until after Christmas 1945. One of the new girls who came over was a little Irishwoman from New York. She used to go to Frankfurt to visit a nurse friend up there. She was coming back and she got killed in a truck crash. I have her second lieutenant bar, brand new.

Mary McDonnell returned home in 1946. She raised a family in Concord and worked at New Hampshire Hospital.

Edith Drake Beaurivage

"YOU FELT THE SORROW OF IT"

When Edith Drake Beaurivage left Pembroke Academy, she had two goals: become a nurse and emulate her childhood hero, Amelia Earhart. World War II gave her the chance to do both. In 1943, she enlisted in the Army and put in a request for flight school.

I had no reason not to go. I felt needed. When I went in, I was an Army nurse. Then the Air Force bloomed out. I went to Mountain Home, Idaho, to the air base where they trained crews for the B-24 flights. Periodically we had a plane crash. When they brought those crews in, we were everything to those boys. You were their mother, you were their sister. You couldn't do enough.

Edith Drake Beaurivage brought wounded men back from the Pacific.

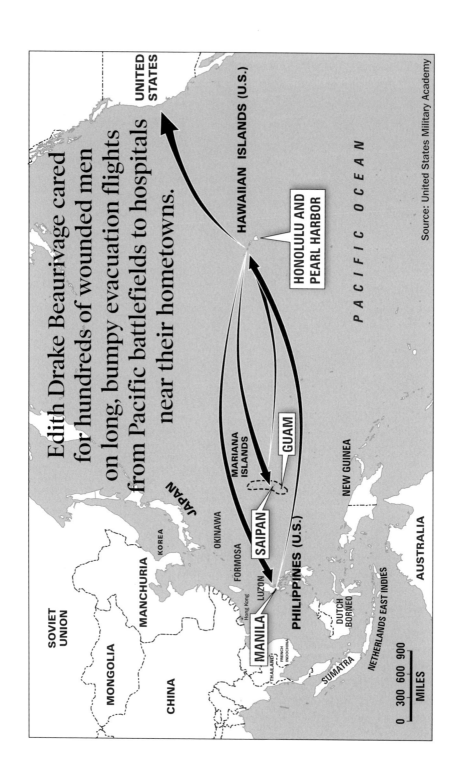

Edith Drake Beaurivage cared for hundreds of wounded men on long, bumpy evacuation flights from Pacific battlefields to hospitals near their hometowns.

Source: United States Military Academy

I met a pilot in Idaho. He was lost when they sent him over to Europe in the raids. His co-pilot wrote to tell me. Heck of a nice guy. He was from Kansas. Another one of my heartthrobs died in the European Theater, too. He was a pilot. One of his crew wrote to tell me. You just accepted it. At least you knew whether or not they were coming back. You felt the sorrow of it. It was part of life like it was then.

They knew when they left what their chances were, but they lived every minute until it happened. That's why we had such good times. At the officers' club at the base every Saturday night they had a dance, and they brought in some of the big bands. We lived for that. They lived for it. When we danced and shared time together, we were on top of the world, trying to forget.

Because I wanted to be a flight nurse, I went to Bowman Field in Kentucky. They made us jump off a fifty-foot tower, feet first! That was part of the training, so if you had to abandon ship you knew to go feet first. They made us go under the barbed wire on our bellies under gunfire. We had to do practically the same thing as the men.

We got more flight training at Randolph Field, Texas. When I left, I was one of fifty that went as replacements for the nurses who were over there. They loaded us on a train. We had no idea where we were going. We went to Seattle. They put us on a ship. We were on the ship for six days. We wound up in Honolulu, on V-J Day. Everybody was celebrating. We didn't know what it was all about, of course, being aboard ship. Nobody had told us the war was over.

I flew patients back to the States. We went to Manila, we went to Saipan. We were flying in B-29s. We carried fifty patients a load. These were all boys on stretchers. Some didn't even know they were going home. If we were lucky, we had two corpsmen to assist us. We had long flights back with these sick boys, eight to twelve hours. Rough. We had hardly anything to work with and just box lunches. But we had medication. We did our best for them.

They had been in battle and they were boys coming back to general hospitals for further care. When our boys came back to the States, they unloaded the planes and tried to transfer them close to home. They depended so much on us. They just had tears in their eyes. They didn't have any therapy or anything yet to help them.

Beauvirage celebrated V-J Day in Honolulu.

Some of them knew they were going home, they knew we were there to take care of them. But some of them—we had at least six that had to remain strapped because they were psycho patients. These boys really needed help. They didn't know where or who they were.

After about six months, I got sick. Exposure. The stress and strain. Some of the places we stopped, we slept on cots. It was so damp. It was just one of those of things. When I took sick, I was supposed to take off on another overseas flight to bring back another load. I knew I couldn't do it, I had such pain. They didn't know what it was. It was some form of rheumatic condition. I was run down, really run down.

Edith Drake Beaurivage spent five months in a Florida hospital before resigning her commission. She traveled the United States, working as a civilian nurse, before returning to New England. She later married and had two children. She lives in Penacook, New Hampshire, with her daughter.

Nothing prepared Warren E. Priest for Buchenwald.

Warren E. Priest

A Complete Surprise

Warren E. Priest was born in Plaistow, New Hampshire, and grew up in Haverhill, Massachusetts. He was a twenty-year-old student at Boston University when he was drafted in December 1942. An orthopedic surgical technician trained mainly to assist in amputations, he served in the 120th Evacuation Hospital. The unit followed General George Patton's Third Army into Germany and entered the Buchenwald concentration camp in April 1945, just weeks before the war in Europe ended.

Our unit consisted of two hundred and seventy-three service personnel—truck drivers, cooks, medical technicians, specialists, surgical units. The nurses and the doctors were generally older and much more distant, with bars rather than stripes. By then, I was a technical sergeant.

We were absolutely not prepared for Buchenwald. We had no concept of it. It was a complete surprise that the Nazis had done such a thing. No one had any idea whatsoever of the life within the camps. We were told: You're going into a camp and it's a special assignment, and it's going to be a good challenge to you and your skills. We'll be going in tomorrow.

We were in Weimar, about six or seven miles from Ettersburg, where Buchenwald was. They took us by motor vehicle and housed

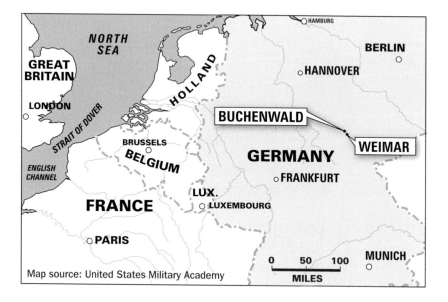

Map source: United States Military Academy

us in Schloss Ettersburg—the castle. We left this lovely summer home and walked up a pathway through the woods. It was spring, and the leaves were just emerging. We saw all the loveliness and color of the season.

We smelled Buchenwald long before we saw it. That whole area was overwhelmingly and intrusively affected by the odor of death in the camp. You couldn't escape it.

Reaching near the top, I suddenly encountered human forms. We had been trained not to fraternize, so I didn't say anything. I held my carbine. They moved to the side of the pathway and got down on their knees and put their hands together prayerfully and looked up and smiled. It was one of those moments when expression was all nonverbal.

Buchenwald was a work camp, not a death camp, although plenty had been killed or died of disease and malnutrition there. Close by was a Karl Zeiss factory, where prisoners worked. They specialized in the assembly of optical instruments—binoculars and cameras. We got quite a few of the things we needed from a supply train that the American troops had captured. We stole, if you will, things from the factory. I had two or three pairs of binoculars and a 35-millimeter camera.

Inside the gates of Buchenwald, there had been a complete abandonment of any effort to maintain basic human living conditions. I took maybe thirty or forty pictures. I was no photographer—I was shooting impulsively—seeing something and deciding whether to shoot.

When I went into the crematorium, there were the ovens, with half-burned bodies in there, and I took pictures of them. I took pictures of the pile of human ashes outside the crematorium. I also took pictures of the piles of bodies stacked outside the barracks because they didn't have the personnel to carry them away. In one pile, I counted eighty bodies—so thin, upper arms you could put your thumb and index finger around.

Mainly we brought hope where there was no hope. Suddenly there was the will to live in some prisoners. I was struck by how little we did with the training they had spent so much time giving us. What we encountered was so different from what we were prepared for. It was all recovery type of medical treatment. For example, the best treatment for dysentery and starvation was whole blood. We all gave blood as much as we could.

Once, I had the assignment to try to separate the living from the dead bodies lined up on the floor in a barracks. There were maybe two or three dozen of them. I had a stethoscope on, and I went down the line of litters listening for heartbeats. I indicated to the litter bearers that the ones without heartbeats should be carried to the morgue. And those with heartbeats we took to try to restore life to them.

Having finished the job, I went downstairs. There were several litters in a row, and I walked by one, and I felt someone grab my leg. It was one I had assumed was dead. I had been unable to pick up a heartbeat. It was startling. I thought, "My God, have I missed some others?"

I met a man who spoke broken English, a minister of bridges and highways in Belgium, a political prisoner. He had found a model boat, and he gave it to me. On the face, it said Santa Maria. On the back was a painting of the virgin and the baby Jesus. There were crosses on the sails. The man who gave it to me said the sails were made of human skin.

While treating Dachau survivors, Priest contracted typhus.

That men could treat men as they did—that men would die for want of food, care, that children would be born in the camp, probably nameless, without identity—it was beyond human comprehension. And it wasn't just Jews. There were Seventh-Day Adventists, homosexuals, political prisoners, people of many nationalities.

After two weeks, we went to Cham to set up a hospital for survivors of Dachau. I had participated in one amputation—a leg—before I got sick. It was typhus. I was treated in the same building, above where the surgery was taking place. If it weren't for sulfa drugs, I wouldn't be here today.

In late May, within two weeks of the end of the war, we were packed up and heading to Frankfurt, and then on to Le Havre for a trip back to this country. We thought we were going to be sent to Japan, but it didn't work out that way.

After the war, Warren Priest returned to his education and became a teacher in Newton, Massachusetts. He retired in 1984. He started a camp for inner-city children and the Center for Affective Learning on Mirror Lake in Woodstock, New Hampshire, where he now lives. He donated the sailboat he was given at Buchenwald to the U.S. Holocaust Museum. Priest uses the website buchenwaldandbeyond.com as a basis for Holocaust lectures in New England schools and colleges.

One of Enoch Perkins's adventures began in Manchester.

Enoch Perkins

O Christmas Tree

In the final weeks of 1944, First Lieutenant Enoch Perkins took command of a new B-17 bomber. Along with his crew, Perkins flew from Lincoln, Nebraska, to Prestwick, Scotland, passing through Grenier Field in Manchester. He remained in New Hampshire for several days while his co-pilot recovered from an ear infection. During the layover, Perkins and a few Red Cross volunteers made sure the crew would experience a little Christmas cheer. Perkins, who died in 2006, kept a journal of his trip and thirty combat missions. Here is an excerpt:

December 16, 1944: Grenier is a pleasant spot, nestled on a hill-side, studded with trees, snow covered. The PX is well-stocked with cigarettes, which is a find these days. The food is fine but expensive. We have run into censorship for the first time here. Officers must sign envelopes in the lower left-hand corner to testify that the letter contains no censorable material. I certainly welcomed the opportunity to stop here and rest before going on. This is our last stopping point before leaving the United States. I wonder how long it will be before we return.

December 17: Of the entire year, probably the worst time to take a crew overseas is Christmastime. These boys have never been away from home much, not to mention leaving the country for combat, and since Christmas is usually a time when family spirit is at its highest, I have felt all along that Christmas Day would find the boys pretty low and lonely. Mother has bought a few little presents for each man on the crew and has wrapped them in bright Christmas wrappings. Just these little packages, though, didn't seem to be all we could do.

This morning, I thought possibly the Red Cross here might get us a little tree. (Navigator William "Bud") Curl and I went down to the canteen and asked what they could do. I think there were five women there, and they all started talking at once. "You can get a nice little tree at the west-side gas station." "You can have some of my ornaments." "What about popcorn?" Suggestions flew like mad.

Finally, one little French lady was dispatched to get the various things they had decided absolutely essential to a Christmas tree. Curl and I went to the PX and bought each man a carton of cigarettes, except (radioman Guy) Shank. Since he doesn't smoke, we got him a scarf. In addition, we bought some candy to scatter around the tree.

By the time we were back to the Red Cross, the little French lady was back with a lovely little tree and a complete set of ornaments. They wrapped up the scarf and the cigarettes for us, and helped us pack the tree. Curl and I then took the stuff out to the ship and hid it as best we could in the tail of the plane.

The kindness of those women, I will always remember. They left no stone unturned. No effort was too great to help us make Christmas Day a little less drab.

December 20 (en route from Grenier Field to Goose Bay, Labrador): At 12:58 we crossed the Canadian border. I called it to the crew's attention and they promptly sounded off with the Star Spangled Banner, jokingly at first but after a few strains there was a sincere tone in their voices, although I doubt if any would ever admit it. I found myself looking back for several moments, wondering when I shall see home again. . . .

The Christmas spirit seems to be most everywhere today. As I made my position reports to the various control stations along the route, the operators have been wishing me a Merry Christmas, good luck and whatnot. I, of course, have answered with "Happy New Year, and thanks." Oh, it's been very jolly. . . .

It is here one finds the real thrill of flying over remote beautiful, challenging country to distant, strange places. This is adventure. What lies ahead might not be, but for me this is adventure. . . .

December 24 (from Goose Bay to Greenland): I'll have to start with yesterday for the full report of events. (Co-pilot George) Pringle, Curl and I had decided that we couldn't possibly get off before Christmas. Consequently, displaying our usual eagerness, we decided to get set for the Christmas party for Christmas Eve.

Commandeering a flight bus, we got the tree, ornaments and presents from the plane. I had the base carpenter make a stand for the tree and then set about to decorate it and arrange the presents. After some three hours, we had succeeded in threading the popcorn into very pretty little strings. Being the cheese-colored popcorn added pleasant yellow to it which contrasted with the red strings we had. Patiently and industriously, we put on the decorations, until finally we had one of the prettiest trees I've ever seen.

I had gone to the usual 8:30 p.m. briefing at which time they told us they might try to send out 20 ships or so to Greenland. I felt almost certain that we wouldn't go, being as we were so far down the list.

Going on with our Christmas plans, I made arrangements for the mess sergeant to have a nice cake made for the party. We also intended to have some hot cocoa, and Pringle had saved half a pint of Jim Beam, which would be enough for each man to have a highball. Our plans were complete and we rightfully expected a fine little party.

The natural thing then occurred. We went to the movies and then for a late snack before going to bed. The public address system announced the departure list and Pringle decided to check it. It's a fortunate thing he did, for we were on the list.

We darted over to our barracks. . . . Curl and I began to dismantle the tree. In an hour we had everything packed away and Pringle took everything out to the ship. Curl, Shank and I reported for the briefing. . . .

Our destination is BW-1, a field in southwestern Greenland, famous for its close-walled fjord through which we must pass to get to the field. Mountains rising abruptly to 4,700 feet from the

In the end, Perkins himself got a Christmas surprise.

water's edge narrowly hem in a plane approaching the field. The runway runs directly into a 5,000-foot glacier. All in all, I don't call it a pilot's dream airport. . . . After a successful landing (thank God) we were parked and brought to operations, where the usual codes, forms, logs and clearances were turned in. Two hours later, after being assigned to our barracks, dismal wooden, outside plumbing shacks with lumpy mattresses and scratchy linen, and a lukewarm meal, we were given a route briefing to Meeks, Iceland.

BW-1 is a dismal outpost. The men here are frustrated souls, some of them having been here close to two years in this wasteland.

December 25: Christmas Day began at 0500 GMT when I was awakened for briefing. . . . At first, it looked as if we were going to get off with no trouble, but the props became cantankerous and, as I thought of that canyon-like fjord I had to take off into, I decided it would be best to wait until another day and have them checked. Thus, we spent Christmas 1944 at BW-1 Greenland.

Christmas dinner in the GI mess hall was sheer luxury in this remote spot: turkey, corn (fresh), peas (fresh), mashed potatoes, giblet gravy, cranberry jelly, fresh strawberries and ice cream, milk, olives, nuts, candy fruit and fruit cake. Pringle, Curl and I had dinner with the enlisted men and all of us fairly gorged ourselves to such an extent that we spent the rest of the afternoon sleeping.

Shortly before dinner, Pringle and I had begun preparations for the Christmas party. . . . We set up the tree in the little bay that connects the two bays of our barracks. A dirty sheet from one of the used beds covered the base and our ornaments were again carefully displayed on the tree. Again, Pringle laid out the presents and I got a fruitcake from the mess hall.

Greenland has not seen many Christmas preparations more ambitiously made or trees more attractively decorated. A strange Christmas that brings the tree, ornaments and presents from 2,000 miles away.

We told the enlisted men to be over at 10:00 for the big event. Without hesitation, I can say our party was a big success. The boys sat and looked at the tree for a full 30 minutes before even opening their presents.

Most surprised of all were Curl, Pringle and I when we found presents for ourselves under the tree. (Engineer Howard) Cochran had sneaked them under without our seeing. Curl and Pringle got a carton of cigarettes, and I got a carton of cigars, and good ones too, which is a real rarity these days.

The boys were tickled to death with their presents and fondled them as they do all new things. After opening our presents we cut the cake and had one drink of Royal Crown whiskey. I tried to think of a toast but, failing, passed the buck to Curl, who likewise thought in vain.

We raised our cups in a silent toast and drank. Somehow, I think our hopes were about the same. I think we all, in our silent toast, hoped next Christmas would find us home again.

Enoch Perkins and his men arrived in Scotland on January 3. The crew completed thirty combat missions before mid-April, with Perkins writing about them all. Fifty years after his tour, Perkins typed up his journal, dedicating it to "the grandchildren we fought to save." His daughter, Edith Perkins of Bow, New Hampshire, shared it with the Monitor.

Like many others, Dick Violette detested flamethrowers.

Dick Violette

In the Rice Bowl

Dick Violette is ninety-one years old and lives in Warner, New Hampshire.
During the Depression, he was a senior leader at the Civilian Conservation
Corps camp on Tory Hill in Warner, helping to build the Mount Kearsarge
road and Wadleigh Park in North Sutton. The Cagayan Valley, where
he fought as an infantryman, was the rice bowl of the Philippines.
Remnants of the largest Japanese force in the islands remained there in
1945 under General Tomoyuki Yamashita, known as the Tiger of Malaya.
After the war, Yamashita was hanged for the massacre of a hundred
thousand Filipinos during the Japanese withdrawal from Manila.

Not long before Pearl Harbor, I went to a dinner party at a hotel in Hartford, Connecticut. There was a Japanese officer there, a naval merchant marine in uniform. At the time I was working in the seventh-floor warehouse of a furniture store, and looking down on the river I had noticed these big Japanese freighters down there. I got talking to this fellow, and I said, "What are you doing down there?" He said, "Oh, we buy scrap metal." I said, "What are you gonna do with all that?" He said, "Ah, you'll find out, you'll find out!"

And I did. I got some in my neck. They shot it back at us.

I got called up in September of 1944. I was scheduled to go to

Source: U.S. Army Center for Military History

OCS (Officer Candidate School). After basic training my orders were changed. I went to OCS—"Over Choppy Seas." We went directly to the Philippines, where I was assigned to the 129th Infantry as a replacement. I was a husky guy, so they gave me the BAR— Browning Automatic Rifle, a semi-automatic with a magazine of twenty rounds.

We were on Luzon. We liberated a town called San Jose and ended in the Cagayan Valley. We worked with tanks, did the Patton tactics, pushing everything off to the side. The Japanese ran into the hills and eventually got cut off from their supplies. They were backing up and trying to kill us. They didn't give up.

Once when we were following our tanks, we got fired on by our own planes. The Japanese had their tanks up around the corner. Our officers called for air support, and we put out smoke signals to mark our position. Four planes came strafing. The last two opened fire early. C Company was in the middle of the road, and A Company— my company—was coming up to take their place. We hit the road when the planes came in. This poor guy next to me took a .50-caliber machine-gun round in his ankle. It blew his foot apart. Six inches over, it would have been my ankle. It gets to you.

I shot a lot of Japanese soldiers with my BAR, and often they didn't die right away. Many of them had high-pitched voices. They emitted a wailing, childlike sound before they died. For years after the war, when I heard a baby cry or whimper or a dog whine, the hair stood up on the back of my neck. I just couldn't stand those sounds.

A lot of the Japanese would sneak in at night. Once there was an eight-foot culvert underneath the road. It rained hard there, and the culvert ran off into a wooded area. There were a lot of bamboo trees down in there. Bamboo is noisy when the wind comes up, so it was a noisy night.

The Japanese must have been there for some time because they had tunneled in underneath the road. They had a chamber in behind us that probably held fifteen, twenty people. They came up that ravine and in under the road and got inside that chamber.

Some of them charged our area. The BAR flashed a lot—the muzzle flash. Rapid fire, you'd give away your position. I threw a lot of grenades. I was a left-handed pitcher in high school, so I had a pretty good arm, and I carried extra grenades. This was one of the best weapons we had.

The next morning, I threw white phosphorous grenades into the culvert with the cave underneath it. That wasn't effective, so we called for a flamethrower. That was napalm—gelled gasoline. The fellow operating the flamethrower stood a few yards from the culvert to get a good view of the opening of the cave. Of course, the men in there were hunkered down. It was horrible. These guys came out screaming, all on fire. There were a dozen or more. They got put out of their misery. We shot them as they came out.

*Violette brought home a cache of photos
of the Japanese occupiers of the Philippines,
including this one of a bayonet drill.*

I'd lost contact with the CP (command post) during the night. We had field wire. About six or eight feet from your hole, you put a tent peg in the ground and made a clove-hitch over that. The next morning I looked out of my hole and saw why we'd lost contact. The Japanese had cut the wire, coiled it up, and put it next to the tent peg.

We went further up the Cagayan Valley. Sometimes we'd find warm food on the table where the Japanese had got out of there just before we came. We were moving pretty quickly. Often when we stopped to eat, we sat among the corpses of Japanese soldiers. In that heat, the bodies rapidly became bloated and decomposed. More than once while I sat there eating, I could see maggots crawling out of their eye sockets.

In those camps you'd find all kinds of things—nice swords with jeweled handles. Of course, we weren't carrying those things around. You'd stick them in a coconut tree and break them off and throw the handle away.

The Japanese also had grenades. They had one they had to detonate by hitting it on something solid. They'd hit them on their steel helmets. You'd hear a sound—tap, tap—and four or five seconds later, they'd detonate.

One place, the Japanese were coming out from under the road again. One of them tapped his helmet, and I hollered, "Grenade!" and we ducked, and we got sprayed. They were small grenades. They'd break up in fine pieces, almost like BB pellets. A buddy and I both got peppered. I got some in the lobe of my ear and in my neck. After we were out of there, I got out my pen knife and dug them out of him, and he dug them out of me. We put iodine on it and went along our way.

In a town called Cordon, we had hot food for the first time in some time. Filipinos started to come out of the woods and mountains. One fellow had a little boy about three years old. His wife had a baby in a sling. We'd just been through the chow line, and I had my mess kit with the American chop suey—boy, that was great. His family looked hungry, so I gave the woman my mess kit. He took it away from her and fed the little boy and then himself. All that was left in my tray were wet pitted cherries—the sour ones they make pie out of. She started eating the cherries and gave one to the baby and the baby puckered up. So she pulled her breast out and washed it down with mother's milk.

The father spoke English, he'd been to Chicago. The first thing he said to me was, "Me guerrilla. When do I get my back pay?" We ran into that often when they came out of the mountains. They wanted to be paid.

We got to the South China Sea, up in Appari, on July 2. The Japanese had gone up in the mountains. They were cut off from their supplies, and they would come in and raid towns—get chickens and goats and raid gardens.

Violette fought in the Philippines until the bitter end, and beyond.

We ran patrols up there. I was on one of those patrols and we took two prisoners in, stragglers. They were in good shape. One could speak English a little bit. I broke out some C-rations and gave them something to eat. I lit up and said, "Cigarette?" The one who spoke English said, "OOOOh, Lucky Strike. Long time, no smoke."

He was a draftee. He had worked in an airplane factory in Kobe. He asked me, "Kobe—did it get bombed?" I said yes. He said, "Our officers tell us no, nobody hurt anybody in Japan." Of course, they were retreating "gloriously." But he was concerned—he had a wife and two kids like I did.

I had a group of Filipinos assigned to my squad, and we went on patrol once. They were trigger-happy. They'd shoot every time a bird squawked, and a lot of birds squawk in the jungle. I called them all together one day and told the squad leader to take all their ammunition and put it in a pile. I said, "Give them one round of ammunition each and put it on lock. The next time somebody fires, I want to see a dead body." We had a good patrol after that.

One time, there were Japanese dug in behind a hill. Our company was on the point. We crawled through the pucker-brush and tall grass into position at the base of the hill. Our artillery fired all night.

At daybreak the Air Corps strafed. Our orders were to take off at seven o'clock. As the artillery raised its fire, the infantry was to follow. It was a successful way of operating. It kept the Japs down until we got up to the top.

The date was August 14. At 0700, we were holding our breath when this jeep came up and blew our cover. It was a wonder somebody didn't shoot the driver. But he was bringing word that a ceasefire was imminent. Word came down, man to man, position to position, that there was to be no celebration and that we were to stay in our positions and await further orders. We lay there until eleven o'clock. Word finally came down that the ceasefire was in process. We leapfrogged out of there, a few men at a time.

Dick Violette's outfit continued to patrol the area until October 1, 1945, taking some casualties. The unit then went to Cabanatuan, where American prisoners, including survivors of the Bataan Death March, had been incarcerated. Graves Registration personnel were excavating bodies for identification, if possible, and reburial. Violette returned home in February 1946. He worked for fifty-six years for the Merrimack County Telephone Company, retiring in 1987 as the company's president and CEO and staying on until 2002 as chairman of the board. He is now chairman of the New Hampshire Telephone Museum in Warner.

Donald Booth said no to the draft and spent the war working stateside.

Donald Booth

Conscientious Objector

*In 1940, Donald Booth of Canterbury, New Hampshire, was
twenty-four years old. Canadian-born, he lived near Boston
and worked in the photo department of the* Christian Science
Monitor. *He was not yet a Quaker, but he had misgivings about
the coming war. That December, Booth wrote in his journal:*

*"I don't want to go along with the crowd. I'd like the Army's physical training
and the relief from personal responsibility and I'd be an American citizen
on my discharge. But I think I'd rather not kill or be killed, and would rather
direct my energies to constructive work rather than destructive.*

*"I've seen too much of the present turning of energies both national
and personal to killing and I don't think the waste is justified. The best
should stay behind; they should have the courage to save themselves to
clean up afterwards. I don't know that I'm the best, but I'm better than
some. Or rather my energies directed to the improvement and constructive service are more services to the world that the energies of a better man
directed merely at operating a bombing plane."*

My mother was respectful and quietly supportive. My father
was convinced I was throwing my life away.

I had read the Selective Service provisions, which
included alternative work for people whose religious training and
beliefs prevented their participation in the military. Being a pretty

obedient boy, I set out to see if I would qualify. The local board said, "No, you're not a Quaker or part of any other church that includes that training. You're on your own, so no, you don't qualify."

There was an appeal possible. The fairly quick response supported the local board's decision. But there was another appeal possible. That included a federal investigation of my life.

When they actually declared me a conscientious objector and took me into alternative service, it was 1942. There was a small camp in central Massachusetts. Fifty people. The Quakers administered it.

The Selective Service felt that the small camps were inefficient and sent men to larger camps in Gorham, New Hampshire. After one winter in Gorham, we were given a choice. We could go to Oregon, which I chose, or New York. I had some mild discomfort about being so cooperative with the Selective Service.

At first I was mostly a cook, but I also did a lot of what the whole camp did, which was timber stand improvement. We were paid a dollar and a half a month. To get to our work we drove a Forest Service truck. It was called "work of national importance under civilian direction," or, in general terms, "alternative service."

It was a marvelous mix of all kinds of men—well, not all kinds, because there was quite a small number. Some men from New York hated being in the woods. I loved it. Having been in office work before, I liked heaving the heavy logs and swinging the two-man cross-cut saw. An important part of our readiness was for fighting forest fires. When we were in Oregon, the work included replacing trees destroyed by fire.

After a few months there, sometime in 1943, there was an opening in a special unit in Florida. I was accepted for transfer. Instead of just taking the train from Oregon to Florida, I asked the administrator if they could cover the cost of hitchhiking. And so I had my first appreciation for the words of "A Hobo's Lullaby." One driver, when he picked me up, asked what I was doing. When I told him I was in the conscientious objector corps he stopped the car and told me to get out.

In Florida, the main project was building sanitary privies and installing them for families that didn't have any. I worked on this for awhile, but I soon became part of a small company that was working at a black high school that needed a lot of basic repairs. We had a marvelous opportunity to talk with the students and the teachers and learn a bit about life in Florida.

When school was about to close, we figured we could have a going-away party for the graduating class. At first, we thought we'd have it in our house in Orlando, but the idea was quickly abandoned. Some of the Southern members felt it would be suicidal to wave that flag in front of the Ku Klux Klan. So we arranged through the principal to have the party at the school.

We invited families of the graduating class, and some of the campers baked muffins or cookies. I had the responsibility of master of ceremonies, welcoming and all that, and leading folk games that mixed people.

I was surprised at my accomplishment at leadership. Before I went to bed that night, I wrote about it. The thing that was impressing me was that I didn't know how to do what needed to be done, but I was the only one to do what I could do.

That was probably the most important experience of my life at that point. It certainly increased my appreciation of Quaker testimony of the availability of inner guidance. That was a long-term influence of awareness.

Later I was called to the principal's office and told that county officials wanted to talk with me about the party. I cheerfully went along and told them how fun it was, how naturally people felt included and enjoyed playing the children's games. But the county officials told the camp administrators we needed to leave Florida immediately.

After leaving Florida Booth served out his service commitment in Delaware and returned to New England, where he met his wife, Lois. The two moved to Canterbury and had six children. Booth worked as a carpenter for many years and says he never suffered socially as a result of his wartime decision. Now in his nineties, he spends each Wednesday morning in front of the New Hampshire State House holding a vigil for peace.

"You could hear the guys screaming," Ted Rydburg says of the Franklin disaster.

Ted Rydberg & Arthur Brown

The Sinking of the USS Franklin

In June 1944, the USS Franklin joined the Pacific fleet, which was creeping closer to Japan. A mid-sized carrier, the ship had eight hundred and twenty feet of waterline, twenty-six hundred men, a hundred fighter planes, and sixty-two machine guns of various calibers. Its job was to weaken enemy forces on land before Allied troops went ashore. The ship's pilots also destroyed cargo ships, downed Japanese planes, and collected surveillance photos.

On March 19, 1945, the Franklin was within fifty miles of Japan, as close as any carrier had been at that point in the war. Its targets were the Japanese mainland and shipping lanes in Kobe Harbor. Accounts vary about what happened that morning. Some witnesses swear they saw a kamikaze plow into the Franklin's flight deck, but a damage analysis later pointed to a pair of bombs. The flight deck, the hangars, and the command center were destroyed, and ammunition stowed in the stern was soon aflame.

Radio was out and the Franklin sat dead in the water, listing thirteen degrees to starboard. Nearly seven hundred and fifty men died, *and two hundred and sixty-five were wounded. The losses might have been heavier still if not for rescue efforts by the surrounding fleet. Here are two accounts of men from nearby ships.*

Ted Rydburg

THE MOST HORRIBLE DAY

A few days after his eighteenth birthday, Ted Rydberg boarded the destroyer USS Marshall and joined the Pacific fleet. For the next fifteen months, his boat chased the enemy, creeping closer and closer to Japan.

We lived in Brooklyn, in Bayridge. My father didn't want me to get drafted into the Army because he remembered World War I, these guys coming back with no limbs. He said, "That's not for you. You go to sea." I was seventeen, so my parents had to sign my enlistment papers.

I was assigned to the USS Marshall. I turned eighteen on March 11, and on March 15, we got underway. We went to the Marshall Islands and worked all the way up, every naval battle, into Okinawa. We were in the Sea of Japan. It was cold up there. We had typhoons.

There were several carriers, three or four, then the cruisers. We were a picket ship, on the outside, our radar always on. We were the first line of defense. We'd chase the fleet for days, sometimes weeks on end, just chasing the Japanese around. Sometimes, at night, the whole sky would look like the Fourth of July.

I could not stay below decks. It was so stifling and confined. I got claustrophobia, so I went under the torpedo tubes and slept there, or I went over to the side of the ship where they had big 20-millimeter ammunition boxes and I would sleep there. I would never go below decks except to eat and go to my locker. At least fourteen full months I lived above decks.

You couldn't walk around. I was a great walker. It was so confining. Twice in fifteen months I was on solid ground.

*Crew members flee the Franklin's
deck. (U.S. Navy photo)*

I didn't fit in with the guys on the ship. Most of them were from the South. Rebels, we called them. There were very few of us from New York. They'd have hoedowns with bug juice—that's like Kool-Aid. They'd put some white lightning in it. One night, they gave me a little cup. I drank it straight down. Couldn't stand up. At least once a week, they'd have their hoedowns, playing their fiddles, singing. They were a riot.

We had a dog on the ship. He moped around all the time, running back and forth. Everybody fed him. His name was Mac.

When we left port, we had five-gallon tins, hundreds of them, full of cabbage, powdered eggs, and other things, all dehydrated. That's what we lived on. I called it corned beef mulligan. It wasn't. It was beef tongue from Australia.

We got our supplies from tankers, frozen meat and canned meat from Australia. Hershey's tropical chocolate bars were the best thing going. It wouldn't melt. It was hard as a rock. You'd have to chip it away with your teeth. One bar would last me an hour. Sometimes, you'd get a Baby Ruth.

Once in a while, the big ships, the carriers, they'd send us some meat. The troop ships would pull alongside and give us fresh potatoes. Sometime the bread had weevils—the bug that gets in flour. They're little. You'd think you were eating rye bread.

I worked four hours on, four hours off. Every four hours, you'd go down, get your sandwich, and eat it. We'd lie down and try to sleep. Then you'd go back on duty. Everybody was gung-ho. Everybody had something to do.

I was on the forward antiaircraft guns. I would pass clips of shells up. We had to be careful that we didn't hit other ships. You could see the planes we were shooting at, see them coming in. They were very smart. They always came in low, and they'd sneak up high and come down kamikaze. I saw ships being hit. I saw planes going down. When our planes went down, we went over to rescue the pilots.

The most horrible day was when the Franklin got hit. It was morning. They had propeller planes and all those planes were on the flight deck, warming up. I was on my duty station, passing the ammunition. Then it happened.

We pulled right alongside. Guys were swimming. A lot of them were blown off the ship. Other ships were there helping, too. There were about ten or twelve of us who jumped overboard. We got as many as we could. We put ropes down. Some of them were just flailing around. We tried to get them in and bring them closer to the ship. You could hear the guys screaming. They ran into the propellers and got chewed up.

This guy I could not rescue, he was a pilot. He had his flight jacket on and everything. He was about thirty feet away, and I went out and started pulling him in. I went alongside and got him within three or four feet of the side of the ship. His flight jacket just weighed him down. He was hurt. He was dazed. I got him close to the ship, but any time I tried to hold him up and get the rope around him, he kept going down. I kept pulling him up, and he kept going down. I just couldn't do it anymore. The water was bitter cold. Bitter cold. I'll never forget that. He went down. Just disappeared.

We had two hundred and twelve that we saved, but some of them died. We didn't have a chaplain, but some officer said a few words. They sewed them up in canvas, put weights on them. They just tilted them up, and they slid into the sea.

After the war, Ted Rydberg returned to Brooklyn. He worked in international and domestic shipping for the company that eventually became

Mobil Oil. He and his wife, Irene, moved to New Hampshire in 1983. They live in Canterbury.

Arthur Brown

MY NIGHTMARE

Arthur Brown was a Concord High School senior when the Japanese bombed Pearl Harbor. President of the student council and an All-State football player, he won a full scholarship to Syracuse University. In 1942, he played right guard, offense and defense, on a team that finished 6–3.

I t bothered me to be playing football when we were losing in Africa and all over the Pacific. I wanted to get out there and win that war myself. That was a spirit a lot of men my age had. Pretty near the whole team left when I did.

I had an offer to go into training to be a pilot. I went with a friend named Paul Davis, son of the state bank commissioner. They

In his nightmares, Arthur Brown sees the burial at sea of the Franklin's dead.

The U.S.S. Franklin burns

HOKKAIDO
SAPPORO

SEA OF JAPAN

HONSHU

JAPAN

MOJI

KOBE

OSAKA

NAGOYA

TOKYO

SHIKOKU

KYUSHU

PACIFIC OCEAN

0   100   200
MILES

PHILIPPINE SEA

Source: U.S. Navy

said we'd go twelve months at Dartmouth for pre-flight and then six months for flight. Paul said, "If I wanted to go to Dartmouth, I would have stayed there." It was a good answer. So we both turned it down. He ended up on a PT boat, and I wound up on the destroyer, the USS Bullard.

I joined the crew in Brooklyn in February of 1943. At first, I did what every sailor does—scrape paint and whatever it took to keep up a metal ship. I was also training aboard to be a gunner's mate. The gunner's mate is responsible for his gun and is supposed to be in a position to fix anything that goes wrong with it—like a jam in combat. You're trained, you know what to do. I loved it.

I was on gun 40-5—40-millimeter dual barrels antiaircraft, gun No. 5. I could see everything—starboard, aft, the port side. The only thing blocking my view was the bridge right in front of me. That's why I saw so much.

We went to Pearl Harbor, which was still a mess from the attack. It made me so angry at the Japanese for doing this and killing several thousand people that I just had to get out there and get on my gun and start killing.

Wake Island had been taken by the Japanese, and we were sent down to soften them up to take the island back. We stayed far enough out—probably three miles—so their guns couldn't reach us but we could lob our shells in there.

I was the first loader, loading the fifty-six-pound projectiles into the five-inch gun. Just six months before, I was in tiptop shape playing football for Syracuse. The requirement was that you had to be six feet tall to get the shells up in there. But I told the gunnery officer, "Give me a chance on the loading machine, and I'll show you I can beat everybody onboard ship." And I did. And so even though I was only five-foot-eight, he allowed me to become a first loader.

We went to Guadalcanal and then Rabaul and Bougainville. We had heavy combat with the Zeroes coming in dropping bombs on us, strafing as they came in. I had bullets bounce all around me. You can see the Zeroes coming in—five or six at a time. You don't have much protection, just a splinter shield maybe three feet high.

And you always had torpedoes. I've stood there at my gun and watched a torpedo's wake and said, "Get ready, boys." But it would be set too low, to hit a bigger ship. It would go right under a destroyer.

We first saw kamikazes in the Philippines. We couldn't believe it—that people would fly those things and give up their lives to hit a ship. We had one take down our stacks and another one hit our antennas, but no direct hits.

At Okinawa, all the guns were firing on the starboard side. I looked port, and there was a son of a gun coming in skimming the water headed right for my ship. I took my gun out of fire control, where the officer runs it, and told my gunners, "Switch it to port—get ready to fire." And they did. We let him have it. He came in and was going to hit my gun. Just as he got there, his plane swerved off and hit the deck. The engine went flying and his bomb went flying off into the water. I could have reached over and grabbed the pilot. He was dead—that's why his plane didn't go where he wanted it to.

On March 19, 1945, the Franklin, an aircraft carrier and our mother ship, was hit. I saw it hit and thought it was a kamikaze, but historians think two shells hit it. It was six in the morning. We were right there. It was absolute hell—an inferno. Our officers told us: "Tell them not to jump." It's combat and you've got to keep moving. You can't stop and pick them up. If they jump, they'll either drown or the sharks will get 'em. I hollered to the sailors on deck, "Don't jump! Don't jump!" But they still kept jumping.

That day, they sent us on picket duty thirty miles in front of the carriers to protect them. The planes would come out trying to get to the carriers because if they got the carriers, that was several hundred planes that can't fight them.

We came back in about 6 p.m. and they put us to fighting fires. We were right beside the Franklin, right under it. I looked up and saw that she was listing. She had taken on so much water. We had the pump aboard my ship. We'd run the hose over, and our crew members would have to go over to fight the fires because so many of their men were killed. I could not leave my gun to help because more kamikazes came out trying to sink the Franklin.

We buried more than six hundred men. You tie a projectile—a fifty-six-pound shell—on their feet, the chaplain or someone would say a prayer, and in the water they would go. I couldn't help with this either because I had to be on my gun, but I watched it.

This is the image I have had in my mind, all these men being dropped into water one by one, my nightmare, ever since I saw it.

When the war ended, Arthur Brown and the Bullard were preparing for the invasion of Japan. Both he and the ship received nine major battle stars. Back in civilian life, he worked as a general agent for forty years for United Life, a Concord insurance company. He also became a football referee, including fifteen years at the New Hampshire-Vermont Shrine Maple Sugar Bowl and many years in Division 1 college football all over New England. He lives in Gilmanton, New Hampshire.

To Edward Mulcahy, Jimmy Stewart was just a regular guy.

Edward Mulcahy

Rear Window

When war broke out, Edward Mulcahy was among the first in his Cambridge, Massachusetts, neighborhood to enlist. "I don't know what you'd call it—crazy, gung-ho or what," he said. Mulcahy, now eighty-seven years old, received orders for the Army Air Corps. He flew a hundred and five missions, including one that brought the first American bombs to Japanese soil. Later, in Europe, Mulcahy's reputation earned him a spot on the B-24 flown by actor Jimmy Stewart.

During training, they offered us positions. One was tailgunner on a heavy bomber. I put up my hand. I didn't even know what a tailgunner was. They told me the average life of a tailgunner in combat is about six and a half minutes. Does that make any difference, they asked. I said, "No, I want to go."

In three months, I was flying combat. They asked for volunteers to go to the Aleutian Islands. The Japanese were coming up the Aleutian chain. They had ten thousand troops on Kiska and ten thousand on Attu.

The first island we went to was Adak. From there we went to Amchitka. We flew B-24s, four-engine heavy bombers. We kept bombing, sometimes two or three times a day. Missions were short, an hour or an hour and half. We would bomb Kiska in the morning,

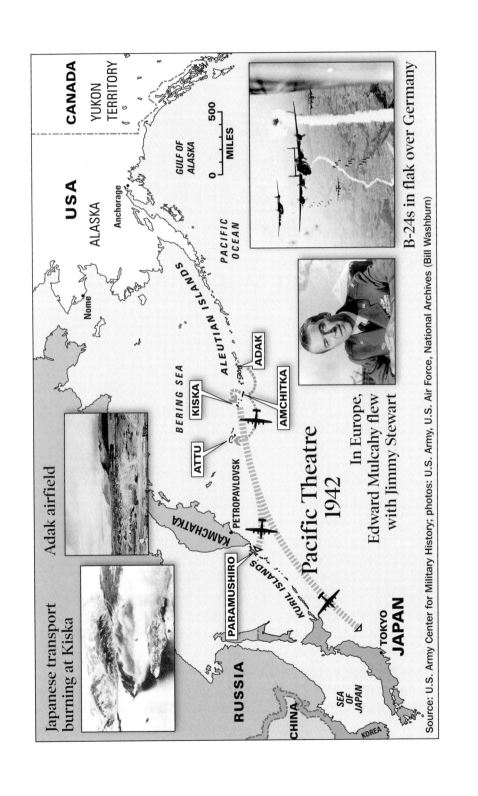

Japanese transport burning at Kiska

Adak airfield

B-24s in flak over Germany

Pacific Theatre 1942

In Europe, Edward Mulcahy flew with Jimmy Stewart

USA

ALASKA

Anchorage

Nome

CANADA

YUKON TERRITORY

GULF OF ALASKA

PACIFIC OCEAN

ALEUTIAN ISLANDS

BERING SEA

ATTU

KISKA

ADAK

AMCHITKA

PETROPAVLOVSK

KAMCHATKA

PARAMUSHIRO

KURIL ISLANDS

RUSSIA

CHINA

SEA OF JAPAN

KOREA

TOKYO

JAPAN

0   500
MILES

Source: U.S. Army Center for Military History; photos: U.S. Army, U.S. Air Force, National Archives (Bill Washburn)

turn around, refuel, and then in the afternoon bomb Attu. We had to contain the twenty thousand troops there, or the whole war would have been different.

The weather was the biggest enemy we had. It was so foggy that if we took off and came back an hour later, we couldn't find Amchitka. There was no way of finding the runway, so we'd have to go up the chain until we found one we could land on.

On maybe the twenty-second or twenty-third mission, shrapnel tore part of the back of the plane out and hit my heat suit. I had to stay in the turret until we got to the base. B-24s weren't pressurized, so I was in the hospital three or four days with frostbite. Couldn't feel a thing. The colonel came through about the third day, stuck a pin in my toe and said you'll be okay. That was the first feeling I had. They thought they might have to amputate both legs.

Finally, they drove the Japs off of Attu. Then they drove the Japs off of Kiska. Then the Aleutian chain was safe.

They asked for volunteers for what they called a suicide mission. It was so far they didn't know if we could get back or not, so we had to have volunteers. I volunteered. The mission was to Paramushiro, up in the Kurils, where the Japanese had many bases.

We couldn't make it from Amchitka, so they built a temporary strip about thirty-five or forty miles northwest of Attu. We took off from Amchitka, landed, and refueled. Then we took off for Paramushiro. It was so confusing—the distance, the time.

I was the tailgunner, and in that position you always feel like a target. I got one Zero, positive, and I think I got another one. It was just horrible suspense until we got a bomb load off and hit the target. When we turned around and went back, the suspense was: Were we going to make it? Did we have enough gas to get back?

We made it, but we just didn't have enough fuel to land. We just pancaked down. It was just tundra, no runway. A meadow, really. When the plane was going down, all I could think was, "Our Father who art in heaven . . ." I've said a few prayers, but I'm a firm believer that when your number is up, you're going to go. I don't care if you're handsome, rich, brave. We couldn't get the wheels down. We just crashed. We all walked away except for the bombardier. He was hit over the target and was dead by the time we landed. Nobody got killed in the crash, not even hurt.

There was a letter I got from my mother. She said, "Dear Edward, I'm so happy you're in the Aleutian Islands, because there's no fighting going on up there." I said, "Oh yeah, I wonder what we were just doing."

I was in the Aleutians for a year, give or take. Then they sent me home on leave on a war bond drive. I'm a charter member of the "I Bombed Japan Club," and the newspapers wrote all sorts of stories about me. I didn't want to talk to them, I wanted to get back overseas. I put in for aviation aircrew training. I wanted to go to Europe. I signed up with another bomber crew in the Eighth Air Force. We picked up a B-24 in Casper, Wyoming, and landed in Norwich, England.

Jimmy Stewart was the squadron commander. He wanted to know if I would fly with him because of my experience. I had probably forty-five or fifty combat missions at that time. I flew at least twenty missions with him.

He was just another guy. No movie star, no colonel, just a regular guy. I was with him quite a bit after because he always came to the Eighth Air Force reunions. He never missed one. There was no saluting. He was like, "We're family. I'm not a colonel, you're not a sergeant." We ate in the same dining room, we went to the plane together, came back together. I even went to London with him a couple of times, just walked with him and sometimes the captain. It was nice to be in his company.

One mission, I flew in the nose turret. The flak was all over the sky. I said boy, oh boy, look at all that beautiful flak out there. He didn't understand it. I said, "Colonel, when you can see it, it's beautiful. It's the one that you don't see that's got you." He said, "Well I guess, you know, it makes sense." He sounded just like he did in *It's a Wonderful Life*. He's not acting, you know. He's just like that.

We bombed Magdeburg, Germany. Flak was damn heavy and accurate, fifteen holes in the plane. They said Hitler had built up a new fort, so we just kept hitting it until we got it.

One day, Stewart called me in and said, "Sergeant, I'm grounding you for anxiety reaction, severe." I said, "What does that mean?"

He said, "It means you're a nut. It's only a matter of time before you get shot down."

That was his joking way of saying I had flown my last mission. It was ten o'clock in the morning. I was on a plane by two o'clock in the afternoon to the States.

Edward Mulcahy returned home with the Distinguished Flying Cross, the Purple Heart, and many other medals. He has been an active member of the American Legion, AARP, and Disabled American Veterans, lobbying to improve benefits for members of the armed services. He lives in Manchester, New Hampshire.

Robert W. Wood shows the scar from one of his wounds.

Robert W. Wood

"This One's Alive!"

Robert W. Wood, who is eighty-four years old and lives at
Havenwood-Heritage Heights retirement commmunity in
Concord, was a freshman at the University of Pennsylvania when
the Japanese bombed Pearl Harbor. His family lived in Vermont.
Wood volunteered for the Army on a delayed-entry program.

At Penn, I got in the first semester of my sophomore year before Uncle Sam decided he couldn't win the war without me. In February of '43, I was called up and did my basic infantry training at Camp Wolters near Mineral Wells, Texas.

I had known since high school that I was a homosexual, but I really didn't know what homosexuals did. When I was in high school, I went to the library to check out the word in Webster's big dictionary. That wasn't helpful because it was a scientific definition. It didn't say what homosexuals did or how you meet one.

So I was closeted. I knew homosexuality was grounds for a dishonorable discharge and loss of all veterans' benefits. I could feel the dirty homo remarks from many of my buddies—stories about queers and pansies and homos and perverts. They didn't know they were talking about me, but I could feel this.

I had occasion to go to part of the camp that I hadn't been to

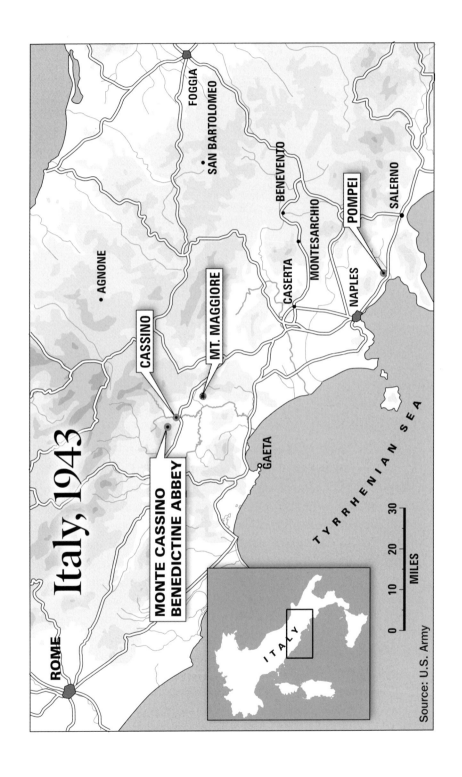

Italy, 1943

ROME

AGNONE

CASSINO

MT. MAGGIORE

MONTE CASSINO
BENEDICTINE ABBEY

GAETA

FOGGIA

SAN BARTOLOMEO

BENEVENTO

MONTESARCHIO

CASERTA

NAPLES

POMPEI

SALERNO

TYRRHENIAN SEA

ITALY

0   10   20   30

MILES

Source: U.S. Army

before, and I passed the stockade. There was a fenced-in place where they could be outside and shoot some baskets. As I walked by, I saw two fellows about my age with a great big capital Q on the backs of their prison jackets. That enraged and frightened me. I thought immediately of Nathaniel Hawthorne's *Scarlet Letter.*

I don't think anyone sensed I was a homosexual. Fortunately I wasn't the fairy type. One event may have come close. We were learning to throw our hand grenades. When I threw mine, the drill sergeant yelled, "Wood, you threw that grenade like a girl." It was true because many gay men can't throw a ball as non-gay men do. That brought catcalls and snickers in my direction.

Eight months later, in the fall of 1943, in hand-to-hand combat with the enemy in Italy, I discovered that nobody cared how I threw a hand grenade as long as it impacted on the enemy. I just tossed mine and they exploded like those expertly thrown by my macho comrades.

We sailed on a troop ship and landed in Casablanca. The North Africa campaign had just ended, and Patton was capturing Sicily. The first invasion of the mainland of Europe was to be at Salerno, south of Naples. The 36th Infantry Division, made up of the Texas and Oklahoma National Guard, was to be the jump-off. I was a sixty-millimeter mortar man. I was a replacement after the initial landing at Salerno, a fellow from Vermont with all those Texas and Oklahoma fellows.

As we were getting ready to go, we heard that the Italians had surrendered. We said, "Oh boy, it's going to be a cakewalk." But the Germans hadn't surrendered. They were waiting for us, and they had the high ground.

The 36th had helped capture Naples, and we were camped just north of Naples in an apple orchard. The German airplanes couldn't see us under the apple trees. One day our battalion was given six-hour passes. Most of the fellows visited the whorehouses in Naples, but that wasn't of any interest to me, so a buddy and I went to Pompeii. Here we were, typical tourists walking around Pompeii. Somebody's bombs had made ruins out of the ruins, and bombs had also uncovered areas the archaeologists weren't aware of. I stopped at a postal card stand. The cards were black and white, and the captions were in German. I realized that just a week before, German troops would have been visiting Pompeii. It gave an odd feeling: We were where they had been—wonder where they are now.

Around the end of October came the battle for Monte Cassino, which had a Benedictine Abbey on top. It was an observation post for the Germans. The objective was to capture that so the Allied troops could go to Rome without being observed.

Italy is so narrow you can't do any flanking. Everything has to be frontal. There were mountains between Naples and Monte Cassino. As the Germans retreated, we occupied where they had been. So they knew exactly where we were.

The weather was horrible. Vehicles were left stuck in the mud. We got stuck, everything soaked. It was cold. You could use battalion mules to carry supplies partway up the mountain, but the last part somebody had to carry fifty-pound packs to get to us on the top. All communications required wires, so there were all these telephone wires on the ground. We tripped over them, and many of them ripped apart. Then as fellows were killed, one of the most horrible things was to trip over a dead body, either ours or theirs, and to land on it and hear it go squish.

We were issued a white mattress cover. That was your coffin. When a buddy died, the first thing we did was check his canteen, hoping he still had some water, and take his weapon, his ammunition, his blanket—we didn't take his dog tag—and then stuff him into one of these white mattress covers. Then we waited for Graves Registration—it must have been the most horrible job in the military. Fellows would carry these dead bodies in mattress covers down the mountain. By then they were wet and muddy and smelly.

The weapons platoon had three mortars and two machine guns. Being the new man on the block, I carried the ammunition. You had a leather vest with three pockets in the front and three in the back. Two of us carried ammunition, so that meant there were twelve shells.

When you fired a mortar, you'd fire one shell in this direction, one in that direction, and one in the middle and hope you hit something. It was called bracketing. Then you would pick up the mortar and get out of there before the enemy could send a shell back on top of you. But you'd used your shells and had to go back down that mountain and bring six more shells up. This was maybe a couple of miles—tripping over telephone wires and occasionally dead bodies and trying to keep under cover because you knew the Germans were observing what they could. If they saw you, they might locate the supply depot.

For me, this routine went on from late October into mid-December. The campaign was fluid. Sometimes you'd have to retreat and fight your way back up again. Artillery shells were going both ways. You never quite knew how close the enemy were, although at times they were close enough that you could hear German spoken. They could be ten feet away or on the other side of the mountain. It kept you on edge.

On December 14, for a change it was sunny. The battalion was the spear-point—the furthest Allied troops into enemy territory. We were on Mount Maggiore. Suddenly an Italian civilian came walking around. And I thought, "Good heavens, he's walking right through no-man's-land. He's lucky to be alive." He said he was a barber. He had clippers and a brush and comb. He offered to cut our hair. Several of us, including myself, sat on a rock, and he clipped and combed. Later I concluded he was a spy—first that he could have gotten through the lines, and while he was cutting our hair he was counting us, seeing where our machine guns were placed, where we were going to sleep. We were glad to get the haircut, but we paid a big price.

At around eleven that night, the enemy attacked. It was pitch black. There was much confusion and you heard the machine guns. Fellows were waking up and grabbing their rifles and hand grenades. It was hard fighting in the dark.

I took a bullet right here [points to area between chest and throat], right between my dog-tag chains, and a few minutes later a bayonet in the right side. The gunshot felt like getting hit with a baseball—a hard blow that knocked the wind out of me. My legs went weak. But I was unconscious when I got stuck. I knew I'd been hit with a bullet, but it was a couple of weeks before I realized I'd been stuck.

An aid man patched me up. The next day, the fighting was over, and four fellows had to carry me down the mountain and keep the litter level so I wouldn't slide off. I was holding on for dear life.

I ended up at a frontline MASH unit—mobile Army surgical hospital. A lot of battles were going on, a lot of casualties. Some person had the task of deciding which patients would get immediate attention and which were too far gone. I was put in the reject pile. It was a tent hospital. I was inside. I had no idea where my arms and legs were, but I knew other fellows were being piled up on my left side. I could hear the moans and groans.

The next morning I could see daylight coming in under the flaps of the tent. Apparently the aid man on the mountain had given me a shot of morphine. I could feel the bandage on my chest, but that was all I was conscious of. And then pretty soon I smelled bacon and coffee. I hadn't eaten for twelve hours or more.

I realized someone was walking along on my right side. All the moans and groans on my left had stopped. I said what I think are the six most important words I ever said: "When do I get some breakfast?"

Immediately, I heard a female voice scream, "This one's alive!"

I was there until after Christmas, then taken by train to Naples to a hospital. In March, Mount Vesuvius erupted—the last time it's blown its top. Naples was blacked out at night, but with Vesuvius that fiery red, the Germans used it three nights to bomb Naples—mostly the harbor, but they also hit the hospital.

The bullet had gone straight through. It came out at the back of my right shoulder. It left a scar like a vaccination in the wrong place. I was fortunate because many times the doctors had to cut you open to remove the bullet or the bullet might break into two or three pieces and they'd have to dig out every piece.

But the fellow who stuck me hadn't sterilized his bayonet, so I got an infection. The blade had broken off the fourth rib and deflated the lung. But it was the infection that kept me hospitalized. It kept regenerating. It's what the doctors called an empyema. This was before penicillin. All they had was sulfa powder for an infection.

After a short stay in Oran, North Africa, I was taken in a hospital ship across the Atlantic. The ship was lit up at night, and it must

*Wood at Camp Wolters, where he witnessed
discrimination against homosexuals.*

have looked like a floating Christmas tree. We were told the radio
operator would radio the ship's position to the German submarines
every hour so they wouldn't mistakenly torpedo us. The Germans
did not sink hospital ships. The Japanese did.

I landed at Charleston on Mothers Day of 1944. I was a chest
case, and all the chest cases from both Europe and the Pacific went
to Memphis, Tennessee, where they had all the chest specialists.

Amputees went to Atlantic City, where they had taken over all those old hotels. Abdominal cases went somewhere else.

On May 21, my twenty-first birthday, they decided they had gotten the last infection out of me and I could now learn to walk again. The military had taken over the Lake Placid Club, a millionaires' playground. That was a rehab station, so that's where I was sent. It was forty miles from my folks in Vermont. I stayed there for exactly one year before I was discharged. This was luxurious, not very GI. I was given the job of assigning rooms when a new group came in.

Then it was that I had my first homosexual experience. One day in January, I was sitting at my desk. I looked down the hall and saw this good-looking fellow about my age. I was getting sexually excited, though I was aware of the danger of being discovered. But as he passed by, I put my left hand out on the desk, and he paused and put his hand in mine—and wow!—the electricity jumped. And he said, "About time!"

He had a roommate, and I had a roommate, but I had this room chart. I looked and I said, "401 is empty—a nice corner room—why don't we meet there at five o'clock?" And he said, "That's chow time." And I said, "That's the idea. Everybody else will be in the dining room. Nobody will be up there." And that's what we did.

He arrived right on time. I had the key. We went in, pulled the blinds down even though it was the fourth story, and locked the door. Both of us were virgins, and neither of us knew what to do. He suggested we show each other our battle scars, which was an innocent enough thing, but that meant we had to take off our clothes, and by then we were figuring out what to do. And so I had my first sexual experience. His name was Scott.

We were able to meet two or three times a week, always very careful. But the war concluded. Scott went his way and I went my way, and we never saw each other again.

Although the bayonet wound was initially more dangerous, now, years later, it's the bullet that causes me trouble. The only bone it hit was the breastbone. It made a hole about the size of a dime. Over the years the calcium has built up to fill in the hole, which was nice, but the calcium, according to the doctors, has continued to build up.

My swallowing capacity is getting narrower and narrower. Now at times I find myself choking not in the throat but down here around the bullet hole.

The Allies bombed the fifth-century Benedictine monastery on Monte Cassino in February 1944 and took the mountain in May. Wood won the Combat Infantryman's Badge, a European Theatre ribbon with two battle stars, a Purple Heart, and a Bronze Star for "heroic achievement in combat." He went on to a career as a United Church of Christ minister. He was an early activist for the rights of gay men and lesbians to live openly and form sanctioned, committed relationships. He and his partner of twenty-seven years, Hugh Coulter, were the first openly gay couple at their retirement community. Coulter died in 1989.

Harlond Perry served as an antiaircraft gunner.

Harlond Perry

It Buries Deep
in Your Mind

New Hampshire's National Guard was federalized September
16, 1939. Nineteen-year-old Harlond Perry, a teenager from Keene,
was inducted in a field near the Concord airport. His unit, the
197th, served thirty-five months, including a stretch when the war
in the Pacific went badly. Bearing mental wounds that afflict him
today, Perry returned home a few months before his buddies.

Eventually they shipped us to San Francisco and loaded us onto the USS Monterey. We headed for the Philippine Islands, but the Japanese had invaded the Philippines, so they sent us to Australia.

While we were in Fremantle, the old Asiatic fleet came in and used that as a base. We saw all the ships coming back from battle in Java—wrecks. We saw the submarines from Corregidor with the nurses they'd been able to evacuate. The nurses were in bad shape. All you had to do was make a loud noise and they would break up.

They shipped us back around to eastern Australia. We pulled

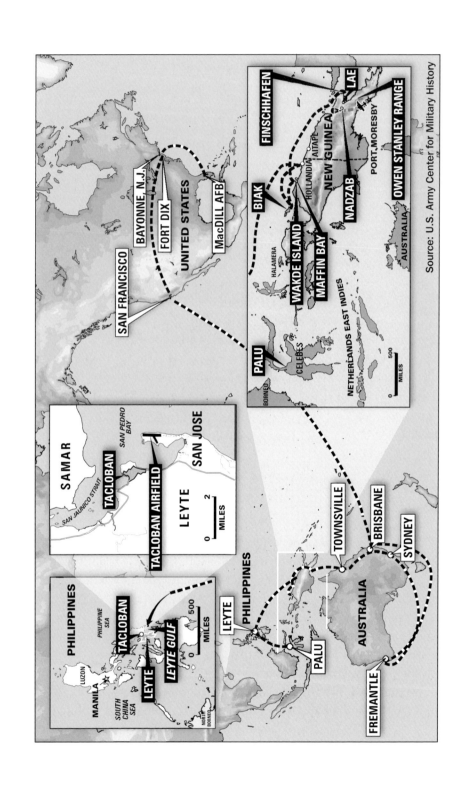

Source: U.S. Army Center for Military History

into the dock in Sydney, boarded trains, and went up along the coast toward Townsville. I was in an antiaircraft unit stationed at the airport. The boys from the 19th Bomb Group in the Philippine Islands landed their B-17s at our base. One of the bombers that came back was named Dyna-Mite. I counted seventy-five bullet holes in that plane.

Next we went to New Guinea. In Port Moresby we were told to set up camp in a slightly open area on a slanted hill. One of my buddies, Pete Prevost from Keene, worked hard building his bunk. Night set in, the guards went out, and all was quiet. Then we heard the wildest scream. A six or seven-foot lizard had crawled into Pete's bunk with him.

We were told we were going in with paratroopers. We put our antiaircraft cannons onto a C-47 and flew over the Owen Stanley Range and into the Nabzat Markham Valley. The paratroopers went down, and the plane went right in after them. They had burned off a strip to let us land near a river, but before we could get our guns off, the Japanese were already bombing us.

The only connections we had to the outside were cargo planes. They'd bring everything—your food, your ammunition. In our time there, they credited our unit with shooting down a hundred and thirty-five planes.

Nearby was the village of Lae. That was Japanese. They were between us and the water, so we had a rough go of it for a few months. Finally, the Australians pushed them back.

Natives showed us the fruit that grew in the valley: bananas, paw-paws, and breadfruit. They were good people and built us a hut near our gun pit to keep out the sun and rain. The valley became a large air base with fighters and heavy bombers.

My crew and I set up our gun on the edge of a bomb dump. We never should have been there, but that's where the officer told us to put the gun. A fire started in the bomb dump, and they couldn't stop it. The bomb dump blew up around me. I spent about four hours on the ground. They sent me to the hospital and gave me a leave.

When I came back to the valley, my outfit was gone, so I had to hunt for it. I searched all along the coast of New Guinea and spent

When the National Guard was federalized,
Perry was in for the long haul.

some time on Biak. I met Lindbergh there at the airstrip. He was doing instruction in the P-38s.

We ran into a colonel from my outfit. He was lost, too. He'd learned that a new Army headquarters had moved into Hollandia down on the coast of New Guinea. We caught a ride there on a C-47 to see if the Army could find our outfit. The Army didn't know where they were, so we asked some Navy men. They took us down a steep area toward a big bay. The Navy guys said, "See that ship out there? That's where your outfit is. They've been on that ship for fifty-eight days, and the Army hasn't come to give them a place to go." Finally they got our outfit off that ship and put us inland.

We missed New Hampshire's cold weather and the milk. You really missed good food, ordinary food. A lot of the food you got was either rations or packaged, powdered. Every time you turned around, something was after you, bugs or snakes, and some of the meanest vines I've ever seen. They had barbs on them like saw-blades. And nothing healed in New Guinea.

They put us on a ship to the Philippine Islands for the invasion at Leyte Gulf, one of the largest I had ever seen. You'd look out and see ships for miles. The battleships were softening up the land for the invasion.

Our guns were on the top deck ready to be taken off so we could get in fast. Leonard Stewart from Jaffrey was sitting on one of them. He looked up and a kamikaze was coming right into us. He squeezed the trigger. You could see the bullets hit the kamikaze. It made the aircraft go up. It hit the bridge, and its bomb slid right across. The airplane smashed to pieces and skidded everywhere. The bomb exploded in the water on the other side of the ship. The fire was bad, but it was put out fast, so we saved the ship. We had one casualty that day, Renee Forest from Keene. He had just stepped out from the bridge onto the main deck. A wing of the airplane wrapped right around him, but he was just wounded.

It was a rough landing with hard fighting. Not long after, word went around that the whole Japanese fleet was right offshore. We just had to hope for our Navy to take care of it, and it did. We got orders to go to the Tacloban airstrip and set up. Every time you turned around, there was a Jap up there to shoot at.

We built up the airstrip and even built a shower. There was a guy from Franklin, Johnny Rogers. He was in the shower one day, and a C-47 landed. Word passed up the airstrip that there was a white nurse onboard that thing. Johnny takes off running down the strip, gets about halfway down, and realizes he doesn't have any clothes on.

While we were on the airstrip, a bomb hit close and knocked me for a loop. I was standing up and didn't realize the bomb was coming down. The rest of the crew ducked into our gun pit.

It got to me then, everything I'd seen. I ended up in a hospital at a big Catholic church in Palu. I spent some time there, got shipped back to New Guinea, and was sent home on the USS Monterey, the same ship that took us over.

I got back to the States just as the European war was ending. I was in a hospital ward and went into a large assembly hall full of soldiers. Officers on the stage were reading soldiers' names and telling them they were lucky to be discharged with only twenty-five or thirty-five points. I knew nothing about points, but I found out later you needed forty-six points to be discharged. When the officer read my name, I had a hundred and forty-six points.

While waiting to catch my bus, I had an attack of malaria and went back to the hospital for another week. I was hit many times with malaria, and what is now called post-traumatic stress bothered me. Treatment was practically nothing. They sent me to a specialist in Boston. He told me I was lying. He didn't believe I was in the bomb dump, he didn't believe I dropped in on the C-47, he didn't believe I went all the way up the New Guinea coast trying to find my outfit. He said I never saw Lindbergh. They didn't believe you. It was frustrating, I'll tell you that. He put me in this room with a special table and gave me a shot. It was a truth serum. After I came out of it, he apologized.

Harlond Perry finished high school and went to the New England School of Art in Boston. He eventually returned to Keene, where he

Harlond Perry

started a sheet metal business. He married in 1954. He and his wife Margaret live in Concord and have five children and many, many grandchildren.

*At Okinawa, Clarence Ashlin's hospital ship
took casualties right off the beach.*

Clarence Ashlin

Love and War

Clarence Ashlin joined the Army in July 1940 at age eighteen. By the time the war in the Pacific approached its height four years later, Ashlin was a warrant officer aboard the hospital ship USS Hope. The crew included nurses, making the Hope one of the few coed ships in the Navy. Together, the men and women encountered the gruesome aftermath of battle and narrowly escaped bombs. They also struck up romances that, by Ashlin's count, produced nine marriages, including his own to Evangeline Perrier, a native of Concord.

The Army decided to put Army hospitals on naval vessels. We ran the medical end of it, and the Navy ran the ship. It was a great working relationship. We traveled over fifty-one thousand miles, carrying seven to nine thousand patients right off the beachheads or island battlegrounds.

Evangeline was a first lieutenant and the head surgical nurse. She'd been trained at the Elliot Hospital in Manchester and the University of Pittsburgh. Our unit was transferred to Camp Anza in Southern California, to a staging area for the Pacific Theater. That's where we became acquainted.

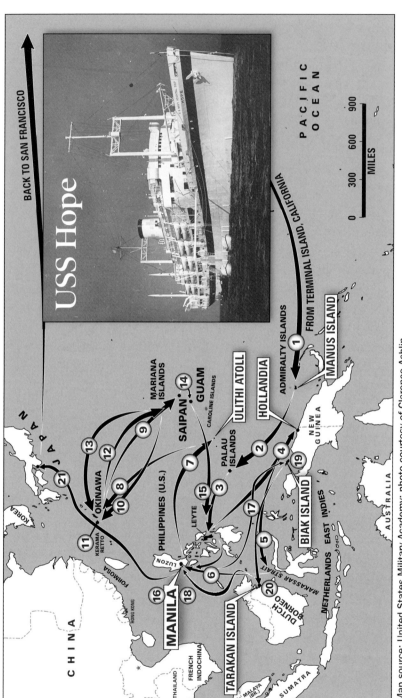

Map source: United States Military Academy; photo courtesy of Clarence Ashlin

As the junior officer of the unit, I became the training officer for all the nurses and enlisted personnel, putting them through embarkation and debarkation exercises, plus taking them out on ten-mile marches with full packs to get them in physical condition. The men and women were together. We had to be able to depend on each other on the ship.

We never lacked for patients in a combat area. We had an average of six hundred men on every trip from an invasion site. We'd take them off the front-line area, and as the battles progressed, we went from dropping our patients off in New Guinea to bringing them to Guam, Saipan, Tinian. From there the patients were picked up and evacuated by air to the States.

Our first large load of patients came during the Philippine invasion. These were first-line casualties, with multiple limbs blown off and sucking wounds in their chests or their abdomens. We lost an awful lot of the wounded that we brought on board. They were all seventeen, eighteen, nineteen years old. A number of them were basket cases, where they had both arms and both legs blown off. They were nothing but a living torso. Burn cases were the worst. The smell was sickening. It lingers long after the patient has left the area. At one point, we had as many as forty burn cases in the operating rooms. To maintain blood flow to the brain, we elevated their feet against the wall, applying burn gauze, maintaining their fluids, just trying to identify each man before he died. They were burned on eighty or ninety percent of their bodies. It was awful.

The Hope had very narrow companionways, only wide enough for one litter, so everything had to move in a circular system, which kept traffic flowing smoothly. Because we had different types of patients, from psychiatric to critically injured, we had to be able to move them as quickly as possible.

We got into some particularly critical areas, especially in the Philippines when we were taking men right off the beach. It got to be a little hairy there. We were a target, the subject of Tokyo Rose broadcasts. We traveled fully lighted day and night, a white ship with nothing else around. You don't have any guns on a hospital ship.

Ashlin and his Evangeline, who met aboard the Hope.

We were at the mercy of the elements and the navigation skills of the captain. He was good, a real cracker jack.

Violations of the Geneva Convention rules were rampant by Japan. We had red crosses all over the ship: the sides, the stacks, the fantail. We were supposed to be safe, but we were torpedoed three times while returning to Leyte. Zeroes would spot us, come down out of the sun, and make their runs, but our crew was alert. Once, as a torpedo was coming at us, the captain turned the Hope toward it. The torpedo went under the fantail, then emerged behind us and disappeared.

On Christmas we were on one of our trips back to the Philippines from New Guinea. The captain told us that a C-46 transport plane had gone down in our general area and asked all hands to scan the sea for the crew. We heard their distress transmitter from two hundred and twenty miles away. At 0200 hours on December 26 we spotted the crew and recovered them. They had floated around for more than thirty hours. Their rescue was a real Christmas present, to them and to all of us on the Hope.

Okinawa was a real bad area because of the kamikazes. That was the last battle area before the invasion of Japan was supposed to take place. At Okinawa, we arrived with our sister ship, the Comfort. It was in the height of the invasion. There were wounded by the thousands. We were in an anchorage where we could only load in total darkness. You'd be surprised how much light there is from natural sources, like the stars. There were a lot of explosions going on, too, and fires in the anchorage. We'd take the patients in through the blackout curtains and triage them there. We were taking them right off the beach. Live fire took place right above us. It wasn't that bad for us, but for those kids on the beach it was terrible.

The Comfort's crew loaded patients about twenty minutes faster than we did. They got under way, and as they were leaving, a kamikaze plane hit their upper decks. They were only twenty-five miles out. They'd just barely turned their lights on. They lost four doctors, five or six nurses, and every patient on the surgical suite at the time.

Evangeline was a real neat lady, extremely well organized. She ran a tight surgical support service. Her friends called her Van, and she was a very caring person. After hours, she would call me. She'd say, "Ash"—that was my nickname—"let's go see how many of these patients need something extra." We'd talk to as many patients as we could. If they were in pain, she'd try to figure out what the problem was. Often, she'd end up probing in a wound and finding metal, either shrapnel or fragments of a bullet.

Evangeline and I worked day and night, side by side, for twenty-six months. That's where the bond began to build. We'd sit across the table from each other at officers' mess. We thought, well, we'll see how it works out at the end of the war.

Aboard ship, we had definite rules as far as fraternization was concerned. The front of the ship was for the men, the back for the girls. We didn't have too many problems. An occasional visitor would leave the ship waving a piece of female underwear, but that was it.

Liberty off the ship was another situation. Van and I ended up as chaperones many times to groups of nurses invited to dine with personnel on other ships. This only happened in the rear areas. Occasionally, we'd have beach parties. The cooks on the ship would come on the beach and they'd cook a BBQ. It was kind of nice.

When the war ended we were out in the Pacific. We were hoping to go into Tokyo Bay for the surrender, but they brought in a new hospital ship that hadn't seen a day of combat. Instead, we were sent to transport a hospital unit to the Japanese mainland.

Some of us went into Hiroshima. It was just something you can't believe. You'd see silhouettes on the side of the buildings, people that had just been incinerated. I wish in a way now that we hadn't gone. It was a pretty sad situation. I hope it never, ever happens again. But we saved one hell of a lot of American boys using that weapon and stopped the need for another invasion.

The Hope arrived stateside in November 1945, and the Ashlins were married in Concord the following February. Clarence Ashlin was recalled to duty in 1949 as a hospital administrator. He spent thirty-five years on active duty, retiring as a full colonel. The Ashlins had two children and were stationed in the United States and overseas before returning to Concord in 1975. Ashlin worked three years for the New Hampshire Hospital Association until health issues forced him to retire. He and Evangeline had been happily married forty-six years when she died in 1990.

Kevin Corbett told the story of his service in verse.

Kevin Corbett

The Poet

Kevin Corbett fought in the Pacific with the Army's 43rd Infantry Division, helping seize several islands, including New Georgia and the Japanese airfield on Munda Point. Corbett, who lived in Henniker and Concord until his death in 2002, was responsible for reconnaissance. While overseas, he recorded his experiences in poems. His widow, Patricia Corbett, shared some of his work with the Monitor. The Rendova mentioned in the last line of this poem is an island in the Solomons that served as a major base for PT boats.

RENDOVA MINUTEMEN

July 2, 1943

How still the sea and minds of men
Before the hour breaks.
The unknown things like where and when
Intrude before the quake.
We walked a muddy road that day
Back out toward the sea,
And straddled in the gentle spray,

From boot to denim knee.
How still the time and palm tree leaf,
Blue clad the quiet sky
While out beyond the rippled feet,
The waves flowed slowly by.

The men and ships along the beach,
In silent mood seek rest,
But well they know 'twas out of reach,
Like home beyond the crest.
So calm those hours in the beams
That fled the daily sun,
Men toiling on and living dreams
Once long ago begun.
The sea comes in and turns around,
Wet sands upon the boots,
Our imprints walked the sanded ground,
The palm tree bared its roots.
Then came the when and dreams were smashed,
And silence was no more,
The island shook and then it crashed,
Nothing was like before.

A sky of blue now filled with death,
Spilled down upon the earth,
And those who ran, ran out of breath,
And ran for all their worth.
Few the seconds from the beach to Post,
The time to dream has gone,
And those who couldn't run, we toast,
Their moment still lives on.
We trudged the muddy road again,
Back where the havoc struck,
And there along the twisted lane,
We found them in the muck.

Kevin Corbett

I stood beside a Paul Revere
And saw a Nathan Hale,
Such stillness, and quite young they were,
So silent and so pale.
I saw Captain Parker lying,
His sinews still yet warm,
With little time for trying
To flee the sudden storm.
You were the where—the world will find
The place wherein you lay,
You are the breed, another kind,
That fell along the way.
They all were there from first to last,
So quiet in the then,
I'll close my eyes and live your past,
Rendova Minutemen.

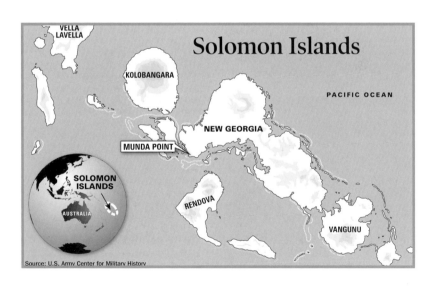

As a Canadian flier, Wesley Megaw made nighttime raids over Germany.

Wesley Megaw

By Guess and by God

As a seminarian at Princeton, Wesley Megaw was exempt from traditional service, but he wanted to enlist. When the draft board ordered him to become a chaplain, Megaw used his dual citizenship to join the Royal Canadian Air Force. He signed the enlistment papers and received a shilling, signifying that he belonged to the king. After arriving in England, Megaw completed forty-one nighttime bombing raids as a navigator and met a member of the Women's Auxiliary Air Force who eventually became his wife.

Aero-navigation was in its infancy. There wasn't any of this push a button and it will tell you where you are. You learned the sextant and shooting the stars. If you made it, you learned by experience: This searchlight was purple, this searchlight that Jerry had was pink, this one was white. And you did a lot of navigation by guess and by God.

The Yanks did the day. We did the night. If you made it, it was a lot of fun. We flew something left over from World War I called a Handley Page. We did nickeling, which was dropping silver foil, by hand, out of a hole in the aircraft. As it floated down, it spread. The German radar thought it was aircraft.

You did five or six of those missions before you graduated and

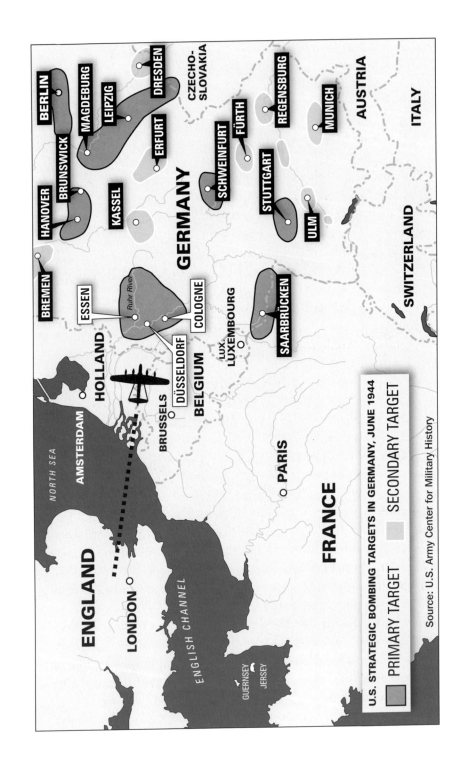

U.S. STRATEGIC BOMBING TARGETS IN GERMANY, JUNE 1944

PRIMARY TARGET

SECONDARY TARGET

Source: U.S. Army Center for Military History

went on bombing runs. The Lancasters were fine airplanes. There's the pilot, the front gunner, the engineer, the wireless operator, the navigator, and the rear gunner. Later on, they put on an upper gunner, but on our plane there were only six of us. There was no co-pilot because the engineer, the front gunner, and myself were trained to bring the thing back. Not fly it, just make a landing you could walk away from.

They needed an engineer for synchronization of the propellers. Our poor little fellow had to work four knobs to keep the propellers going the same RPMs. He wasn't along for a joyride, the engineer. If anyone got tired on a trip, it was that lad.

When the Yanks flew off in the day, they spent maybe an hour and a half getting in their formations that looked so beautiful. That's why the Yanks didn't go very far into France and didn't go into Germany for a long while. Being in formation was their salvation in the daytime, whereas we took right off. We didn't have a formation. We had a line that would be like a box in the air, eight miles long.

If there was turbulence, if you were bouncing around feeling miserable, you were quite happy because you were in a stream. The agitations of the air were one of the safety factors. If a fighter went through that, he'd get all fouled up, too. If you're having a nice, quiet trip, you're worried sick.

I only did one trip to Big B. That's Berlin. Most of my trips were to the Ruhr: Duesseldorf, Essen, those towns. Since we didn't spend any time in formation, you could go to Duesseldorf and back in a little under three hours. When you got near the target, they had something called pathfinders. They were the boys in a stripped-down plane that could go like Billy-O. They would find the target and light it up with flares.

One night our rear gunner got credit for knocking down a night fighter, which happened very seldom. Just think, he's flying by. It's night. How far can you see in the dark?

When it's all over, that's the interesting part. You're alive.

How did I meet my wife? Poland comes into that story. The Polish Air Force was in disarray. They asked for volunteers to train with the Polish boys, people who had at least twenty trips in, to buck up their morale. I volunteered and flew under Polish officers.

Megaw outranked his wife, but she had more time in than he did.

I arrived at this new station with my best friend, who was also a navigator. We went out to see my plane, which was called "O for Obo." It needed an awful lot done to it. It was a Lancaster Mark 1. We were on our bicycles coming back from the dispersal unit to our barracks, and there's this big crane coming down the taxiway. It was used to lift the plane out of the mud and put it back on the tarmac. The tires were at least four feet in diameter. There was a big wheel and, with her hat cockeyed, there was this damned little WAAF driving the thing.

The thing shouldn't go more than eight miles an hours. She had it going thirty. It was swaying coming toward us. I went off in the ditch to avoid her, and my friend went off the other way. Oh, did we cuss that damn little WAAF.

Then we found the nearest pub, and there's this brunette WAAF who nearly drove over us. Sitting beside her was a good-looking blonde. I said to my friend, I'll flip you for the blonde. I lost, so I sat beside the brunette. And I married her.

When a girl became seventeen and a half in England, she had to do something for the war effort. She had two friends from school and they all went in as airwomen first class. They stayed together for all their time because they refused promotions. They were in motor transport because they were from wealthy families and knew how to drive.

When it was all over, she had half a year in longer than I. Of course, I had rank and pulled it. Then she would say, "Get some time in!"

After the Germans surrendered, Megaw and other RAF fliers prepared to ship out to the Pacific for the invasion of Japan. Their orders changed after Americans dropped the atom bombs. Megaw flew medical supply missions into Europe. He and his late wife, Joyce, were married July 14, 1945. They returned to the United States, where Megaw worked for many years as a Presbyterian minister. He lives in Concord.

For Jim Grosvenor, joining the Army was like moving to Georgia.

The Red Ball Express

Jim Grosvenor is eighty-five years old and lives in Concord. He grew up in Boston's South End. As a member of an African-American quartermaster company, he landed at Normandy shortly after D-Day. He drove the trucks that supplied the advancing armies, was involved in five major battles, and transported injured soldiers, German POWs, and concentration camp survivors out of the war zone.

I was drafted in 1943. They sent me to Fort Eustis, Virginia, for basic training. We learned the manual of arms, learned to march, pulled KP duty. That was a segregated unit with black officers. The white and black soldiers weren't together at all. The further separation was that we had Southern black soldiers in our battalion, and they were in one barracks and we were in the other. I never knew why.

In training, we began to work with field artillery and antiaircraft. As far as I knew, our training was the same as the white soldiers'. White officers came to inspect us and ask us questions about maps and other topics.

I didn't go to town the whole time I was on base. I wasn't acquainted with the mores and the culture in the South. We had some dances where the girls would come from local black colleges. The squad leader would pick out those interested in going.

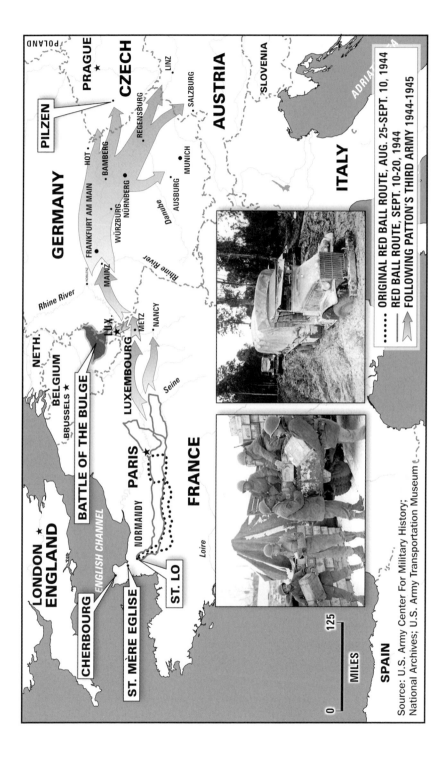

ENGLAND
LONDON ★

NETH.
BELGIUM
BRUSSELS ★

GERMANY

POLAND

PRAGUE ★
CZECH

PILZEN

CHERBOURG

ENGLISH CHANNEL

BATTLE OF THE BULGE

LUX. ★

Rhine River

FRANKFURT AM MAIN

HOF •

BAMBERG •

REGENSBURG •

LINZ •

ST. MÈRE EGLISE

ST. LO

NORMANDY

PARIS ★

LUXEMBOURG

METZ •

NANCY •

KOBLENZ •

MAINZ •

Rhine River

WÜRZBURG •

NÜRNBERG •

Danube

MUNICH •

AUSBURG •

SALZBURG •

AUSTRIA

SLOVENIA

ADRIATIC

Seine

Loire

FRANCE

ITALY

SPAIN

MILES
0   125

ORIGINAL RED BALL ROUTE, AUG. 25–SEPT. 10, 1944

RED BALL ROUTE, SEPT. 10–20, 1944

FOLLOWING PATTON'S THIRD ARMY 1944–1945

Source: U.S. Army Center For Military History;
National Archives; U.S. Army Transportation Museum

After Virginia, I went to Camp Gruber in Oklahoma, where we joined the quartermaster corps. This was a supply unit—you moved things from one place to another. I hadn't driven before, but there I learned how to drive and maintain a six-by-six army truck.

We went overseas from New York and landed in Liverpool. They were gathering men and bombs and all the things for the invasion. I was in the 399th Quartermaster Corps. We camped in tents near Stratford. They thought we were going to be part of the invasion, so we waterproofed the vehicles. We collected bombs stacked in ditches beside the road and put them on the trucks to be loaded onto planes.

In the end, we went across the channel a couple of days after the invasion. We didn't have any trouble getting ashore. We went onto the beach in a landing craft and drove the trucks right off.

We got involved with the war right away. They were still fighting to take control of the beach, and the Germans were fighting for Saint Mère Église. I saw dead paratroopers with their parachutes caught on church steeples and tree branches. The troops were still fighting, trying to push the Germans out, so they couldn't take the bodies down.

We drove standard army trucks with canvas tops. In the cab we had a carbine—or we were supposed to. We'd move out in convoys of ten or twelve. The leader would be in a jeep, and he'd tell you where you were going.

Once they took Cherbourg, we would go in and they'd unload stuff from the ships in port, and we'd take it out to the troops—ammunition, supplies. Most of the people unloading the ships were black troops. In the harbor, you'd see a lot of bodies—they were still trying to clean it up. Because the Germans made a stand in Saint-Lô, you'd see a lot of dead bodies there, too.

Seeing all that death, I just hoped I would get through this. But you didn't spend much time worrying about that because you had to take care of yourself. You followed all the things you'd learned in training so you could survive.

Saint-Lô was the bottleneck. Once the Air Force and the artillery came in and destroyed the Germans and chased them out, we began to go through there and drive food, supplies, and ammunition down to the troops as they went farther into France.

We drove through Paris the day after the liberation. The people stopped and waved and shouted. People were happy on the outskirts, but there was still fighting, too. We saw members of the resistance walking out Germans with their hands up.

We moved with the troops. When Patton came in, we became part of the Third Army. We followed the Red Ball Express. We had to get things to the front right away.

When combat came near towns, civilians would move out of danger and come out onto the roads and block them. You had people with bicycles and cars and on foot with their possessions. But the Red Ball Express was just for troops and tanks and our trucks.

Even so, civilians were a hindrance at times. The military put up red balls and signs to warn them to stay off the road, but they would get on it anyway. The Germans seemed to have a technique of pushing the civilians into the way of the Americans advancing, to slow us down.

On the road, sometimes when you had a break, kids and grown-ups would come up to you. I knew a little French because I had studied it in school. I was the translator. They would just be asking, "How are you?" and basic conversation, and some would ask for food. The children would want chewing gum and candy. They would say, "You speak good French."

The Battle of the Bulge was terrible. That was winter—really terrible. It was so hard to stay warm. You couldn't turn your motor off. The ground troops had it worse. The Germans broke through the lines. Because a lot of our troops didn't have winter gear, their feet froze and turned black. Some were just stiff all over. You'd see them staggering in together, trying to keep each other warm. You had to get them in the truck and get them out of there. We'd bring them back behind the lines and then load ammunition and go back to the lines.

It got so tough during the Battle of the Bulge that Eisenhower wanted some black soldiers to volunteer for the front. Not many did.

The commander of our company was from Texas. He was white—all our officers were white after we left the States. He was a taskmaster. He was also standoffish, not a friendly guy. One time we were going up to the front, and he wouldn't let us take our carbines with us. A couple of soldiers in the outfit didn't like him. We figured he

Grosvenor once found himself in a battle without a weapon.

was afraid they would shoot him, so sometimes he wouldn't give us our guns. And I don't doubt that someone would have shot him.

This one time, we wound up at the front with people shooting all around us. The commanding officer up there wanted to know what the heck we were doing in the middle of a battle without our weapons. He gave our commander a bawling out.

When we first got to Germany, we had to wait on the border, on the riverbank. They had to make sure the bridges were safe for the troops. When they had done that, we crossed into Germany. Wherever the Third Army was—and sometimes the Seventh Army—we went. We were going straight across Germany. We were diverted once to Bavaria because they thought the German army in Italy was retreating and would come up through northern Italy and France to join the rest of the Germans. The people in Bavaria were interesting with their hats and leather pants, but we didn't have any time to enjoy that.

Patton's headquarters was close by. I saw him a couple of times, with his two ivory-handled revolvers. For Patton, you had to be in military dress. He was all about rules and regulations. You couldn't walk around without your hat on or be lackadaisical in any way.

We had Germans to do KP. When you went to empty your tray, they would say, "Can I have that?" They took the leftover food because they didn't have any.

After we drove ammunition and supplies to the front, we would drive loads of German prisoners to the rear. They spoke German so we didn't have a chance to interact with them, but they seemed disgruntled—they didn't know what to expect.

We also transported men and women from the concentration camps. These were people they wanted us to take out to an Allied camp where they would be identified and deloused and so forth. We'd pick them up right outside the camps. We'd squeeze as many as we could into the trucks—thirty, forty, more. Most of them had their prison uniforms on, and some were half dressed. Some were emaciated. We had to help them into the truck. Sometimes when we stopped in a town for a break, German people—usually women— would point up the hill and say, "That was a concentration camp." The idea seemed to be that the bad people were up there but the women telling us didn't have anything to do with it.

We didn't know much about what had happened in the concentration camps until later when *Stars and Stripes*, the Army newspaper, came out with stories about it. It was terrible to see what condition the people in the camps were in, but it was only later that I really knew what happened there and could relate it to my experience.

All in all, for me, serving in the Army was like going from Boston to live in Georgia. It was a whole different kind of life.

From time to time, some woman would come up and say she

was raped by a black guy. They would call up the company, and the company would have to line up and this woman would come by with the white commanding officer and stop and look at every soldier to see if he was the one. Then she would go away, and nothing ever came of it. That happened three or four times, in both France and Germany. I had spent my time in camp, so I always knew I wasn't in trouble. But it became a routine, and men who had been in town would be concerned that they would be chosen by mistake.

Another time, one of our soldiers was shot dead. He had gone to a canteen where there were men from a nearby white engineering company. Officers from the Third Army came down because they thought there had been a fight between the white and the black soldiers. They made us line up so they could find out who was there.

When the war ended, we were in Pilzen, in Czechoslovakia. We were happy, of course, that the war was over. We didn't get killed, we didn't get frostbite—lots of bad things could have happened.

Even with the war over, we were instructed not to fraternize with the enemy. They would come into the camp and beg for food. Our officers would come out and chase them away and tell us we weren't supposed to have anything to do with them.

We left Czechoslovakia before the Russians came in to take it over. We went back to France. I spent my time there learning to type because I was thinking of going back to school. Because I could type, I was transferred to headquarters.

After the winter of 1945–46, I went home. In addition to a good conduct medal and the stripes of a T/5 (equivalent to corporal), I had earned five battle stars—Normandy, Northern France, the Rhineland, Central Europe, and the Ardennes.

Jim Grosvenor used the GI Bill to go to Boston University, where he majored in American history and English and earned a master's degree in remedial reading and psychology. He became a teacher in Cambridge, Massachusetts, and later at Manville School, a private elementary school for children with emotional and learning problems. He came to New Hampshire during the 1960s to help turn a tutoring program for troubled students at Spaulding Youth Center into a certified elementary school. He worked for the state until his retirement, and he and his wife lived in East Andover. After she died in 2004, he moved to Concord.

Ruth White with a photo of her dad, a chaplain from Greenland, N.H.

Ruth White

Life without Father

Ruth White was the eight-year-old daughter of a Baptist pastor when the Japanese bombed Pearl Harbor. Her father, Charles Blakeney, went to Europe as a chaplain, and she never saw him again.

My father was a Canadian citizen. He had tried to go into the service in 1938, when the British began mobilizing, but he was too old, way over six feet tall, didn't weigh enough, and had bad teeth. They wouldn't take him.

My mother didn't want him to go, but my dad was determined. You couldn't stay home. You had to fight for what you believed in. He said, what good would I be here?

When we got to Greenland, New Hampshire, he tried again. I'm not sure he gained any weight, but he got his teeth fixed. Eventually they needed chaplains so desperately that they took him. They sent chaplains to Harvard. The college changed in the summer to train specific groups.

Within six months, he was sent to Wales, where they were massing for D-Day, as a chaplain in the 112th Infantry Regiment. The chaplain acted as a liaison with the town fathers. They would talk about the medical, the water, sanitation, and so forth that this huge American camp was going to be imposing on the English countryside. He became close friends with the mayor in Camarthen.

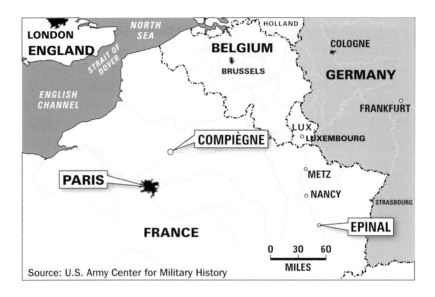

Source: U.S. Army Center for Military History

My mother took his place as pastor at the Baptist church when he left. She didn't preach the sermons. An interim minister came over from Kittery on Sunday. But my mother visited people in the hospital, she was in charge of the church youth group, she kept my father informed through letters. They wrote each other almost daily.

Greenland was a town of about six hundred people. We had blackout every night. There were dark curtains in the house, and you had to cover the top half of the headlights on your car—if you were still running your car. We had air-raid drills in the elementary school where we went down in the basement. They taught us songs—"Old Molly Pitcher"—I still know the words—and we would sing while we were down there.

We were near Portsmouth, which was considered a prime target because of the Navy yard. Many of the men in Greenland worked there. They were building submarines, and we knew there were German subs off the coast.

There wasn't much to buy. The men working were making good money, but factories all around the country changed what they were making. They weren't making refrigerators, they were making jeeps.

The war didn't affect our diet much because we had lived through the Depression. We had ration stamps for coffee, canned goods, meat. Every week they would tell you which stamps you could use because they might have more eggs or whatever.

I remember the meals, and I still like them today. Corn chowder, beans and hot dogs, macaroni, fish chowder, grilled cheese sandwiches. I still have some of the recipes—here's one for a milkless, eggless, butterless cake. It had a third of a cup of lard plus raisins and nutmeg, lots of spices, and you put it all together and made like a moist molasses brownie. The soufflé—without any eggs, you made cheese sandwiches and put them in a casserole and covered it with milk. Tomato-oatmeal stew: tomatoes and carrots and onions, but instead of meat, there was a cup of oatmeal.

I don't remember feeling deprived. One of the good things about rationing was that you didn't have any less than anybody else.

We had maps on the wall for both theaters of war. Almost everybody did. We got the news from newsreels, and a lot people did go to the movies—Saturday matinees, double features. They did a lot of propaganda through Hollywood, though we didn't think anything of it at the time. Mickey Mouse and Donald Duck had uniforms on to get people to enlist. They used the media to try to convince you that the Japanese and the Germans were bad—you've gotta teach people to hate them if you're going to kill them.

The 112th Infantry went into France after D-Day. They marched down the Champs Élysées after the liberation of Paris and then went northeast toward the German border. They were going along near Compiègne, and there was sniper fire. Some people were hit. They wanted a chaplain, so my father went out with the medic, and that's when the sniper hit him. It was September 1, 1944.

That night, a taxi driver from Portsmouth brought my mother a telegram saying my father was critically wounded. Then we waited. It was a terrible, terrible time. My mother and my aunt wrote everywhere. They wrote to Governor (Robert O.) Blood. She wrote to Washington. She called people.

Two and a half months later, we were down at my aunt's house in Massachusetts for Thanksgiving weekend. The morning after Thanksgiving, the phone rang, and it was our neighbors. They said, "We've got a telegram here. Shall we open it?" And we said yes. After the call, the adults were in shock, I guess, and just sat in the living room. I thought, somebody should cry, so I did, and then everyone else did.

We went to North Station to get the train for Portsmouth. My cousin, who was in the WAVES in Boston, came down to the station to give us hugs and support. Trains were crowded in those days, and there were no seats together. I thought, I should be with my mother, but I was a seat behind her. It was a long trip home.

He died the day after he was shot. There was never any explanation of why it took so long to inform us.

After my father died, my mother went back to work as a teacher. We had to leave the parsonage. It was tough—everybody else had dads, and I didn't. It was just the two of us, my mother and I. I didn't have any brothers or sisters. My mother was so distraught. She would cry and I would cry, and after a while we didn't talk about it much, which was probably a mistake. I remember thinking I'm never, ever going to do anything to give my mother any grief because she's had more than she needs already. I still miss him.

I was eleven years old. I didn't want to go to school after he was killed because I was afraid they were going to tease me. Nothing happened, of course. But when you're little, you don't want to be different. And I was different. I felt really different for a long time. I felt that I didn't have a complete family almost until I got married.

The people in the church loved my mother. The town was supportive of anybody who had anybody in the service. After the war, people would invite me up to their camp on a lake and that sort of thing. It was nice to go, and I knew they were being nice, but I knew I was there because I was different.

For us, the end of the war was bittersweet. I didn't feel the same sense of excitement when the war ended that everybody else did. I was glad the war was over, but for me it had already been over.

My mother was a quiet woman, very soft-spoken. When the 112th Regiment came home and landed, imagine how everybody would have been so hyped and so excited and so delirious to have made it. My mother went down amid all that happiness to talk to the chaplains who knew my dad and find out what they knew about his death. I can't imagine anybody doing it at that point, but she did.

She learned the story of his death. He was shot in the abdomen and probably knew he wasn't going to make it.

I had two cousins in the Canadian army. They were both killed. Everybody but those two was a daughter, so the Blakeney name is gone except that my granddaughter has it as a middle name, which is wonderful.

My father was buried in a temporary cemetery, and he's now buried in the Vosges Mountains, in Epinal. I went in 1986. When you go in these military cemeteries, as far as the eye can see, there are crosses and Stars of David. When you come, there's a place where you get the book out to see where your family member is. And there are three books of just names starting with "Bl." Then you think that's just one of so many cemeteries.

It's gut-wrenching even if you don't have somebody there. I hadn't cried for a long time, but when I got to the cemetery, I lost it completely.

The stone is just chiseled granite, a blah white stone with a name on it. They take flowers down, and they take black dust and put it in the carved letters so the name stands out, and you can take a picture. It's extremely well done. Both my sons have gone.

I started watching the Ken Burns series (*The War*), but when they got to the Vosges Mountains, where my father is buried, I turned it off and never turned it back on.

Just before my mother died, she said, "I wish we'd brought the body back." But she'd originally said he would want to be there because it was so important to him. When you read his letters, it's clear he felt so strongly about being part of the support for the men.

On her stone I put "Charles Blakeney, buried in France." In Greenland, on Memorial Day, they put up a flag, as if he were there. She'd be pleased.

Ruth White went to the University of New Hampshire on a war orphan's scholarship. She wrote her master's thesis on the American chaplain. A retired teacher who worked for many years in the Kearsarge Regional School District, she lives in New London, New Hampshire.

"The Japanese bombed us every night," says Gerard Joyal.

Gerard Joyal

A Marine on Bougainville

On December 7, 1941, Gerard Joyal was a sixteen-year-old attendant at the New Hampshire State Hospital in Concord. When he learned of the attack on Pearl Harbor, he hitchhiked to Franklin to ask his mother to sign his enlistment papers. She refused but allowed her son to join the Marines a few months later.

We ended up going to the Russell Islands, above Guadalcanal. We had an airfield and we would service the planes to bomb the other islands. That place was loaded with parrots. When they took off, it was pretty, like a flying rainbow.

We were taking a lot of islands, but the biggest one was Bougainville. They wanted to take it because they could bomb Rabaul, a big Japanese naval base. When we got Bougainville, we could arm the planes and bomb the Japanese.

We hit the beach, the front of the LST (landing ship, tank) opened, and we drove out with our equipment. All we had was ten square miles. The Japanese had had an airstrip, and we built two more, another fighter strip and a bomber strip.

We had Douglas dive bombers, Corsair fighters, and Grumman torpedo bombers. That was about it. A couple of B-24s came in that

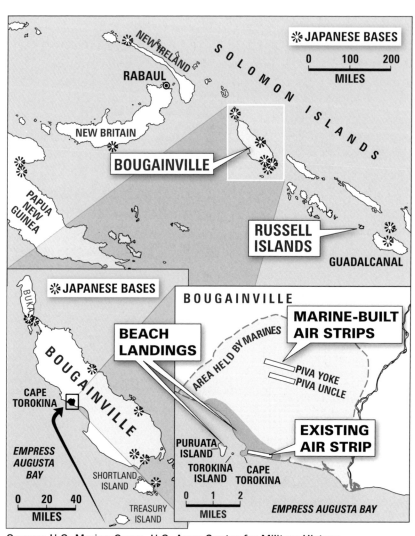

Source: U.S. Marine Corps, U.S. Army Center for Military History

we serviced, but they weren't part of our squadron. Some of them were shot up. I saw one that looked like a sieve, but it came back.

The rest of the island was Japanese. We turned all our planes around so the machine guns would face the lines. The Navy came in with a destroyer and a light cruiser and shelled the Japanese all night long. You could hear the guns fire and see the flames, hear the bombs go overhead and see them land.

We were on Bougainville about fourteen months. It rained two hundred inches a year. It was all swamp. There weren't any parrots on Bougainville, just snakes and wild boars and jungle. Once, swimming in the water on the edge of a reef, I saw an octopus. I got one look at him and I got out.

I was a crew chief, responsible for about sixty men. The Japanese bombed us every night. We would dig a hole and put our cots in it, so when they came we didn't have to get up. One night, I lay there and watched a rat and a centipede on top of my mosquito net, fighting. The rat won.

We would put bombs together and store them on small trailers for other squadrons. We might have a thousand trailers loaded and ready. We had a bomb dump where we'd bring the bombs in and stack them. One day, a Japanese shell hit the dump and set off two hundred and fifty bombs.

We had different types of bombs. Some would go off if you just dropped them, so you had to be careful. In our spare time we used to make up bombs called daisy-cutters. We'd put in nails, scrap metal, and boosters to make them explode quicker. When they exploded, they would shred everything. The planes used to drop them on Japanese gardens. We didn't want them to get too healthy.

I got a fungus. It was like blisters—they'd break and run. It got to be like a big scab. My hands, my feet, my head were all scabbed over. I couldn't bend my fingers. They evacuated me to the Russell Islands to a hospital. They couldn't cure it. I had to go down to Guadalcanal, and they couldn't cure it either. I didn't get rid of it until I got home.

About once a week we got letters. My mother was born in Canada and had trouble writing English. I'd get a letter that would be half French, half English, but I knew it took her all night to write

Joyal had several encounters with Pacific island wildlife.

that letter, so it meant a lot to me. They'd load a sea bag with mail and call your name. It was worth waiting for.

We didn't eat too good: Spam, Vienna sausage. The rats would eat up the food dump, so three nights a week all the squadrons would get together with clubs and chase rats. They'd chew right through a can. The most I ever got in one night was forty-three. That's a lot of rats.

The torpedoes ran on alcohol, and they put what they called pink lady in it to make you sick if you drank it. If the planes didn't use the torpedoes, we were supposed to dump the liquid out. We dumped it out, but not back in the barrel. We made torpedo juice instead. We had copper tubing and guys from Tennessee. They knew what to do. At night in the foxholes, we'd run the stuff through a still and get the pink lady out of it. I didn't drink it. It was a hundred proof and a great bartering tool. We could barter for stuff we didn't have, food from the Navy and the Seabees: peaches, pears, powdered eggs, butter.

Transportation was hard to come by. We stole a jeep from the Army. We went up to our place, threw the top away, painted it Marine green, and wrote "USMC" on the side. We had it a couple of weeks. Then we got a call from the captain.

On one island, we found a brook with trout, but we didn't have fishing poles. So we went back with hand grenades and block TNT, threw them in, and the fish came to the surface.

It's survival. You did whatever you could to make it easy for you or the other fellows.

Gerard Joyal returned to the States with his unit during the summer of 1945. He was on a thirty-day leave when Japan surrendered. He returned to New Hampshire and married his childhood sweetheart, Beverly. They were married for more than fifty-seven years. He worked as a tradesman for the state for nearly four decades, surviving near-electrocution in 1953 and helping drive President Eisenhower around the state in 1955. Joyal recently received a medal from the government of the Solomon Islands thanking him for helping to capture the region from the Japanese.

Elwood Thompson witnessed the Rangers' ascent at Pointe du Hoc.

Elwood Thompson

D-Day, Omaha Beach

Elwood Thompson is eighty-eight years old and lives in Franklin, New Hampshire. When the Japanese bombed Pearl Harbor, he was living in Andover, New Hampshire, and working as a carpenter. He landed on Omaha Beach on June 6 with the 618th Ordnance Ammunition Company.

In 1942, I was working on a government project in Springfield, Vermont. One weekend I came home to Andover to visit my father. He had been in World War I. He started in Franklin in a machine gun company, but they changed that to a field artillery company. He never got a chance to go to France. He wanted to make a little bet with me. He said, "I'm going to be in the service before you are." I said, "How do you figure that? They aren't going to take you. You're almost forty years old." All my friends were in, and I told him I was going to join, too. About the middle of the next week I got a card from him down in Fort Devens—already in. He was training troops as a corporal, his old rating.

I took the oath December 5, 1942, and joined the engineers, the 90th Heavy Pontoon. I shipped to northern Alberta the next spring. Six months later, they deactivated that outfit and sent me to Camp Pickett, Virginia, where I joined the smallest outfit in the Army,

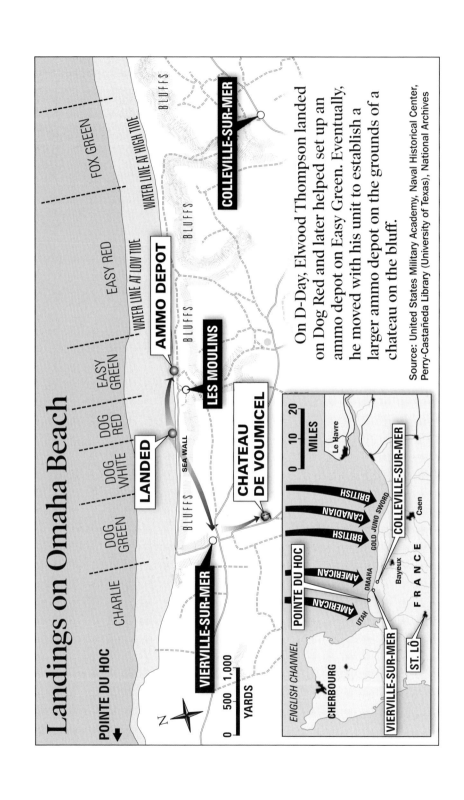

Landings on Omaha Beach

POINTE DU HOC

CHARLIE

DOG GREEN

DOG WHITE

DOG RED

EASY GREEN

EASY RED

FOX GREEN

WATER LINE AT LOW TIDE

WATER LINE AT HIGH TIDE

BLUFFS

BLUFFS

BLUFFS

BLUFFS

BLUFFS

SEA WALL

LANDED

AMMO DEPOT

LES MOULINS

VIERVILLE-SUR-MER

CHATEAU DE VOUMICEL

COLLEVILLE-SUR-MER

N

YARDS

0   500   1,000

On D-Day, Elwood Thompson landed on Dog Red and later helped set up an ammo depot on Easy Green. Eventually, he moved with his unit to establish a larger ammo depot on the grounds of a chateau on the bluff.

Source: United States Military Academy, Naval Historical Center, Perry-Castañeda Library (University of Texas), National Archives

ENGLISH CHANNEL

CHERBOURG

POINTE DU HOC

AMERICAN

AMERICAN

UTAH

OMAHA

BRITISH

CANADIAN

BRITISH

GOLD JUNO SWORD

Le Havre

Bayeux

Caen

COLLEVILLE-SUR-MER

VIERVILLE-SUR-MER

ST. LÔ

FRANCE

MILES

0   10   20

forty-nine men, the 618th Ordnance Ammunition Company. We shipped over to England in December of 1943.

They took over a whole town in England on the channel and moved everybody out. They took the bulldozers and carpenters in there and built the waterfront so it looked like Normandy. It was known as Slapton Sands. I made two practice landings there, and it was scary. Before D-Day, we marched down to Southampton, where they had a shingle—a stone beach that projects out into the water. There were six LSTs (landing ships, tank) there. We had several dry runs out into the English Channel.

On June 6, we were already on our LST in the channel. They got us up at four in the morning. My outfit was supporting the 29th Infantry Division, so we had a lot of men from that unit on board with us. There was a combat engineer outfit, too, the 202nd. I was up on the deck, but you couldn't see much because it was dark. The boat was heaving up and down because of the weather.

I had my M-1 carbine, and I was carrying two grenades. I had two clips of fifteen for my carbine and a box of ammunition to replace the bullets in the clips. I had a combat pack that was supposed to weigh twenty-six pounds. Inside were an extra pair of socks and one blanket, a raincoat, and rations for three days. We had D-rations, which were nothing but a chocolate bar, C-rations, which were cans that made up a meal, and K-rations, which were in a waterproof container. And of course, I had a couple of cartons of cigarettes.

We had to wear our ODs (olive drab uniforms) to show we were American soldiers. They soaked that thing in some kind of impregnating stuff, to stop gas from going through your clothing. We also had over-alls over the ODs, and they were soaked in that stinking stuff. Our boots were covered with it, too. It was a terrible smell. And we were hot—pretty bulky outfit. And they had this oily stuff that you smeared over your hands and face, also for gas.

Our LST stopped about a mile off the beach at Normandy. We waited up on deck to climb down the rigging into the landing craft. Visibility still wasn't good, but you could see the beach. Our first wave went off, and we got all belted up and ready to go. The six boats that were supposed to come and pick us up got lost. So the commander of the ship said, "I know you guys have got to get in there, so I'm going to take you in." He started in with that LST. We got in about a hundred yards from shore, and the shells started dropping right around the ship. The doggone naval commander ordered him to get that thing the hell out of there.

He couldn't take it in reverse, so he swung it to the right. He took us right in there and we saw the Rangers going up that cliff—Pointe du Hoc. They had this sixty-foot extension ladder mounted on a barge, and they got that thing in under the rocks along the shore. They ran it up, but the cliff was about a hundred feet, so they were forty feet short. They had a small-caliber rope gun, and the rope got wet and heavy so they couldn't even throw a grapple rope. They had an awful time. We could see the Germans on top shooting down at them.

By the time we got back in position, it was clear, but all you could see was smoke and fire on the beach—terrible smoke. The big boats, the Texas and the Nevada and the others, were firing away.

Our section of the beach was supposed to be Easy Green, but it was so plugged up that the coxswain had to get out of there and land at Dog Red. We didn't know where the hell we were. They had told us we wouldn't have to dig in after we landed because the bombers had gone over earlier in the morning and there would be all kinds of bomb craters. There wasn't a bomb crater within a mile and a half of the beach!

We climbed over the rigging. We knew this was it. We knew we were in for something, but we didn't know what.

We had fifteen men on our landing craft. Some got sick on the way in, but I didn't. Coming in, they had these railroad irons welded together in a "V." On top there was a mine to blow up boats. They called them Belgian gates. Here was this guy from my outfit, his arms wrapped around the gate, hanging on and hollering, "Help! Help! Help!" He was from our company, but we couldn't stop to help him. I guess his landing craft had been blown out from under him. I never saw him afterward.

I pushed way up to the front of my landing craft because I wanted to get out of there as quick as I could. When that door went down, I was the first one out. The water was up to my knees, and I was maybe thirty feet from land.

The first thing I saw was just wet sand, and right away I looked for cover. I saw a seawall to my left, and I said, "I guess that's my best bet." We were taking machine gun fire from the right, nothing from the left. There were bodies in the water and on the beach, and you had to get over them. I could see maybe twenty men down. You weren't supposed to stop. No matter what, they said, keep going. And I never looked back either.

There had been two photographers from *Life* magazine on my LST. They had dark green uniforms. One of them went in with the first wave. Just as I got to the beach, there was his camera on the ground. I had to kick it out of the way, for crying out loud. I don't know whether he got killed or whether he just lost his camera there on the beach.

I had about a hundred yards of beach to cross. I could see bullets hitting in the sand and hear them going past me. A lot of guys made the mistake of hitting the ground there. Then they made a good target. I just kept zigzagging and kept going, which wasn't easy because I had water rushing out of my boots. I might have fallen down a couple of times—I don't know. I was just running as fast as I could with those soggy boots.

I made it to the seawall—and then wished I hadn't. A medical outfit had dug in there, and the casualties were terrible. There were maybe half a dozen of them, arms missing, faces blown in. It made you sick. I went around to the other side of the seawall and dug in there. I couldn't go much beyond there because there was a long double-apron barbed-wire fence there, probably six foot high and twelve foot across and thirty or forty feet away.

I was alone at first. I didn't know where the rest of my outfit was.

I stayed by the seawall until they got the barbed wire cut. It was risky going near that barbed wire because the Germans had that all zeroed in. The engineers came down with Bangalore torpedoes. A Bangalore torpedo is a piece of thin tubing, about two and a half inches in diameter and probably six foot in length, and it's full of TNT. The first one has a pointed end so it will keep going through, and the next one that goes in has a blunt end, and they push the first one through with it. When the first one reaches the other side of that barbed wire, they put on another one with a detonator in it. And then you use a fuse. I saw the German machine guns kill the first man who tried to get the torpedo through, and another man took his place. They got him, too. The third man got the torpedo through, and it blew a hole through the barbed wire.

By this time there were about six men waiting where I was, none of them from my company. We all crawled through the hole in the wire. We dug in again and waited for people to come along and group us up. We had no business there—it wasn't where we were supposed to set up. Finally we moved down to where we were supposed to be—Easy Green.

There we set up our ammunition supply point, the first on Omaha Beach. Our job was to provide ammunition to the men after they moved in off the beach. We unloaded the ammunition, sorted it and put it where we could find it even in the dark to load onto the trucks. We were on a good flat place about fifty yards from the water. We were at the base of a hill so the Germans couldn't see us—they would shoot over the top of us from the big bluff.

They set up the morgue right beside us. As they brought the bodies in, Graves Registration took care of them. They stripped the bodies, all the packs and everything, and put them up in a pile. Some were in body bags, mattress covers. Some were just laid out.

A couple of Rangers who had scaled the cliffs at Pointe du Hoc came up and wanted us to fill their jeeps with grenades and small-arms ammunition. They still had their faces blacked up. One of them told me how the people who ordered the taking of that point were damned fools. He said there wasn't a gun up there.

We stayed on the beach for maybe three days. Once the troops had moved inland far enough to make it secure, we set up a new ammunition supply point on a field up on the bluff. We got up there on a crisscross trail that the engineers cut. The Germans were shooting at us, so we dug in twice along the way. I was digging in, and my helmet was in the way, so I set it on the sand pile, and the next thing I knew a bullet hit that helmet and threw it ten feet. I had to go get it. There was no hole in it, just a crease.

There was a large area with barbed wire around it with signs hanging on it with the skull and crossbones and the word "Minen"

In the sand of Omaha Beach, Thompson
saw a Life *photographer's camera.*

(mines). We supposed there were mines all across that field. The engineers went through with a mine sweeper and cleared a path wide enough for two men and marked it with engineer's tape—white tape. You're supposed to stay inside the tape. These two guys, they just got off the boat, gung-ho, and they got behind us, and they said, "You guys are going too slow." And we said, "If you don't like it, go ahead." They plunged out there, goll dern it, and one of them stepped on a mine.

We got up to the top of the bluff in the evening and probed for mines up there all night long. Didn't find any. I guess Rommel (Erwin Rommel, the German general) had time to put the signs up there but no time to put in the mines. We set up our big depot there. The DUKWs (six-wheeled amphibious trucks, called "Ducks" by the soldiers) came in all day bringing ammunition, and it was sorted and hauled up to us.

It was my job to help set up the bivouac area on the grounds of a big chateau. We went to set up the CP (command post) near the gate. Up in a tree, buried in the trunk, was a projectile—could have been one of their 88s or one of our 105s. Every time you went by that thing, you wondered if it was going to go off. Right where the captain wanted his tent set up, there were two German bodies buried with helmets on the graves. We had to dig up the bodies and move them so we could set the CP up. They weren't in coffins—we figured they were guards and were the first to die when the bluff was taken.

They moved in two big shower units with hot water. We'd been wearing that stinky clothing for days and days by then. They said. "Okay, boys, strip everything off and throw it in that pile there." They told us to keep our boots. And after the shower, they gave us a new issue of clothing.

About that time the rain started—a big storm—and it must have rained twenty days after. The only way the vehicles could move in the mud was to get one across and winch the rest across. You'd get back to your foxhole at night and there'd be six inches of water in it. You'd have to take your helmet and bail the water out and get some old ammunition crates and put them in the bottom. You were tired enough that you slept anyway. We didn't have our shoes off for three or four days at a time.

The big storm came on June 19. It wiped out our operation down on the beach. We had breakwaters down there, Mulberries (artificial harbors), and a regular dock to unload ammunition. Since no more ammunition could come from the water, we took a bulldozer and scraped an area flat up on the bluff and laid down steel matting, and they brought the ammunition in by air to supply the troops.

We stayed there a couple of weeks and then moved up to Saint-Lô. After the breakthrough at Saint-Lô, they pulled us out.

Elwood Thompson served out the war at several outposts in the south of France. After the war, he built his own house in Franklin and had a long career as a carpenter. Of his war experience, he now says: "I wouldn't have missed it for the world, but I wouldn't do it again for a million dollars."

Colonel Robert Fortnam made an unscheduled landing.

Robert Fortnam

Shot Down and Captured

*Colonel Robert Fortnam of Pembroke, New Hampshire, was five
years old in 1927 when Lindbergh flew the Atlantic, and from then
on, he yearned to fly. He joined the Army on January 2, 1942, and
got his wish. After training stateside, he was shipped to England
to join the 365th Bomb Squadron of the 305th Bombardment
Group. His first mission as a B-17 co-pilot was uneventful. "I wasn't
smart enough to be scared," he said. Then his luck ran out.*

The second mission was October 8, 1943—I'll never forget that
date. It's an eight-hour flight, and you're carrying a dozen five-
hundred-pound bombs, bringing the total weight of the plane
to fifty-three thousand pounds. It takes three hours just to take off,
climb to altitude, get into formation, and get to the enemy coast.
Then you've got a couple of hours flying to your target and three
hours back to base. The fighters left us at the European coast or fifty
miles inland. The P-47s didn't have the range to go farther.

We were over the German border when enemy fighters hit us,
but I wasn't aware of the attack except that the window beside me
broke. I looked out and No. 3 engine was on fire. I looked over to
reach for the fire control, and Wally Emmert, the first pilot, was
gone. So I pushed the fire control buttons, and the fire went out. I

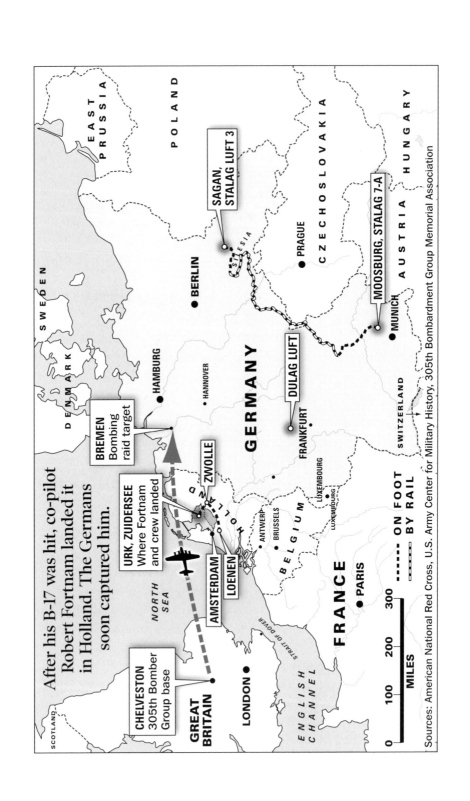

After his B-17 was hit, co-pilot Robert Fortnam landed it in Holland. The Germans soon captured him.

CHELVESTON ● 305th Bomber Group base

GREAT BRITAIN

● LONDON

SCOTLAND

NORTH SEA

ENGLISH CHANNEL

STRAIT OF DOVER

BREMEN Bombing raid target

URK, ZUIDERSEE Where Fortnam and crew landed

ZWOLLE

AMSTERDAM

LOENEN

HOLLAND

● HAMBURG

● HANNOVER

GERMANY

● BERLIN

SAGAN, STALAG LUFT 3

SILESIA

DULAG LUFT

● FRANKFURT

SWEDEN

DENMARK

EAST PRUSSIA

POLAND

CZECHOSLOVAKIA

● PRAGUE

MOOSBURG, STALAG 7-A

MUNICH ●

AUSTRIA

HUNGARY

SWITZERLAND

LUXEMBOURG

● ANTWERP

● BRUSSELS

BELGIUM

LUXEMBOURG

FRANCE

● PARIS

- - - - - **ON FOOT**
━━━━━ **BY RAIL**

MILES
0   100   200   300

Sources: American National Red Cross, U.S. Army Center for Military History, 305th Bombardment Group Memorial Association

asked the navigator—"Where's Wally? Has anybody seen Wally?" Nobody had seen Wally.

I tried to figure out how to keep the airplane going. I added power to the other engines. No. 2 engine malfunctioned, and I had to shut it down, too. So now we were losing speed and falling back in the formation.

I decided we had to turn back and try to get to the coast and ditch in the North Sea. If we could make that, our chances were good. The Brits had set up an excellent air-sea rescue system. Crews had been rescued within an hour. I asked the navigator to send out his best estimate of our ditching position based on the amount of time I thought we might be able to fly.

The navigator found Wally and revived him with a portable oxygen bottle. He was turning blue. He had been shot in the abdomen. Under the cockpit there's a crawl-way to get to the nose. He was lying down there, but at twenty-five thousand feet you shouldn't do that. You can't breathe—there's no oxygen. He left his oxygen mask when he left his station.

He got back into the cockpit, and we discussed the situation briefly and decided to land in the Zuidersee in Holland. We could see it ahead. We decided we couldn't make it to the North Sea after all.

I ordered everybody back into the radio room into crash-landing positions. I realized at about eight hundred feet that I didn't have my seatbelt fastened. It was too late to take my hands off the controls, so I put my feet up on the rudder bar to brace myself.

We were over drained land. I picked a place straight ahead. I couldn't put the landing gear down because it would dig right in and cause the plane to stumble, maybe even flip over. I just made a normal landing without wheels. The ball turret plowed a four-hundred-yard trough in the ground. Anyway, it was a good landing—everybody walked away from it. I call it an "off-airport landing." I climbed out through the co-pilot's window. Everybody else went through the rear door.

Only when we were on the ground did I realize we still had the bombs. I had pulled the red handle to release them, but that only opened the doors. Because I had had so little training on the B-17 and because I wasn't the first pilot, I didn't know you had to pull it a second time to drop the bombs. We landed with a full load of bombs, although they're not fully armed until the little propeller on them unwinds.

Drainage canals crisscrossed the whole area. The tailgunner had also been shot, so we had two wounded crew members. Some people came out to help, but they couldn't get to us because of the canals. A couple of the fellows told them we had two wounded people. They said they would take care of them, get them to a hospital, which we later learned they did.

The rest of us split up in pairs. You traveled easier in pairs— it's too hard for people to make decisions in larger groups. Also, if you're traveling in a group, you'll never get picked up by the underground. One or two might. I paired up with the navigator, Ernie Shelander, and we started walking. That was the last I saw of any of the others in the crew.

We came to a drainage canal. It was chilly, but we stripped and swam across, holding our clothes up. We dried off and put our clothes back on. We came to a bigger canal. It was too wide to swim and it was getting late. Across the canal a barge was tied up against a pier. We stayed low and figured we'd try to cross in the morning. We curled up together for the body heat and slept that night in the bushes.

The next morning, we heard a fellow whistling, "You are my sunshine, my only sunshine." He had seen us in the weeds, and he had whistled that song, which any American would recognize and no German would. He said, "Stay there till noontime, and I'll get a boat and get you across the canal somehow." He brought a couple of apples and some other food for us. He rowed us across and pointed us toward the mainland.

The next town we came to was Zwolle. We kept walking. We slept in a haystack. We were looking for food and also looking to swipe a couple of bicycles, but we never found two together. We walked through villages where the houses were built right up to the sidewalk. Children were sitting on the steps watching us. We couldn't avoid the towns because it was all rural land, and wet.

The third day we were walking through a town called Loenen. It was about three o'clock in the afternoon. The Dutch police stopped us. We didn't have any papers, of course, so we were arrested and turned over to the Germans. One German guard came over and said, "Follow me." I thought about leaving, but I was scared. I didn't know the people or the language. Here's somebody who's going to take care of you, and being a human being, you expect that someone else might be a human being, too.

They took us to Amsterdam, and we ended up the next day at Dulag Luft, the interrogation center just outside of Frankfurt. The Germans knew all about the air crews—they had crew lists, they had spies in England. But they didn't have anything on us because we were a replacement crew. You told them name, rank, and serial number, didn't give them any information. I was held in a cell for two days and they put me on a boxcar to prison camp. They split Shelander and me up and I never saw him again.

They took me to Stalag Luft 3 in Sagan (now Zagan, Poland), ninety miles southeast of Berlin. You walk through a fence and you're back with a bunch of Americans who look on you with suspicion because they don't know if the Germans have put a spy in there. Everybody was interviewed, asked personal questions, sports questions—things only an American would know.

We settled into the routine. There was an existing government under Colonel Delmar Spivey, the senior American officer. We were segregated by nationality. We had double bunks. There were maybe twelve hundred men in the camp, a hundred in each building.

The Germans gave us bread and potatoes and some kohlrabi. It was like a turnip. They gave us barley every day and a ration of roast beef every three weeks. Red Cross food packages saved our health. They came by train, and we were supposed to be given one package per man per week. But when the fighters began shooting up the transports, it went to half a package.

We were treated better because we were all officers. All the German guards were older men, no longer fit for front-line service. They knew which way the wind was blowing. Germany was a signatory to the Geneva Convention of 1929 on the care and custody of prisoners of war. So they thought if we take care of these guys, they'll take care of our prisoners over there.

We had almost no contact with Germans. Only designated people could speak with them. I've never been a smoker, but in the Red Cross package there was always a pack or two of cigarettes. The Germans would bring in anything, especially in winter. They'd strap a chicken underneath their greatcoats. So these four or five designated prisoners were barterers. They'd trade one cigarette to get an egg, which I would give a whole pack for.

In camp, you started the day by trying to wash up. You'd go to the cookhouse to get hot water for coffee. I kept a little for myself to shave with. I had barley for breakfast and a little toast. We had some margarine—the colored stuff, which we didn't have in the States, even after the war—and jelly that came in packages from home.

After roll call every morning, we'd settle down and play cards or read books. We had a library of about a thousand fiction and a thousand nonfiction books, all supplied by Switzerland, the YMCA. Sports equipment came from there, too. I enjoyed reading. I took a walk around the compound every day, wrote letters. There were people who taught. I took German, Spanish. I took a class in celestial navigation. I received several college credits after the war.

We weren't allowed to work. Under the Geneva Conventions, officers don't work. They had about a hundred enlisted types there for menial chores.

The Germans were shooting down airplanes all the time, so the population of the camp grew, and they converted the bunks into triples. By the end of the war, there were more than twelve thousand prisoners.

The Great Escape occurred in another part of the camp. I didn't know about it until a senior officer came in afterward and announced it. In the next couple of days, fifty of the seventy-three men who were caught were shot. We knew what had happened.

We knew everything that was going on in the war. We had a BBC news broadcast every day. We had a crystal radio with earphones, and the Germans never found it. They tore the barracks apart trying. I never knew where it was until after the war. It turns out they

This U.S. bomb had Hitler's name on it.

took a leg off a table and hollowed it out and put it in there. I don't know where they kept the headset. Somebody would copy the news down, we'd gather in the middle of the building, and he'd read it. We'd post somebody at the end of the building, and if somebody hollered, "Goon coming!" we'd start talking about a baseball game or a movie.

When we heard about D-Day, the first thought was "Home by Christmas!" It didn't happen.

The Germans moved us out on January 27, 1945, because the Russians were coming. Hitler decided we were bargaining chips against unconditional surrender. He wouldn't let the Russians capture us. They moved us all down near Munich.

We made sleds to haul our belongings. I lugged this scrapbook with me about my experiences in prison camp, but I saw many such things discarded along the road. We hadn't been allowed to store foodstuffs—they punctured every can that came into camp. You could keep chocolate bars and things like that.

We started walking at four o'clock in the morning and hiked all the next day. We straggled along—no formation—in ten to twelve-degree temperatures—bitter cold. I slept in a tank garage one time and a brick factory another time, up in the loft where all the flues came up from the stoves down below. I had some dried soup with me and that was a treat.

Older people, injured people, fell by the wayside. People inactive for a year—you can't just set out and walk fifty miles.

We walked three days, and then they put us on trains. When there was an air raid, the engineer stopped the train under a bridge so the fighters couldn't destroy the locomotive. We'd walk up to the locomotive, and there was a little condensate drain valve. We got a cup of hot water and made tea or coffee. It's surprising what you can do when you need to.

We wound up at Stalag 7-A, north of Munich. Conditions were stinking there. We were stacked in, and more men kept coming from everywhere.

On April 29, General Patton's army came through. First thing in the morning, there was a skirmish for the town—Moosburg. Then a tank came rolling down the road in front of our entrance gate. You couldn't see anything but the barrel of the gun. There were men all over it—men on top of the track guard, men on top of the tank itself. Our reaction was, "Oh, boy!" But then there was a better reaction because at lunchtime a truck showed up with a big Red Cross on the side and three girls serving coffee. Three girls! Real American girls!

A couple of days later we were trucked to an airfield. The next morning they said there'd be fifty airplanes there. Not five minutes later, I looked up and saw a couple of specks and two or three more in trail. By nine o'clock there were fifty C-47s on the ground. They were delivering fuel in five-gallon jerry cans for Patton's tanks, which were running ahead of their fuel supply. We had to unload the fuel so we could get on the planes.

We were taken to Reims and then to Camp Lucky Strike, a collection center where they made manifests for troop ships going home. When we arrived in New York Harbor, a couple of fireboats came along and there was another boat that had women all over it. That ship was listing our way and our ship was listing their way.

I got home at just the time my girlfriend, Marion Johnson, was graduating from the University of New Hampshire. She found out I was coming home and ditched the guy who had invited her to the prom. I got to escort her to the dance. We were married forty-eight years before she died in 1993.

Bob Fortnam, now eighty-five, stayed in the service and continued to fly, remaining in the Reserves until his retirement as a colonel. He graduated from the University of New Hampshire in two and a half years and became a mechanical engineer, designing machinery for the food industry. During a 2000 trip to Holland, he met Bart Bos, the man who whistled "You Are My Sunshine" and helped him across the canal the morning after his crash. Fortnam and his second wife, Janet, live in Pembroke. He still flies rental aircraft.

*From ship holds to prison camps, Bill Onufry
suffered the horrors of captivity.*

Bill Onufry

Under the Japanese Thumb

Bill Onufry is eighty-six years old and lives in Freedom, New Hampshire, a perfectly named town for a survivor of the Bataan Death March. He lived in Topsfield, Massachusetts, in 1940 when he turned eighteen and joined the Army Air Force. Six weeks after his enlistment, he was on his way to the Philippines.

In the Philippines, even a private could live like a millionaire. Things were cheap, and by local standards we made a lot of money.

I was stationed at Nichols Field. We got off work at one o'clock every day because they thought we couldn't handle the heat. We were free to ride cavalry horses at Fort McKinley or go to Manila whenever we wanted. There were all kinds of cafés and dance halls there. The Filipinos loved Americans and catered to us.

At Nichols Field I went to school to become an airplane technician. When I started, we had a little airplane called the P-26 with an open cockpit. [Laughs.] That was the state of the Air Force. P-40s were shipped in just before things got started. I became a crew chief, which meant I was in charge of two airplanes, a P-35 and a P-40.

We had no sense of any growing problem with Japan. The attack came on the same day as the Pearl Harbor bombing, and it was a

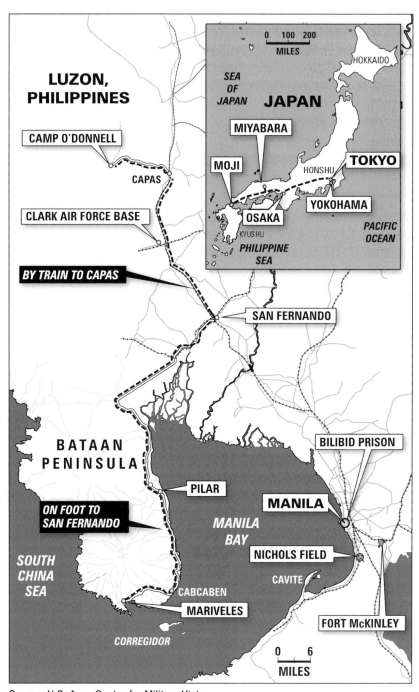

Source: U.S. Army Center for Military History

complete shock. I had been in town the night before raising heck with everybody. I was sound asleep. The charge of quarters came in and shook me and said, "Get up! Get up! Get down to the hangar line. We're at war." It was still dark out. I went back to sleep. He shook me again. This time I realized what he was saying, and I could hear all the commotion downstairs in the mess hall.

I went down to check on my P-40. I took the cover off and got it going. My pilot finally came and took it up, but he saw nothing and came back.

The next night at nine o'clock, we heard sirens and fires broke out all around the field. We could hear a hum in the distance. The Japanese had spies who had marked the fields with bonfires. The Japanese bombers came right down the line.

With the drone of those airplanes coming over, our first instinct was to run—get off the airfield. But then the bombs started to come down. We didn't get a chance to run. Another fellow and myself made it just off the field to some jungle where we felt a little bit protected. We turned around and watched. I saw my airplanes blown up almost instantly. A few planes got off, but not many.

They had blown big holes in the barracks, and we were instructed not to go back there. I did go back to get what I could. I had bought tailored suits in Manila, and I saw them hanging there and wondered if I would ever need them again.

There was not much in the way of orders about what to do. The officers seemed lost in spite of all the training. Everything was a confused mess. From that day on, we lived outside. We didn't even have tents much of the time. We'd be down working on what airplanes we had, but we had air raids almost every day. By the time the war was about a week old, we had fourteen airplanes left.

They used to bring down a truck with lunch. One time, the chow hounds lined up waiting for their sandwiches and coffee, and we heard airplanes again. I said to the fellow next to me, "Boy, if they come over now, they'll get a whole line of us." We could see some coming, and some guy says, "Oh, those are our P-40s." They had that antenna sticking up in the front that we didn't have. I said, "P-40s? Hell, those are Zeroes." We had no place to go. Four or five of them came over the field strafing, and we rolled into the tall grass along the sides. The bombers—about twenty-five of them—we called them Bettys—came after that.

Once when the Japanese came strafing in, I got underneath the wheel of a big road scraper. One of the planes shot a tire out. I got up and saw a piece of metal sticking out of the tire. It said "Ford V8" on it. For shrapnel, they were using scrap iron they had got from us.

This was just before Christmas. Not long after that, we abandoned the field. We loaded food, medicine, and ammunition, blew up everything we couldn't carry, and left for Manila. We loaded some inter-island steamers at the pier there. While we were in the harbor, the Japanese bombed it, even though we had declared Manila an open city so they wouldn't.

We left by ship for the Bataan Peninsula across Manila Bay. I didn't have much with me—no change of clothes, almost nothing. I went to a little airfield at Pilar. We camouflaged the field to look like a rice paddy. While we were waiting for planes, we built so-called revetments around the field to hide the planes. About eight planes came.

There was a report of Japanese aircraft in the area, and the planes all took off. A Japanese airplane came over—we called him Photo Joe, and we figured he took pictures of the field. The next morning, they blasted that field. We repaired it, but then our planes took off to Mindanao, to the south, and that was that.

That's when we found out we were being transferred to the "flying infantry." We were issued 1903 Springfield rifles, World War I equipment. We had shot a little bit in basic training, but not much. We also had .30 and .50-caliber machine guns that had come out of the airplanes. In the air they were fine, but on the ground they got too hot.

We were on beach defense, to keep more Japanese infantry from coming in. We were on our way back to a rest camp one day when a general came buzzing down in his jeep and told us some Japanese had landed. He wanted us to get back and get them out. There were more than a few—we were there twenty-two days.

We knew the situation was deteriorating. We had so little food that we tried to get food out of the jungle. One guy shot a wild boar, but it was so awful-tasting I couldn't eat it. They would shoot monkeys. They ate all the cavalry horses. I have a picture of one I used to ride. I didn't eat that either.

I was defending the beach near Mariveles at a place we called Monkey Point when I heard we had surrendered. We were instructed to destroy everything. We threw our .50-caliber machine gun into the ocean. One of the officers told us to march down to Mariveles.

Thousands of us gathered there, and we stayed there all day April 9 and all day the next day and never saw a Jap. We were instructed by our own officers to get into groups of a hundred. When the Japanese did arrive, we marched out.

We knew by hearsay and what we saw that the Japanese would not honor us as prisoners of war. I was in terrible shape, hungry, weak. I had had malaria, and I didn't have any medicine. We had no food, no water, and they didn't care to give us any. We didn't know where we were going.

The Japanese grabbed you to steal whatever you had—money, rings, cigarettes, though most of us had run out of those by then. They loved eyeglasses, whether they could see through them or not. My watch didn't last ten steps.

When they pulled us aside, they broke up our groups. There was also confusion because men were running out of the jungle along the way. Half of them had blood all over them from being hit or shot by the Japanese. As they came out to the road, the Japanese would just shoot them.

When we started out, half my outfit was with me, but we were soon separated. The Japanese mixed us up so much and stopped us so many times that, three hours into the march, I suddenly didn't see anybody I knew. I was all alone—a very bad feeling.

Finally I ran into a fellow named Brown I knew from our armament section. He was worse off than I was, and I tried to help him. I couldn't carry him, but I let him lean on me here and there, and we'd stop at night together. We buddied up.

I was on the road maybe eight or nine days. Every night we'd stop and rest in a yard or near a building with a fence around it. Plain ground, no food, no facilities. Men just used the ground to urinate and defecate. It was filthy. Then we'd start out again in the morning.

I got water now and then. Brown was with me once when I saw

a spigot and went to get some water. A guard jabbed me with his bayonet—a slit in the back of my leg. I wrapped it up.

A lot of men died during the march. A lot died while we were resting at night. You'd see bloated bodies all along the way. I never saw a beheading, but I did see the results. I saw heads. And I saw guards just nonchalantly shoot men. In fact, they shot Brown.

He and I always started the morning at the beginning of the line. He was so weak that about a half hour into the march we were at the tail end—a dangerous place. There were guards there. One day, Brown said he just couldn't go on anymore. I said, "You know what's going to happen." He said, "I don't care." So a guard came by and jabbed me—the second time I'd been jabbed with a bayonet. Brown dropped, and I had to let him go. I wasn't far up the road when I heard two gunshots.

You never knew what might make the Japanese mad. One might be looking for something, and if you didn't have it, he'd get angry. The Filipinos along the way tried to help us. They threw us rice wrapped in banana leaves, but if the Japanese saw them do it, they'd cut their hands off or something. The Filipinos would put a bucket of water beside the road, but if the Japanese saw it, they'd kick it over.

I never thought of giving up during the march, but I also thought it would take a miracle to get out of the mess I was in. We were so desperate that an officer with us, a colonel, I think, offered thousands of dollars when we got home to anyone who would help him. Who the hell was going to help him? We couldn't even help ourselves.

When we reached San Fernando, they packed a hundred and twenty-five of us in a boxcar. Some of the cars were steel, some were wood. Guys in the wooden cars were lucky. There were cracks between the boards where some air could get in. I got lucky. I was stuck in a corner, but I could get air from outside. It was hot in the Philippines—really hot. The steel cars, when they packed a hundred and twenty-five men in there, the air gets a little short. We were on the train three or four hours. By the time the steel cars got to our destination, a lot of the men in them were dead.

When I reached Camp O'Donnell, there were thousands of men there—maybe forty, fifty thousand Filipinos and ten, twenty thousand Americans. O'Donnell had been a Filipino military training camp briefly before the war. Everybody was looking for water. We hadn't had any food. They set up a kitchen area and brought in rice. That's all you got. You got in line to get rice. You even got in line to get water—one spigot, and a thousand people trying to get water. You stood as much as all night to get a canteen of water.

People were dying all the time. One building was referred to as the hospital area, but we called it the death house. I got on a couple of burial details. We'd dig a big hole and put in thirty men. We didn't know who they were, and this has always bothered me. I buried a lot of people that nobody knows. How do they know who's who?

I had been at O'Donnell about three weeks sleeping in a crowded Nipa hut (a thatched-roof bamboo house) with a dirt floor. They were looking for a work detail, and I said to myself, "If I stay here, I'll die."

They took me to Clark Field, where I stayed for more than two years. We had a two-hundred-man detail. There were buildings there that our enlisted men used to live in. There were facilities with water. You could take showers. We had decent conditions, but food was still a problem. They had the idea we could survive on rice. In my time in captivity I went from a hundred and sixty pounds to ninety-eight.

We worked at the airfield extending the runway with shovels— very crude equipment. I worked on kitchen detail. We moved bombs. We moved gasoline drums, fifty-five-gallon drums, all from the United States. Either we'd left it there or the Japanese had stored it there somewhere.

I was sick in the beginning at Clark Field and could hardly walk. I had fever and malaria attacks. This is when I came to know what dark is, what black is. There's another color besides black—blacker than black. I was in such misery and despair. The danger was that they'd send me back to O'Donnell and replace me at Clark. A fellow I had befriended bargained with the Filipinos and got an egg or two. He mixed it with the rice and fed me. I started to get a little stronger. They held me up and I'd walk out to the shower and they'd rinse me off.

My name showed up on the detail to leave for O'Donnell. My friend went and saw the fellow who made the list and told him I was going to work tomorrow and to take me off the list, which he did. I went back to work the next day. We were carrying bombs for small planes. My friend made sure there were two to carry the bomb, and he gave me the thin part, which was light.

Then I got on another detail, working in the kitchen feeding five thousand Japanese. Of course, I could steal a lot of food. I started to put on a little weight.

It's strange. We had no idea what was going on beyond the camp. Your mind thinks in a small circle, inside a fence. The next thing you know, all you're thinking about is what's going on in there. You don't know what's going on outside.

We received no mail. Once in a while, they let us write a multiple-choice postcard home. "I am well" or "I am fair." And you better tell them you're fine. We got two Red Cross packages in the time I was there—canned food, chocolate, cigarettes. Even guys who were starving would swap food for cigarettes.

I got to know some of the Japanese guards. Some spoke a little English. One gave me some Japanese cigarettes. One even brought me a bottle of Golden Wedding whiskey—American whiskey. To take it back into the camp, I tied a string around the neck of the bottle and hung it under my shirt. Sometimes the guards didn't check closely, and fortunately they didn't that day. I was so scared I decided I'd never to do that again.

The Japanese used to tie men up by their hands with their toes barely touching the ground and leave them there for hours, some for days. Some Japanese trucks burned alcohol. We had a guy who was a real alcoholic. He got a hold of some of this alcohol, got drunk, and started yelling at the guards. The Japanese brought him into the little house where they stayed and beat him to hell and left him hanging. He died.

In mid-1944, American planes from aircraft carriers began to strafe the area. We got a little cheered up by that. They kept coming back, and we knew things were going better.

Not long after that, the Japanese sent us without warning from Clark Field to Bilibid Prison in Manila. We stayed a few weeks in a holding tank, and then they marched us through the streets of Manila down to the same pier I had left for Bataan.

Onufry is still haunted by the memory of comrades
who went to their graves naked and nameless.

We were put on one of the last ships to leave the Philippines. They were called "Hell Ships" for good reason. The guards opened the hatches and piled six hundred men into the forward hold, six hundred into the rear. After we went down the wooden steps into the hold, they tell you to sit down, but you can't—there's no room. Then they pull up the stairs and batten down the hatch. There's an iron ladder and one man at a time can get out. You had a Japanese machine gun on top pointed down into the hold.

We said, "We're not going to stay here long." Rumors were going around that they were going to take us out to a bigger ship. Big ship, hell. This is where we were going. I was there thirty-eight days, chased all over the Pacific and the China Sea by American subs. This was near the end of the war. The ships weren't marked as POW ships, and Americans had control of the seas.

I had an old army blanket that they never did steal from me. I had a piece of rope. They had apparently shipped animals in this ship because they had boarding on the sides. I climbed up and made a little hammock with my blanket and sat up there above the crowd.

I was on burial detail there also. There was a chaplain in charge, and every morning he'd say, "Check the man next to you and see if he's dead." There were always a few. Another fellow and myself would pull the bodies up through the hold with a rope. The Japanese insisted we take the clothes off the corpses. Then we'd take the dead back and throw them over the fantail.

We did this every morning for about ten days. We'd throw them into the wake of the ship. Legs would flop or arms would flop. I'd salute them and say a little prayer. Every once in a while, I still see those bodies with their legs kicking in the churn of the ship.

Sometimes these were men who had been beaten up by the men next to them. If prisoners thought you were hoarding water, they'd go after you. If anybody rattled a canteen at night, that was dangerous. A lot of men went out of their minds, screaming and yelling. I had men grab my feet a couple of times, and boy, I did some kicking.

The days were a little better than the nights. When I was done with burial detail, I used to throw a bucket from the gangplank and bring up water and pour it over my head to refresh myself a little. Still, men were so thirsty that their tongues would swell up and roll back into their throats. I used to reach in and pull their tongues free.

For food, they'd lower a five-gallon bucket of rice into the hold. The chaplain was in charge of doling it out. He had established himself as a leader by calming the men down. They were jumping around screaming, and their body heat was making things worse. He was very good.

We stopped in Hong Kong. We didn't get off, just stopped. We were in a convoy of about twenty ships, only two with prisoners.

In Formosa, they took us off and we worked for several months. We filled freight cars with crushed rock. You'd walk up with a wicker basket full and dump it in. You'd look down and say, "We never could fill this car up." But we'd do about two cars a day.

We began to see more American bombers. It was kind of mean. Every day the bombers came over, we didn't eat. They punished us. We'd just as soon have them come over.

We got on a ship leaving Formosa. Although we got bombed and strafed before we left the harbor, the ship was a little bit better. We had bunk beds and more room, but the hygiene facilities were the same. They lowered a bucket for us to go to the bathroom. I used to say to guys, "It's the same bucket they send the rice down in." And it was.

They took us to Moji, Japan. It was February 1945, and it was cold. We were used to warm weather. The first place they took us from Moji was an abandoned schoolhouse in Osaka. The camp commander made us all line up outside in the snow. "Take all your clothes off," he said. We all stood there bare naked until they came out with a big pile of new Japanese clothes.

I was there when Osaka was bombed. The walls were too high for us to see the bombs land, but we could see the bombers and see the bombs dropped and hear them explode. They did a job, I'll tell you. Osaka burned for five days.

We were shipped north to Miyabara, my last stop. It was a railroad head. Our job was to drain a lake. We dug a tunnel with shovels to get the water to another lake. And it worked.

One day we didn't go to work, which we thought was strange. Then another day, no work. That afternoon, the camp commander lined us up and told us the war was over and Japan had lost. He had instructions to keep us there until the Americans came, but he let us walk out and around. They opened the gates. Pretty soon planes started dropping food and cigarettes and clothes.

I was so relieved that I had made it. Some of the others went kind of wacky. Some took revenge.

A fellow named Heinz from New Mexico, who spoke excellent Japanese—he'd learned it as a prisoner—he said to me, "Let's go to Tokyo and watch the Yanks come in." I said, "Are you crazy?" It was several hundred miles. But I went with him to the railroad station, where a guy was collecting tickets. Heinz pushed him aside and said, "We don't need tickets." He didn't stop us.

There were people hanging all over the train. We got inside somehow, and two Japanese got up and gave us their seats. Here we were, two stupid Americans on a train with four or five thousand Japanese, most of them servicemen. All they had to do was break our heads and throw us off the side.

We got to Tokyo. There was no roof on the train station. We saw cars rushing around, but no Americans. It was dark, and there was one building with lights on. Heinz said, "Where are the Americans?" The guy there said, "They haven't landed yet." I looked at Heinz and he looked at me. We had nothing with us. The man there had heard that paratroopers had landed about fifteen miles away in Yokohama. We decided to go to Yokohama.

We got to the railroad station, and here come two guys out the door. They didn't look Japanese. Of course, they didn't look like Americans because the uniforms and helmets had changed. We had had those little porkpie World War I saucers, and we had never seen fatigues with side pockets. Heinz said, "I think they're Americans!"

We ran down to give them a hug, and one of them yanks on his .45, ready to pull it. He didn't realize who we were because we were in Japanese clothing. He waved down a big car with his flashlight. The car stops. It has a big flag and a star on it. This Japanese driver gets out and starts raving away. Heinz says, "He's saying this is his admiral's car and he has to get it back."

They made him take us to the Imperial Hotel. We went inside, and the only ones there were sixteen or eighteen reporters from around the world. They had the whole hotel. We didn't have any money, but we didn't need any. We owned the place.

We went to the airstrip the next morning, flew to Okinawa, and stayed there two days. There was still gunfire in the hills—Japanese in caves. We caught another airplane to the Philippines, but I got a malaria attack and passed out on the flight. They carried me off and wouldn't let me go any farther. I stayed there fourteen days.

When they finally let me go, I couldn't get a plane. I went down to the same pier in Manila where I had left for Bataan and later for Japan. I got a ship home. In San Francisco they put me in the hospital for a few days and then put me on a hospital train to Fort Devens in Massachusetts. There were just POWs on the train.

I was supposed to stay at Devens, but I sneaked out the gate and went home to see my mother, who lived in Ipswich, Massachusetts. She was shocked. She was president of an American Legion Auxiliary chapter and she was going to a meeting. So I went with her.

I had been a prisoner of war for three and a half years. When I got out, the government people told me I'd be taken care of, but I got nothing. I even paid for my own psychiatrist.

I hated the Japanese and swore I'd never go back to Japan, but my wife Lorraine talked me into returning there in the 1980s. When we flew in, I recognized Fujiyama, and I had tears in my eyes. It brought everything back.

The second day there, I went for a walk by myself down into town. I realized that gee, these people all looked the same as they did forty years before. Then I saw these little kids going into school, all dressed in uniform, and it hit me. These were not the people I had my problems with. These kids weren't even born then. Why was I mad at all of them?

I think it got me through a lot that I did go back.

Bill Onufry's older brother Ed, whom he had followed into the service, was killed during the takeoff of a bomber in 1942. Onufry left the Army Air Force in 1946 and began his career selling Chrysler-Plymouth automobiles in Massachusetts. He retired in 1978. He and his wife have had a home in Freedom since 1984.

Join the Navy and see the world? Bob Davis did just that.

Bob Davis

Fish Bait

Aviation improved dramatically during World War II, but most cargo
still traveled by ship, making freighters and tankers prime targets.
Protecting the freight convoys fell to Bob Davis and the other members
of an obscure branch of the Navy called the Armed Guard. Davis, of
Contoocook, New Hampshire, quit high school at seventeen to join.
By the time he turned twenty, he'd visited fifty-one foreign ports.

We probably saw more of the sea and more of the world than the guys in the fleet because anywhere these merchant ships went, they had to have a gun crew. On most ships you had at least eight Navy men on lookout duty around the clock. We stared at a lot of water, hoping we wouldn't see anything. If we did see a periscope or a submarine or an aircraft, we were there to sound general quarters and man our battle stations.

We usually traveled in convoys of ships of all types from Allied countries. At first, we were escorted by Canadian corvettes because America wasn't into anti-submarine work. We didn't have the knowledge the Canadians and the English had. We were latecomers. The lessons were hard sometimes, but America did learn about convoy duty.

The German U-Boats were within two miles of our shores, the

Cargo ships were prime targets for German subs and Japanese planes. Protecting the freight was a harrowing job, one that fell to the Naval Armed Guard

The Naval Armed Guard kept lookout for German U-Boats like this U-570, which surrendered to the British in 1941.

NEW YORK

ARUBA

MEDITERRANEAN PORTS

TRINIDAD

ABADAN, IRAN

SUEZ CANAL

PANAMA CANAL

MAPUTO, MOZAMBIQUE

CAPE TOWN, SOUTH AFRICA

Source: U.S. Naval Historical Center; National Archives

wolfpacks a little farther out in the Atlantic. About the time we'd clear the submarine nets in New York Harbor, we'd have contacts with subs. We always felt they were out there somewhere, waiting for us. When we got over into the combat area, aircraft got to be a problem.

I've been in convoys as large as a hundred ships and as small as four or five. It depended on where you were going and what you were carrying. We carried everything from bombs to toilet paper. One time we had steel matting on board that they used for runways. The first ship I was on, we had a locomotive and a couple of railroad cars. They'd put airplane engines on the decks.

When we started out, it wasn't wise to go directly across from New York Harbor to the Straits of Gibraltar, so they sent us down by way of Trinidad over to Cape Town, South Africa, then up the Indian Ocean, through the Suez Canal, and out into the Mediterranean. Long way around to get into the war area, but they thought it was safer. We eventually emptied our cargo in Italy.

Everyone called us fish bait because a lot of our ships were torpedoed. The merchants ran the ship. We provided the expertise on the guns. One of the galley boys was my loader on my first trip. They were civilian ships, but they were all under the War Shipping Administration. I was on the Hugh Williamson, a Liberty Ship in the Atlantic, and I was on the Frenchtown, a tanker.

Mozambique was a neutral port, Portuguese. When we went in there, we had to take the firing mechanisms out of our guns to make them inoperable. They had to be covered and pointed up to the sky. There were Germans in there, too, at the same time. The Portuguese were sympathetic to the Allies, so they never placed the Allied ships in the same place as the Germans. However, the German subs would wait outside the two-mile limit for the Allied ships.

Once a few of our guys got to whooping it up on shore, and they got acquainted with a couple of Germans. The Germans grabbed our two guys and took them to a house and tried to interrogate them. Four or five other guys from our ship followed, broke in, had a scrap, and got our guys back.

My ship was pretty lucky. We didn't get into anything other than nuisance raids that got us out of the sack and into the guns. The big

When the war ended, Davis's ship was in Iran.

thing was the constant pressure of waiting for something to happen. We were looking for torpedoes, looking for German planes, looking for submarines. We were the hunted. We weren't the hunters like the men on the cruisers and destroyers.

In the fall of 1944, we got into a wicked hurricane. We were on our way to Aruba for oil. We lost two lifeboats. Our deck cargo was fifty-five-gallon drums of a special grease for the tropics that wouldn't melt. We lost all of them. They tried to tie them down, but the captain was worried guys were going to get killed.

We picked up the oil, went through the Panama Canal and out into the Pacific. I probably missed a few of those islands out there, but I hit an awful lot of them. I was glad I was in the Armed Guard and not one of those poor fellows on those islands. It would rain every day and then it would steam when the sun came back out. Those poor Marines and soldiers there.

I made five or six trips back to the West Coast to load up with oil. Each time we went back out, the war had gone up a little farther, so we went to a different group of islands. Thankfully the only planes I saw in the Pacific were ours.

We stood watch in dungarees and blue shirts. Only in port did we have to be in the uniform of the day. They called us the dungaree Navy.

I ended the war in, of all places, Iran. We were on our way to the Persian Gulf to load up oil for the invasion of Japan. One of the boilers blew up, and we were stranded there for two months waiting for parts. The temperature was averaging a hundred and twenty in the middle of the day. One day it got up to a hundred and forty.

The port we were in was Abadan. It was a nothing place. I don't think the people there knew the war had ended or started. They knew very little of the outside world, but there was one fellow there, he wanted to come to the United States pretty bad. Everybody did. All the people we came in contact with, they all wanted to come to the United States.

Bob Davis left the Navy in 1946 and asked his girlfriend, Marcia, to marry him. After a brief engagement the couple parted ways and led happy but separate lives. Decades later, they were reunited and finally married in 1996. They split their time between Contoocook and Florida. Between them, they have sixteen grandchildren and two great-grandchildren.

Robert Foster saw war's carnage, but he also saw Marlene Dietrich.

Robert Foster

"When the Tanks Moved, We Moved"

In 1943, Robert Foster graduated from the University of New Hampshire with a degree in engineering. As an Army second lieutenant, he landed in Normandy eighteen days after D-Day and soon joined General George Patton's march through France and across Germany.

They had expected ten percent losses on D-Day, and we were replacement troops. When we landed, there was not a shot fired.

Because casualties were only four percent, they didn't need us as urgently as they thought they might. They gave me my eight feet of hedgerow between Caen and Saint-Lô, Patton's takeoff point. We'd go to the beach every day, load German ammunition onto a barge, take it out, and dump it by hand into the English Channel. Or we'd help store gasoline they brought ashore. There must have been ten thousand five-gallon cans.

One time, we got a lorry to take us to the edge of Caen, where the British had been fighting Panzers. A guard stopped us, but we talked him into letting us walk down one side of the street and up the other. We saw the British soldiers sitting in pubs having tea

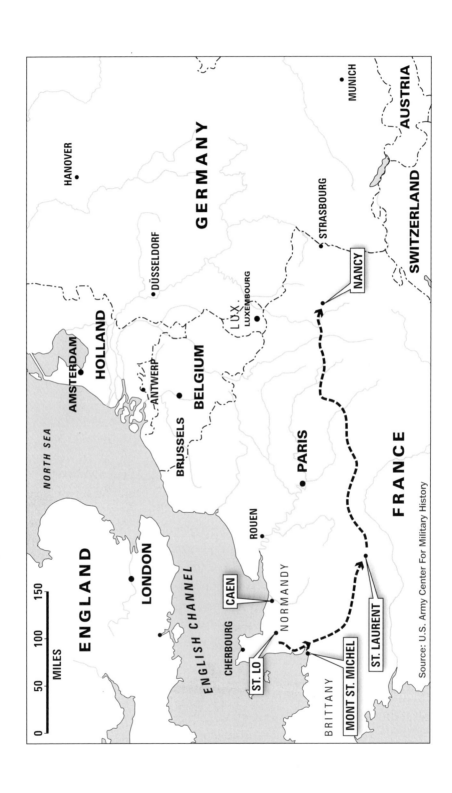

Source: U.S. Army Center For Military History

and crumpets. They had dusted off their puttees and put their steel helmets aside, and they were *enjoying* life. I said, "My God, those British know how to fight a war."

Meanwhile, we were moving stuff all over the place to give Patton enough push to go through, and we were sick of it. We wanted to be assigned to a unit —be family. Finally we joined the 128th Ordnance Battalion of the Sixth Armored Division.

They loaded us in two-and-a-half-ton trucks and took us from Saint-Lô down the road Patton had taken. There were ruined tanks and trucks all along the way, and they just bowled them aside. They took us toward Brittany, and finally that beautiful monastery, Mont Saint Michel, showed up in the distance. At Saint Laurent, we began our work. The job was maintenance of tanks and any other equipment used by an armored division.

The Germans had us beat on every element of armament. We were going for a lighter tank, and sure, we had a lot of them. Patton's idea was to get there firstest with the mostest. A Sherman tank on a blacktop will go like hell, but just get off the road and see what happens. I had the fun of pulling them out with wreckers.

The Sherman had only a twelve-inch track. The German Tiger had an eighteen-inch track. On the roads of France and Germany, you were going to go through mud. You needed a wider track. The Germans were ready for it, but we had to use hacksaws and metal dowels to weld iron strips onto the Sherman tread to widen it by three inches.

With 88-millimeter and 76-millimeter guns on their decks, the Tigers and Panthers could just sit there and watch the Shermans go by and pluck them off like ducks. The German shells had that high trajectory, and the cannons had muzzle brakes to cut back the recoil.

I was never assigned to a fighting unit, but when the tanks moved, we moved. I had my own jeep, and I wheeled all over the place looking for trouble. If I could find the maintenance officer of a combat command, and he said, "Get me some ammunition," or, "Get me a couple of more tanks," I'd run the liaison back to headquarters to get it done.

So I saw some things. One time there was a guy in the road. All

I could see was his two legs, his boots, sticking up out of the mud. The rest of him had been buried by a tank rolling over him. I didn't know if he was a German or one of ours or what.

They used to bring all the tank wreckage into a dump. Geez, I'm moseying around this dump, and in the turret of a tank I see a guy, a redhead, who's burnt away from the middle of his chest down. Just his head and torso had been lodged in by the 37-millimeter cannon on this light tank. His face was charred black, and all you could see was a little red in his hair. And they had pulled that tank up and put it in the junk pile with the guy in it. Eventually, I guess, the Graves Registration people came and got him.

We moved up to Nancy in Alsace-Lorraine to prepare for a major offensive. There were three hangars there—wooden buildings. I occupied the second floor of one of them. One day they came in and told me Marlene Dietrich was going to perform a show in my hangar. They built a stage for her downstairs, and I had to get out of my loft and give it to three or four of good-looking babes in her troupe.

It was my hangar—I thought I ought to get a good view of the show, so I sat right in the front row. Dietrich wore a split skirt. She sang the song she always sang, "Lili Marleen." She and these gals put on about an hour show. The guys were bughouse. I mean, just to look at a woman.

Sherwood Young was my boss, a first lieutenant. Everybody loved him—six-foot-two, a swashbuckling guy, always working side-by-side with his men.

I was out on a road, not a cement road, but a well-packed country road. Young was up in front of me by half a football field. He's got a wrecker with ten, fifteen guys. I've got a wrecker, ten or fifteen guys. We're trying to get damaged Sherman tanks back on the road.

I looked up ahead, and there was Young saluting somebody. I said, "It must be some field-grade officer looking for his troops." [Laughs.] And I thought, I'll get ready for this guy. I'll give him a snappy salute. I didn't know it was Patton until he was about twenty-five feet from me. There were three jeeps—a jeep in front with a .50-caliber machine gun, our boy Patton in the middle, a jeep behind with a .50-caliber facing back.

Foster had an unexpected encounter with General Patton.

He stopped, and he said, "Lieutenant." I said, "Yes, sir!" He said, "Are you in charge of these men?" I said, "Yes, sir!" He said, "How come they haven't got their winter galoshes?"

Now there's the general of the Third Army worrying about whether the soldiers have galoshes. He said, "Lieutenant, you make sure your men get galoshes." My thinking was, what about the poor infantryman sitting in a hole somewhere? He needs the galoshes, not me. I'm going back to a cement floor that's not wet.

But of course, everybody got trench foot. I had it myself—I was laid up for two or three weeks waiting for my tootsies to be cured. We were supposed to carry extra stockings—couldn't find the stockings. And we had a hard time getting those galoshes, the old-fashioned rubber ones with the buckles on them. In the winter, it was not the bullet but the environment that took out a lot of American soldiers.

I think everybody liked Patton in spite of the fact that he was killing a lot of them. He was a maverick, but he was effective in his routine. You've got to have somebody who's going to go charging. He didn't care what was in front of him—it was just, "Go!" Well, if you can keep the enemy off balance, eventually you're going to be in better shape.

Not long after we saw Patton, Lieutenant Young was out patrolling. He wanted to drive, so his driver sat in the passenger seat. Young went off the blacktop onto a farm to get to a Sherman tank that was knocked out.

The damn Germans had been around, and they were clever enough to plant Regal mines in the ruts of the farmer's road. The Regal is about three feet long and looks like a light fixture. The mines were staggered on this road, one in the left rut, one in the right.

Young was driving like hell up that road when—blam! It blew him out of the driver's seat, practically tore off his leg, and threw him down the road thirty feet. It turned the jeep sideways with his driver still in it. And Young was saying, "Hey, I want my pistol! Give me my pistol!" The driver got down there. Young was blinded. He wanted his .45 to shoot himself. The driver put a tourniquet on as best he could and went for help. They got Young to an evac hospital, but he died that night.

The next day, I was assigned with a couple of guys with mine detectors to figure out what had happened. You could see the mines in the road. The Germans had planted them only two or three inches deep, and they'd gotten exposed. But Young hadn't seen them.

We went out to the tank in the field, the one Young had been trying to reach. You talk about crazy things in a war. On a big field, there had been an advance of three or four Shermans. Down on the road, a German 88 field piece was firing up at this echelon of tanks. So the men in one of the tanks say, hey, let's get out and get behind the tank, let's not stay in it.

The driver was the last one out. He gets off the back, walks thirty feet, and falls dead in the rut the tank made. It turned out one of the shells fired by this 88 had slapped the ground and, without exploding, bounced into the bottom of the tank, the weakest part of the armor. It had split the armor and shoved a piece of steel up the aluminum seat and right up this guy's ass. When he got out and moved, apparently, he just aggravated it so that that piece of steel cut his spinal cord or something.

I found his body under a tarpaulin on the field. I also saw the seat inside the tank. When I got back to the hangar, the rest of the crew was still crying their eyes out.

Robert Foster's unit crossed Germany with Patton's army. When the war ended, his commanding officer learned that Foster was from a newspaper family and instructed him to oversee production of the 128th Ordnance Battalion's unit history. It was written by others, but Foster found the material for it, oversaw its production, and had it printed by the newspaper company in Wiesbaden, Germany. Back home, he went to work at Foster's Daily Democrat *in 1946 and still spends time on the job. He has long owned the paper, which has been in his family for a hundred and thirty-five years. He and his wife Terry live in Dover.*

"When the fighting was fierce . . . you prayed a lot," says Barbara Hauck.

Barbara Hauck , Donald Hall
& Gertrude Hankins

The Home Front

World War II dominated lives on the home front as well as on the war fronts. "What do newspapers write about when there's not a war?" the poet Donald Hall remembers thinking. With many young men gone, the war often meant work for women, as it did for Barbara Hauck, a "war wife" from Portsmouth. For Hall, a teenager who spent summers on his grandparents' farm in Wilmot, rural New Hampshire remained a place apart, but newspaper maps and radio broadcasts kept the war ever-present. Through her job, Gertrude Hankins of Contoocook had an inside look at the transformation of Washington, D.C., into a war capital.

Barbara Hauck

A GIRL WORLD

Barbara Hauck grew up in Portsmouth and summered on Odiorne Point until the government seized the land and turned it into an Army fort. During the war, she worked for several Boston-area companies and the Portsmouth Naval Shipyard. While her new husband, Bill, was serving in North Africa and Italy, she wrote to him each day.

Wre were all very young. I think you adjust to things no matter what happens. Bill and I were married while he was serving a year commitment in the Army. He was in nine months and war was declared.

He was at Camp Edwards on the Cape. I remember driving back to Boston when the news flash came over the radio that the U.S. had been attacked in Pearl Harbor. "Oh, now we're in it," I thought. "There's nothing we can do." But there was much we could and did do. We all worked in some capacity for the war effort.

We "war wives"—that's what they called us—traveled to wherever in the country the service sent our man, to be with him until he was shipped overseas. There were long hours of train travel, going alone to strange places, finding housing, a job if the stay was going to be long enough, and the joy of being with him once again. And always the dread of hearing, "We're shipping out tomorrow." When it happened, there was the long, lonely journey back home, filled with worry.

He was over there two and a half years. He was part of the African and Italian campaigns. His division spearheaded the drive to the Italian Alps and accepted the surrender of the Germans in the Alps. They were just a little unit, and an enormous German unit was there. He said you were marching people down the hill that you had been shooting at the day before. By the time you got partway down, you were giving them cigarettes. Humanity is a great thing left to itself.

He wrote every day, and so did I. In some letters he would say, "I know you're writing, dear, but I haven't heard anything." Then sometime later it was, "Oh, how wonderful it was to get a whole bunch of letters." He could write more on a postcard or one of those little V-Mails legibly than anyone I knew. Mostly it was concerning personal worries and thoughts. I think all the men's letters were about how much they longed to be at home. He would describe a day as long as there wasn't any fighting in it. They had to be careful because all of it was censored.

When the fighting was fierce, the communications were poor. You tried not to imagine where they were. You prayed a lot, and that was the way you carried through.

At home, we just accepted things. It was hard to get nylons.

Gas, especially, was rationed. It was wonderful when the soldiers came home on furlough because you got extra gas. Meat, butter, soap, sugar, shoes were rationed. I can remember friends saying how quickly their kids' little feet grew and how difficult it was to get shoes.

Everybody worked. I was working for Raytheon in Boston and E.I. du Pont in Pennsylvania in the purchasing department. Later, when Bill was overseas, I planned to go home to Portsmouth. I was informed that if I was leaving, I had to work at the Portsmouth Naval Shipyard. You couldn't move and just quit a job and not do anything. You had to be in the workforce. So I worked in the purchasing office at the Navy yard until the end of the war.

Most of the young men were in service. It was kind of a girl world. You got up, got ready, went to work, and did your job. Then you either went out with the girls and had dinner or you went home. Maybe you'd go to a movie.

Ours was a purpose. The whole nation had the feeling that we've got to end this war. We girls all knitted for the Red Cross, sweaters, socks, mittens. We had the USO. We served in the canteen. We had a big one in Portsmouth. It was a large brick hall with a kitchen. It was used for entertainment so servicemen could have a place to go. There were card games, dancing, just friendly communications for the fellows stationed at the naval base and Fort Dearborn (gun batteries installed at Odiorne Point). There was food and a reading room.

Bill was home when Japan surrendered. He was home on furlough, getting ready to ship out to the Pacific. He said, it's so good to be home to sit at a table with a tablecloth and linen napkins and all I have on my plate is meat and vegetables! He was glad the dessert was served in a separate dish instead of on top of your dinner in your helmet.

You had the greatest feeling of thankfulness that they were all right and at the same time more joy than anything else. You know what young love is like. You're exuberant.

I can remember the night we heard Japan had surrendered. My sister and I owned a cottage at Great Bay, inherited from our parents. We were there with our husbands when the news came over the radio. We piled into the car and went into Portsmouth. Haymarket

Square was just one wild gathering of people, horns tooting, people laughing, hugging people they didn't even know. Everyone was just so thrilled, so thankful. Everywhere you heard, "It's over. Thank God, it's over!"

Eventually, the state bought what is now Odiorne State Park for $91,000. Barbara Hauck's family home became part of the Seacoast Science Museum. Hauck, who lives in Gilford, is thrilled that people from all over the world visit the park to enjoy the scenery and learn. Barbara and Bill Hauck celebrated their sixtieth wedding anniversary five days before he died.

Donald Hall

FARM SUMMERS

As a teenager, Donald Hall lived in Connecticut, where his father ran a dairy business, and spent his summers with his maternal grandparents, Wesley and Kate Wells, on their farm at Eagle Pond in Wilmot, New Hampshire. He was thirteen years old when the war began.

I don't remember when I started reading newspapers, but I was young, certainly before the war started. Not long after, I remember thinking, what do newspapers write about when there's not a war? Every newspaper headline, every front page was the war. It was the Pacific and Europe. It seemed to me there was nothing else for four years. All journalism, radio and print, was consumed with this.

When I came up here in the summer, we got the *Boston Post* two days after publication. It came up by mail to the post office in West Andover, seven-tenths of a mile from here. We would read that and find out about baseball games two days ago. There was baseball still, but the war, the war. Newspapers were full of maps, and we became aware of the Marshall Islands, or the Solomon Islands, New Guinea, Australia. We learned about North Africa, Sicily, Finland, and Norway.

Airplanes were incredibly romantic. It was like space travel a few decades ago. I read aviation magazines even before the war. I could

Like many, Donald Hall listened for the radio voice of Gabriel Heater.

look up and identify a single-engine monoplane or a Waco, which was a biplane. Any flight over an ocean—Wrong-Way Corrigan, Amelia Earhart's disappearance—was big news. My poems, especially early ones, were full of airplanes. That's where it comes from.

I was sixteen when World War II ended, almost seventeen. So my parents and grandparents always assumed that when I turned seventeen or eighteen, I'd go in the Army. I just missed.

I usually came up here right after school ended and went back right before school started. In New Haven I would take the New York, New Haven & Hartford to South Station in Boston, and then take a taxi to North Station and take the "Peanut." Originally it was the next-to-last—the penultimate—train, hence the Peanut. The Peanut morning and night was the cheap passenger train. I'd go from the Streamliner to the old chugging, coal-fired train of the Boston & Maine and come up to the West Andover depot—no building there anymore—and my Gramp would be waiting for me.

My grandfather never had a car or a tractor. He would take me back here by horse and buggy. Route 4 was a macadam road but much narrower than now. It had been paved in 1928, the year I was born. It was two-way—Model A's would pass us, and Model-T's.

There was electricity in this house, and we had kerosene lamps. There was a telephone—"Hello, Central!" It would ring in every house, and my grandmother would pick up the phone and listen in.

Rationing didn't have much of an impact here. My grandparents didn't buy much. They bought coffee and salt or traded eggs for goods they couldn't grow. They didn't need sugar because they had honey and maple syrup. They spent so little. They had chickens and sheep and an enormous garden. They lived off the land.

I think they'd buy a hundred chicks—they wouldn't all live. They'd sell the little roosters and keep what remained of the chickens, and maybe there were twenty-five or thirty chickens throughout the year. When a hen stopped laying, she got her head cut off. Then she was boiled for an hour because she was so old, and then—fricasseed chicken!

The whole year was devoted to the cows. Sheep and chickens didn't take that much time. In summer you were haying all day and growing corn for ensilage. In winter he'd take ice out of Eagle Pond, and that was for the cattle. You had to chill the milk overnight or it would go sour. We also used it out here in the icebox. Sometimes Gramp was paid ten dollars a month for the milk. He had seven or eight Holsteins, sometimes one Jersey or Guernsey to raise the cream level because he was paid partly on that.

Gramp was a terrific baseball fan, and I was. I was for the Brooklyn Dodgers because spring and fall I listened to them down in Connecticut, and he was for the Red Sox. But we couldn't listen on the radio because although we didn't hay when it rained, if it was raining here, it was raining down in Boston. On Sunday you couldn't listen because it was the Sabbath. They were Congregationalists—old Calvinists. They went to the little church in South Danbury.

My great uncle, Kate's older brother, preached down there every Sunday. He had retired from a parish in Connecticut. He was born in 1856, and I remember sitting on the porch with him and him telling me about the boys coming home from the Civil War.

My grandparents would get up at five and start the fire—get kerosene and pour it on the logs in the stove. My grandmother would bring black coffee to me at six. My Gramp would go up to the barn and milk. I'd have breakfast and feed the chicks—they were my job in the summer. Then I sat down in that room, where my study is now. I had a bed and a brown drop-leaf table, and I'd sit at the table and read and write all morning. At fourteen, I got serious about work, and this became the poetry place.

About noon we'd have lunch and my grandfather would lie down on the sofa and close his eyes. In about ten minutes he would leap up from the sofa and say, "Boy!"—surprising me—and we'd go out and fix up the horse to the rake and rake the hay into piles. Then we'd hitch the horse up to the hayrack, take it into wherever he'd been cutting, and load the hay.

If I had to mow, I'd walk down Route 4 in the gutter carrying a scythe and keeping the point tilted down toward the ditch in case there was a German escaped prisoner of war. I had read in the paper about German prisoners of war in Canada and some of them escaping. I was ready. Preparedness.

Before supper we'd milk the cows. Then my grandfather and I would read, and my grandmother would knit or sew, darn socks, until nine o'clock. Every night before bed, my grandmother would have her little cheese glass of Moxie, and my grandfather had his bread and milk.

Over there in the corner there was a big cabinet radio—I still have it in my study—and we would listen to Gabriel Heater. He had a deep, dramatic voice, and he told the news on the radio every night at nine o'clock. It was probably fifteen minutes. "The skies are dark tonight with young Americans flying over Germany. . . ." He had a voice like Gabriel's horn.

Since 1975, Donald Hall has lived on the farm. His study now was his room then. Hall was the nation's poet laureate in 2006–07. In poetry and prose, he has written extensively about Eagle Pond Farm.

Gertrude Hankins

WAR CAPITAL

At the time of her interview, Gertrude Hankins lived in Contoocook, where she grew up in a family of eight children. After graduating from business school in Concord, she went to work for the Selective Service System in Washington, D.C., in May of 1941.

There were about thirty people in my office typing, filing, doing general office work. There was a one-year draft. I had all the records to take care of for men from all around the country. They put the fear of God in you. You were not to say one word about your work to anyone.

The Sunday Pearl Harbor was bombed was horrible. My roommate worked for the Navy Department. We were sitting on the bed listening to music when the news broke in. Some got called back to work that day, and they canceled our leave for Christmas.

Before long, records came in from Pearl Harbor—the records of the men there. Some were a little charred, some had a little blood on them. We were all so upset.

Washington was nice until war was declared. Then life became hectic. We worked overtime, no holidays. The city grew so much

Gertrude Hankins learned from her files that Clark Gable had false teeth.

that no matter what you did, you had to stand in line—get your check cashed, stand in line, everywhere you went, stand in line. I learned a lot of patience.

Before, you hardly saw anyone in uniform, but suddenly everybody was in uniform. They seemed to come out of the woodwork. They put up barracks all over the city. The Pentagon was being built, and we had to go through it by bus on the way to the city.

We did some things for fun. Through churches, we invited both Navy and Army men to our house for dinner. Sometimes we went to the bar where Kate Smith got her start. My girlfriend had a lovely voice, and they'd ask people to get up and sing, and one night she did. And we went to the movies. They used to have a stage show before the movie. One night we were there and Ronald Reagan and Jane Wyman were the actors. They performed and then announced their engagement right on the stage. And I thought, "How nice!" Little did we know he would be president one day.

I looked at his record in the Selective Service office. One time, out of curiosity, I also looked at Clark Gable's record. He was an enlisted man. I liked him because I was young, too, you know, but when I found out he had false teeth, that did it. People with false teeth, when you're young—they don't seem so young anymore.

I had met my future husband, Albert Hankins, in 1940 in what used to be the drugstore down in Contoocook, a hangout for kids. We could get sodas, and they had a little table and chairs right by the river. His cousin introduced us. We had been going together for a few months when he was drafted for a year. Pearl Harbor ended the idea that he would only be in for a year. He was in for the duration.

After Pearl Harbor, Albert was assigned to a ship, the Borinquen out of New York, and went to Iceland. They brought prisoners back from different countries. He went all over the world and wound up in New Guinea. He was an aircraft warning plotter and rose to first sergeant. We wrote each other throughout the war, but with censorship he couldn't say much about what he was doing. After the war, he never talked much about his service.

In time they made me a supervisor of my office. I had a lot of people doing clerical work for me—colored, Asian, men and women, all kinds of people. I think the government was more willing to hire different people because the war had taken all the men away.

After about three years in Washington, I went home to Contoocook. My mother got sick, and my father wanted me to take care of her. There weren't many young men in town. Many were gone off to war, and some had gotten killed.

Albert called one day and said he was back in the States. I was in seventh heaven. The next day was VJ Day—the war was over. They rang the church bells all over town and blew the sirens, the whole works. They had a big bonfire down by the railroad station in the village. People were dancing around the fire, and everybody was so happy.

Albert and I were married December 7, 1945—Pearl Harbor Day. He had contracted malaria in New Guinea. It took him years to shake it for good. He had a recurrence on our honeymoon in Montreal, and we came home early. The headaches and high fevers were awful.

From the war, Albert had brought home some Atabrine, the preventive medicine for malaria. I used it to dye my kitchen curtains a lovely shade of yellow.

After the war, Gertrude Hankins became a mother and homemaker. Albert Hankins was postmaster of Contoocook for more than thirty years. He died in 2001. Gertrude Hankins died on September 1, 2008.

Russell Elwell never used a parachute before the day he had no choice.

Russell Elwell

Over the Hump

Russell Elwell was a senior at Pembroke Academy when the Japanese bombed Pearl Harbor. He joined the Army Air Corps with a friend, Paul Muller of Allenstown, New Hampshire, in the fall of 1942. He trained to be an airplane mechanic and flight engineer but wound up as a waist gunner on a B-29 bomber. With the 20th Air Force, he made bombing raids on Japan from India, China, and the Mariana Islands. On one mission, his plane was hit and the crew bailed out.

I shipped out to Casablanca on a Liberty Ship and then flew off in a C-54 cargo plane. We stopped at Tripoli, Libya, and Abadan, Iran, on the way to Chakulia, India. When they opened the exit, it was like opening the oven door. I was in India for about a year.

The B-29 was the biggest bomber made at that time. It was pressurized and heated, as today's airliners are. It had double bomb bays, one forward of the wing and one aft, and could haul forty five-hundred-pound bombs. With fewer bombs, it could carry auxiliary fuel tanks.

The island airstrips in the Pacific weren't yet available. We flew our missions out of both India and the forward base in Cheng-tu, China. Because there were no roads for trucking in China, we had to fly "The Hump" from India—over the Himalayas—to bring in

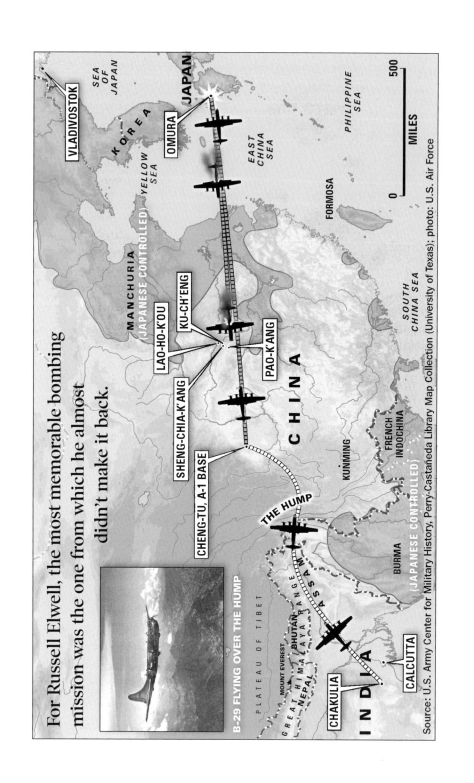

For Russell Elwell, the most memorable bombing mission was the one from which he almost didn't make it back.

B-29 FLYING OVER THE HUMP

VLADIVOSTOK

SEA OF JAPAN

KOREA

JAPAN

OMURA

YELLOW SEA

MANCHURIA (JAPANESE CONTROLLED)

EAST CHINA SEA

FORMOSA

PHILIPPINE SEA

LAO-HO-K'OU

KU-CH'ENG

SHENG-CHIA-K'ANG

PAO-K'ANG

CHENG-TU, A-1 BASE

CHINA

KUNMING

SOUTH CHINA SEA

FRENCH INDOCHINA

THE HUMP

PLATEAU OF TIBET

MOUNT EVEREST

NEPAL

BHUTAN

GREAT HIMALAYA RANGE

ASSAM

BURMA

(JAPANESE CONTROLLED)

INDIA

CHAKULIA

CALCUTTA

0   500

MILES

Source: U.S. Army Center for Military History, Perry-Castañeda Library Map Collection (University of Texas); photo: U.S. Air Force

everything we needed: the food, the fuel, the bombs. Flying over the Himalayas was unbelievable. You'd be flying at twenty thousand feet and you'd look out, and there was a monastery.

Our missions varied from ten to seventeen and a half hours. The mission I remember most is the one I almost didn't come back from.

They loaded the bombs, and we flew out of India over The Hump to A-1 (Cheng-tu). We refueled there and got a night's sleep and headed out on a mission to Omura, Japan. We were in formation and made our bombing run at maybe twenty-two thousand feet. All of a sudden the pressure—just *psshu-u-u*—went right out of the airplane. We never knew what hit us.

It's foggy in the plane right away, and we put our oxygen masks on. Then we started to lose altitude. The pilot was severely wounded in the lower back. The flight engineer, who sat at his instrument panel with all the controls of the engines and everything—he had a helmet on, but he got hit in the head and it scalped him. I went up to the front of the plane, and he was lying on the floor unconscious, and I could see his wounds. I saw the pilot's wounds also.

In the confusion of getting things leveled out, we lost a lot of fuel. Apparently a fuel line was hit. So now we were wondering if we had enough fuel to get back to our base.

They talked in the front office, as we called it—the front of the plane—about whether to go back to our base in China or to Vladivostok, Russia. But if you went up there, the Russians interned you until the end of the war. To get there, you had to fly along the coast of Japan and over areas where you might run into more trouble. So they decided to try to make it back to China.

They called me up and wanted me to take over the flight engineer's panel. I didn't have any experience, but the tailgunner—he was an old-timer—he came up to do it.

The airplane was flying nicely. To save fuel, we started throwing weight out. We had a bomb-bay tank or two—we dropped those. We threw out radar equipment, an auxiliary engine in the back that was used to start the engines, flak suits—anything we didn't need. But the navigator did some work and determined we weren't going to make it. We had flown four hours when we ran out of fuel, and we were at about ten thousand feet.

The area we bailed out over was a lot like the White Mountains. The only way the guys in the front office had to get out was through a hatch in the floor. You drop the nose wheel and lift this hatch, and you've got an opening of about three-by-three feet. The pilot was wounded, the flight engineer was still alive but unconscious. The pilot's parachute was all shot to hell when he got hit. Fortunately we had an extra parachute on board. We had flown a mechanic from India to China, and he left his parachute on the airplane. The guys in front took the shroud lines off the pilot's damaged parachute and tied them to the ripcord of the flight engineer's chute. They tied the other end to part of the plane inside. They dropped the flight engineer out. Right afterward, the pilot jumped. He did a freefall of about five thousand feet before he opened his chute, so he would reach the ground before the flight engineer and know where he landed.

In the back end of the airplane, we jumped out of a side door, maybe four feet by two. The top gunner was in front of me. He stood there and tried to fall out, but the slipstream nailed him right to the door jamb between his backpack and his body. He couldn't go out and he couldn't get back in. I wanted to get out, so I gave him a push. And then I backed up and dove. I had never been shown how to use my chute, but it was simple. All I could think of was, just do it—you had no fear of doing it because you had no alternative.

The ripcord is just a handle with a cable on it that went around to the back and pulled the pins that opened up your little pilot chute. The pilot chute was on a spring arrangement. It was square and it had these wings on it that were folded. When the wings opened, it shot out, and the wind would catch it and pull the big chute out.

When I went out that door, I rolled over and I looked up and I saw the plane's tail go over me, and I pulled my ripcord. That was too soon. I was still in the slipstream, still going along at the speed of the plane. When that chute opened, it snapped so hard it knocked me unconscious. There's a period of time I don't remember. I got blood all over the back of my neck where it hit me. The top gunner must have pulled his ripcord fairly soon, too, because before we got to the ground—it took eight or ten minutes—I could talk to him. We didn't say anything, but that's how close he was. On the way down, I got sick and vomited. I don't know if it was from the injury to my head or what.

The top gunner landed on the tile roof on a little peasant's house. His legs went right through the tile, and he straddled the roof beam. He didn't get hurt. I landed in the garden about fifty to seventy-five feet from the house. The cornstalks were sticking up. I landed on my feet so hard that my head went right down between my knees.

This little farmer with a goatee and a white clay pipe in his mouth came out. He walked over to the corner of his house, looked up on the roof, disappeared, and came back with a bamboo ladder. He set it up on the roof and turned around and went back inside. He acted as though, hell, this happens all the time. I gathered up my chute and put it back in the pack.

The guys in the back of the plane and the guys in the front had bailed out at different times, so they were on one side of the mountain range and we were on the other. We never saw them again till we got back to our home base. That's where we learned that the flight engineer had died shortly after landing.

We weren't sure whether we had made it to free China, but it turned out we had just got past the Japanese-controlled area when we bailed out. There were six of us, including the bombardier, a lieutenant. We walked down along a nice little mountain stream just like we have here in New Hampshire until we reached a farmhouse where the Chinese let us sleep in a shed.

During the night one of the local people sneaked in and took one of our jungle packs. He took off with it toward the major village eighteen or twenty miles away. He went on trails—there were no roads. Apparently he took it to prove we were there.

The next morning when we woke up, there was a commotion outside. There were fifteen or twenty Chinese soldiers out there with their leader, a major. We went out, and they pointed their guns at us. The lieutenant went ahead, and the Chinese major could speak some English. They prepared to lead us out.

The lieutenant had landed on the rocks in that mountain stream. It was hard for him to walk. When the Chinese saw that, they went

*In Chinese villages, Elwell and his fellow
crewmen were treated as heroes.*

out and chopped down bamboo trees and took vines and made up sedan chairs, not just for him but for all of us. The Chinese soldiers carried us, but they had to get farmers to help. They drafted these guys right out of their gardens. I saw one guy who didn't want to go, and he got a gun butt right in the ribs. He went.

They carried us down this trail by the river. About halfway through that day, they came up to a rise in the trail. The person carrying one end of a sedan set it down and took off over the mountain. Two or three Chinese soldiers took off after him, and an hour or so later we heard a gunshot. We assumed they shot him.

At some point we decided we wanted to walk because the sedans weren't that comfortable. They insisted, no, we want to carry you. And we insisted, no, we want to walk. So we did.

We came to a walled village—Pao-k'ang. All the people were outside the gate lined up on each side—the whole village. The town dignitaries were walking toward us. The guy in front in the blanket suit that a lot of the Chinese wore stuck out his hand and said, "Hello, Joe, am I glad to see you." They took us into the village. We're heroes! They couldn't do enough for us. We had a banquet with the local magistrates, the whole bit. They gave us cakes—and maybe dog? I didn't know. We spent the night there.

The next day they wanted to show the Chinese village people how the parachute worked. I put my chute on and went out to the center of town, and all the people gathered round. One of the other crew members pulled the chute way out of my pack. The interpreter explained to the Chinese people how it worked, and they applauded, and the flags came out—American flags that they had made.

When we left the village, they supplied us with two or three mules, with crates of live chickens and other supplies, and they sent soldiers with guns to protect us. We walked for another day down another trail to a river. We came to a little village on the bank and spent the night there. They gave us doors to lie on, and we used our parachutes for blankets.

The next day we all got into a sanpan, a good-sized boat, and started drifting down the river with a crewman on the bow and one on the back who poled. We went as much as a hundred miles. It was beautiful, with the mountains rising right up out of the river, and the cliffs. We had armed soldiers with us, and we found out later we were in bandit-infested territory.

We landed close to a town on flatter ground. They had rickshaws, and they took us into town. People were all over the streets—like a big parade around here. We walked down the main street, and everybody was applauding and yelling—and firecrackers!—the street was knee-deep in blue smoke from the firecrackers going off all around.

They had a show for us that night in their theater, a ramshackle building with a tin roof and a stage with wooden benches. They put on an opera and all kinds of entertainment—sword duels, fire batons, songs. The Chinese boy scouts and girl scouts got together and sang a song in praise of America. Their English wasn't very good, but they did it.

Before we left the next morning, they wanted to take our picture. We gathered out front of the town hall with all the dignitaries— twenty or thirty people—behind us. The six of us were sitting there with bundles of chopsticks they had given us.

Somewhere along the way we went to a nice house where some sort of magistrate had a small automobile. All six of us got in, and he drove us to a point where there was a bus to pick us up, an old dilapidated school bus. It smelled awful because of the fuel they were using. The fuel was what they drank—jing-pow juice, that's what they called it.

Finally, we came to a Norwegian mission in Lao-Ho-K'ou, where we stayed for about three days. Japanese fighters sometimes strafed the airfield nearby, so it took three tries for the C-47 to come in and pick us up. Finally he made it, but he didn't even shut his engines off. He threw his doors open, we bailed in, and boom, off we went. We flew back to A-1 base and stayed there a few days before they took us back to India.

In early 1945, they moved us to the Mariana Islands because they had the airstrips ready for us there.

One of several missions I flew out of Tinian still remains in my mind, and it bothers me some. It was near the end of the war, about a twelve-hour flight to a fire-bombing mission over Tokyo at five thousand feet. Going in at that low altitude, we saw the whole city as just one huge ball of fire. That's what we were doing dropping bombs. We were burning the whole population of Tokyo.

The demolition bombs were five hundred pounds. With the fire bombs—magnesium, gelled gasoline, stuff like that in them—they were also five hundred pounds, but several of them were wrapped together with tailfins on them. When they came out of the airplane, the clusters would burst open, and they'd go down separately and scatter and set fires wherever they landed.

I did more than one raid like that. Sometimes these raids had three hundred airplanes. The one I remember best had probably that many. We hit there at nighttime, so you can imagine what the fire looked like. Each airplane went in individually over the target at a different altitude and a different time—this had to be so coordinated because at night you don't see the other airplanes.

It didn't bother me then. At the time, it was just bomb, bomb, bomb. It was never referred to as a campaign to burn the city. We knew we had fire bombs, we knew we were bombing, but it was just "Let's kill Japs. Who cares how?" But as I got older and thought about it, my feelings changed.

I had thirty-two missions. I had flown on my unit's first mission to bomb the mainland—Yawata, Japan—on a plane called the Twentieth Century Unlimited. I also flew the last mission—when the B-29s flew over Tokyo Bay on September 2, 1945, during the signing ceremony. I could see battleship Missouri down there.

After the war Russell Elwell became a builder of homes, boats, and pop-up campers. He worked as superintendent of properties at the former Saint Mary's College in Hooksett, New Hampshire, and retired twenty-four years ago as a licensed electrician. Now eighty-five, Elwell lives with his wife in a house he built in Pembroke.

When the chance came to kill a German, Tony Hyde missed.

Tony Hyde

Mountain by Mountain

Tony Hyde spent two years training for Alpine combat with the
fledgling Tenth Mountain Division but didn't join the fight until
the final months of the war. In Italy, Hyde and his men captured
mountaintops, villages, and tunnels from war-weary German troops.
Although the enemy was tired, Hyde didn't escape unscathed.

I t was a romantic outfit, one that had people talking. The Army
could always say, "Hey, we've got these ski troops over here." We
had all this training and white uniforms.

I was commander of a heavy weapons company. The people we
had to train were supposedly outdoor people and, if possible, skiers.
The heavy weapons companies, when they hike, carry a machine
gun and a mortar, which are heavy. Skis are not handy when you
carry that stuff. So we didn't have much to do with skiing in combat,
but the rifle company did.

We were in Camp Hale, Oregon, for at least two years. A nearby
hill had a T-bar, and we skied on weekends. We had rock-climbing
classes, which were more for fun than anything else, because when
someone is shooting at you, you don't want to be climbing up a cliff
or dangling from a rope.

The government didn't know what to do with us. There were

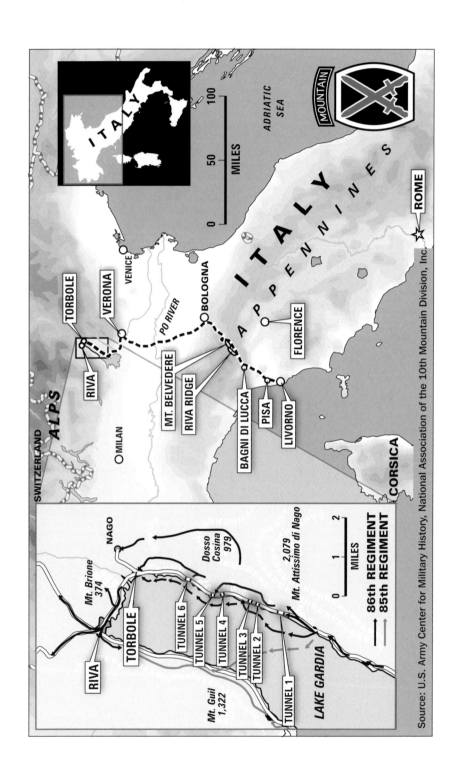

MILES

0   50   100

ITALY

ADRIATIC SEA

TORBOLE

VERONA

VENICE

RIVA

ALPS

SWITZERLAND

MILAN

PO RIVER

BOLOGNA

MT. BELVEDERE

RIVA RIDGE

BAGNI DI LUCCA

PISA

LIVORNO

FLORENCE

A P P E N N I N E S

ROME

CORSICA

MOUNTAIN

RIVA

TORBOLE

NAGO

Mt. Brione 374

Dosso Cosina 979

TUNNEL 6

TUNNEL 5

TUNNEL 4

TUNNEL 3

TUNNEL 2

TUNNEL 1

Mt. Guil 1,322

Mt. Attissimo di Nago 2,079

LAKE GARDIA

MILES

0   1   2

86th REGIMENT
85th REGIMENT

Source: U.S. Army Center for Military History, National Association of the 10th Mountain Division, Inc.

rumors about going to Borneo and who knows where. It finally came that we were going to Italy. I was thrilled to go. We had a nice boat going over, a luxury liner. The war was on its last legs when we arrived in late 1944.

We went into Naples and on up to Livorno—"Leghorn," they called it—near Pisa. That was where the front lines were. We were in meadows. All our weapons came, and we had to clean off the grease they had put on them to keep them from rusting on the ocean. All of a sudden this airplane comes over us, maybe forty or fifty feet off the ground, and does a barrel roll. It was an American plane. We're all standing there, our mouths open, thinking, "This is the greatest place in the world."

I was on the front for at least three weeks before I heard a shot fired. We were about a half mile from the Germans. It was wooded. No big mountains. The war was at a stalemate because it was cold and there was an inch or so of snow on the ground.

We were getting organized and meeting the natives. I was annoyed that the guys in the outfit were complaining because they went downtown and the people there couldn't speak English. I had to say, "Look, you're in Italy now. . . . They're not going to learn your language. You've got to learn their language." I hired a little old lady who was a schoolteacher, and in exchange for butter and sugar from our mess halls, she gave me Italian lessons and an Italian grammar book. Pretty soon, I could speak enough to get by.

Our baptism by fire came when we went to capture Mount Belvedere, a good-sized mountain. It was night. It was a walk up, no steep mountain, maybe a scramble here and there. Wooded. Open fields. We got to the top, or virtually the top, enough where people could shoot you from the other side. The Germans were so surprised.

From then on we captured one little mountain after another. We would attack during the day, starting at dawn. The Germans were not enthusiastic. As soon as they knew we were serious, they would skedaddle. We'd go to the next mountain. My job was to make sure my machine guns were positioned in the right spot to help the infantrymen.

After the fight was over, I would walk around to see if they were okay. One day I was walking with my messenger along the side of a hill. One of the guys says, "Hey Captain, there's a German over there smoking a cigarette." I said, "Really?" I went up and looked over the edge and took my binoculars out and, sure enough, there was a German leaning against a tree smoking a cigarette.

So I said, "Gee, maybe we ought to do something about that. Why don't we shoot him? Anybody got a rifle?" Someone gave me a rifle. Guys were watching, of course, so everything had to be by the book. I squeezed off a shot. Nothing happened. He's still smoking a cigarette. Another shot.

Now, I'm not the worst shot in the world and I'm not the best, but as you live with your rifle in the woods, you bang it here and there and the sights get a little off. I asked one of the guys, have you got a tracer round? A tracer is a machine gun round and there's a little red spark in the back of it so you can see where your bullets are going. We loaded up with a tracer round and squeezed off a shot. Sure enough, I'm landing about twenty or thirty feet to the right. I squeezed off one more shot. This time, the German put his foot down, looked around, put his cigarette out, and walked out of sight. That's my whole war effort of trying to kill a German, and I missed.

A little later, I was in the back of the command post talking to the officers, and a message came up that I was wanted for a meeting. We were in a steep gully. I jogged down the path. I could see the farmhouse ahead, and I was about to break out of the woods and into a grassy meadow maybe a hundred feet across. I guess I was the first one to go down there after the Germans had left, because there was a tripwire across the path hooked up to a German hand grenade. I never saw it. Because I was running, by the time the grenade went off, I was about seven or eight feet beyond it. It went off with a great bang, hit me in the middle of the back and knocked me down.

Very easy wound. Shrapnel. In fact it's still there. I was surprised. It was more of a shock than anything else. The medics got me out and put me in a hospital in Florence. I was in a ward with ten people. One day, all of a sudden, up comes this orderly pushing this wagon between our bunks. He takes a Purple Heart medal and tosses one at each bunk as he goes by. That's not exactly the ceremony you'd expect getting a Purple Heart, but that's how they handed them out.

The next day, I called the company and told them I was ready to

Hyde's war booty consisted of a fascist's silver spoon.

return. They were at the foot of the Alps. We started up along the shore of Lake Garda. The Germans had blown up the shore and ruined a bridge, so we had to go by boat, only about two hundred yards. Our top speed was five miles, maybe four. Nobody with serious intent was shooting at us, so we made it out of there and went up this road, with the Germans holding every tunnel.

We had to get them out, get a gun in the right place, and when they learned we meant business, they got out. Until we got to the last tunnel. This was an interesting spot, mountains all around, pretty country, and here's this cliff coming down and a tunnel coming out of it to where the towns were. A German 88 (88-millimeter artillery) was shooting at the mouth of the tunnel.

I was sitting in the sun outside the tunnel. Along the edge of the road was a fence to keep the cars from falling in the lake and a stone wall, beautifully laid. A shell went over my head and exploded in the tunnel. My company was in there, as well as some others, waiting for headquarters to decide what to do with us. This shell did a lot of damage. I must have lost three or four guys.

I was an impatient guy. I don't think the colonel knew what he wanted to do, so I decided there must be another way out of there. I went to the other end of the tunnel, and there was a path. I walked up, my messenger with me as always. The two of us were going along this path with bushes on either side. All of a sudden, out in front of us jump two Germans. They'd had enough of the war and they'd given up, so we captured them. We went on a little further and the path continued to the village below. I went back and told the colonel that if you go up that path, you'll be able to get into town without that gun shooting at you. I brought (the Germans) back and handed them over to intelligence. That night we walked up that path and down the other side and into Torbole.

Now we're getting into the end of April, and you could see the Alps up ahead. We're walking down the main road, and the town in front of us had been captured. The Germans obviously had just left it. The Italians were outside, yelling and screaming and giving us wine and fruit. We were the first Americans they'd seen. It was just great.

The fascists had left with the Germans. I went into a fascist house, a beautiful house. I came upon a sideboard with some silverware in it. I thought, "Hyde, you're gonna have some loot!" So I picked up one silver spoon. I've lost it since then, but I brought that back as my only loot from the war.

The next day, I was called to a company commanders' meeting. The colonel got up and said, "I've got something to tell you. I want you to treat this information like anything else I would tell you. I want you to tell your lieutenants, who will tell your sergeants, who will pass the information down in a normal military manner. There will be nothing unusual about it. But . . . the war is over."

I went back and had a lieutenants' meeting. I told them, "Look, I'm going to tell you something. No shooting of rifles, nothing like that. Treat it like any other information. Tell your troops and have them be quiet: The war is over."

Everybody looked at everybody else and said, "Whew. I made it."

Tony Hyde and his company spent the summer of 1945 in Yugoslavia as part of a show of American might meant to prevent violence among local political parties. He returned to the United States and eventually moved to Warner, New Hampshire.

"Being scared out there most of the day is no fun," Will Gundlach says.

Will Gundlach

Avenger

*Will Gundlach joined the Navy shortly after Pearl Harbor. His iron
stomach got him into flight school, but at six-foot-five, he was
too tall to pilot anything but the Grumman Avenger, a torpedo
bomber based on aircraft carriers in the Pacific. Gundlach, of
Concord, flew ninety-nine missions but landed only ninety-eight.*

It was a pretty powerful plane. There was one pilot and a crew of
two: a radioman and, behind him, the gunner. Our carrier was
called the Sargent Bay. There probably were twenty pilots, plus
the people to run the ship and man the guns in case we got attacked.
We were an escort carrier. They're so small that in a choppy sea
they're doing this [bobs his hand through the air] and you're trying
to land, which is difficult.

We had a hook on the back of the plane. If you landed properly
at the right place and time, that hook would catch on a cable across
the carrier deck and stop you from going into the barrier, which
was in place to keep you from going into the other planes. You took
off only with a catapult because you didn't have enough room to do
anything else. You were just heaved out over the ocean.

Our first duty was an anti-submarine raid. We had to escort a
parade of ships going out west. You'd go out, make a ninety-degree
turn, fly a short way, make another ninety-degree turn, come back,
and hope to find your ship. We never saw a submarine.

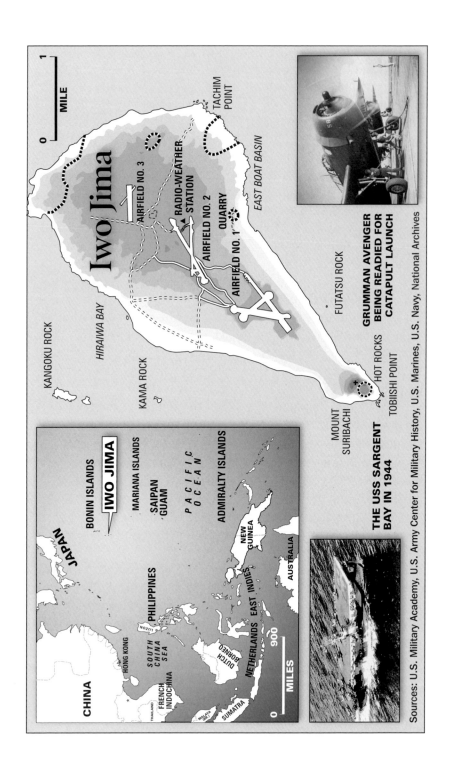

Iwo Jima

KANGOKU ROCK

HIRAIWA BAY

KAMA ROCK

AIRFIELD NO. 3

RADIO-WEATHER
STATION

AIRFIELD NO. 2

QUARRY

AIRFIELD NO. 1

TACHIM
POINT

EAST BOAT BASIN

FUTATSU ROCK

HOT ROCKS

TOBIISHI POINT

MOUNT
SURIBACHI

0   1

MILE

**GRUMMAN AVENGER
BEING READIED FOR
CATAPULT LAUNCH**

BONIN ISLANDS

IWO JIMA

MARIANA ISLANDS

SAIPAN
GUAM

*P A C I F I C
O C E A N*

ADMIRALTY ISLANDS

JAPAN

CHINA

HONG KONG

*S O U T H
C H I N A
S E A*

PHILIPPINES

LUZON

FRENCH
INDOCHINA

THAILAND

MALAYA

BORNEO

DUTCH
BORNEO

NETHERLANDS EAST INDIES

SUMATRA

NEW
GUINEA

AUSTRALIA

0   900

MILES

**THE USS SARGENT
BAY IN 1944**

Sources: U.S. Military Academy, U.S. Army Center for Military History, U.S. Marines, U.S. Navy, National Archives

Then we got into landing support in the islands. While the Marines and the Army would land, our job as pilots was to shoot and bomb the Japanese defense of the island. It sounds gruesome now, but my whole duty over there was to kill them if I could and, if I couldn't, to keep them busy.

Our commander had been an Annapolis student in peacetime. He was excellent in his task and a fairly nice guy. He was with the first flight that went out for landing support. He never came back. He got shot up. This business of looking for a submarine that wasn't there, that was benign, but his death brought the war home to me.

From there on, it was more of the same. Fly a flight. Sometimes it was daytime, sometimes nighttime. Then you'd fly back to your ship and fuel up and out you go, sometimes two or three times a day.

Being out there scared most of the day is no fun, but everyone tried to be helpful. Camaraderie, they called it. The whole year that we were over there, we had an ongoing, never-stop game of hearts in the ready room. You try to make some fun out of something. We'd play for a nickel, day and night. They were men you'd like to think you were going to be lifetime friends with, and some of them didn't come back.

One landing, I was coming in and the ship was going like this [holds his hand sideways] and they waved me off. The deck officer thought he had me in safe conditions, and we made another attempt at a landing. We shouldn't have. The boat was pitching, and my hook caught the cable while I was gunning it to get away. The hook held and the plane fell over the side of the ship and broke in half, right behind the radioman's seat. The front half, which included me and my two crew guys, went into the Pacific Ocean. The rear half stayed on the boat because of the hook. Fortunately, the wings were still with us. They acted as buoyancy, but we were sinking. We had a lifejacket, but you wanted to be darn sure to get unstrapped.

Behind us we always had a destroyer escort whose whole job was to scoop up anybody like me who was in the water and shouldn't be. We got rescued, and because the seas were so rough, we spent three days on the destroyer until it was possible to get the two ships together. I wasn't hurt, the radioman wasn't hurt, the gunner had a slight cut on his hand where he pushed out of the plane before it sank.

It was like driving a truck. Not much maneuverability. We were getting attacked by fighter planes, the Zeroes. They would come at

Gundlach and his plane once took a dip in the Pacific Ocean.

us and shoot us up to the extent they were able. In the latter parts, the kamikazes came in. We had a couple go right through our rigging and crash into the water on the other side.

Pretty soon, you don't care if you are killing human beings. It's the terrible part of war.

During the time of Iwo Jima, the U.S. had control of the air. There was no need for a radioman or a gunner, so I was alone in the plane. It's a nice little island, mostly flat ground. It was just this small place with all these people: twelve thousand of them and fourteen thousand of us. I knew what I was to do: You push this button to drop the bomb, this button to get the rockets. I could shoot the guns. I was getting some good shots in, but I was also getting shot at.

By the grace of God, no bullets came into my pilot's area, but I started to see more and more holes in the plane. I still had a job to do, so I couldn't go home to the ship yet. Then I couldn't make left-hand turns. My left wing had been shot up, and that had destroyed or done damage to the equipment that lets you tip the plane. If you can't tip the plane, you can't turn. On my carrier, you can't land if you can't make a left-hand turn.

I radioed down to the island. By that time there were two teeny-weeny grass airstrips where there were no Japanese left alive. I said,

"You got any Seabees who might be able to fix this thing?" They said, "We can fix anything."

So I landed on Iwo Jima. Just a few miles away, you could hear the battle going. A bunch of the guys jumped out and replaced some of the wires. I thanked them nicely, took off, and went back to my ship and landed. Good landing this time.

Everybody ran out to see the plane, because there were holes everywhere except in me. That was a nice feeling to look at that plane and to know that I hadn't even gotten a bloody elbow. They took off the radio, the propeller, and anything else that could be used for spare parts and pushed the rest of the plane off into the Pacific Ocean.

The only shore leave I had was when our ship went in for a one-day fix-up. We had one overnight on dry land. Somebody found some gin, and we got our first mail in six weeks. I'd been waiting and waiting and waiting for mail because my baby was supposed to be born. We were married shortly after I was commissioned, and my wife was pregnant when I left.

I knew the time of the birth was past, but how did it go? Was it okay? Was it safe? Did I have twins? Was I a father? When I got to Okinawa for our mini shore leave, I had one letter from my father. All it said was, "Congratulations! It's a boy."

There were maybe fifteen of us, and we started taking bets on how big this kid was. I was the biggest guy in the group. I'm not a drinker. I don't think I've been drunk more than once in my life, and that was there. I can remember standing up on the bed, taking the bets coming in. I started out with one of those little medicine cups. By the time we were well into the betting, I had a big glass that somebody gave me. We got the bidding up to nineteen pounds.

We always called him Skip because he was the little skipper of our Navy time.

The next morning we were all back on the ship, going at it again.

Will Gundlach was home on furlough when the war ended. Within days, he and his wife enrolled at Cornell University. He graduated and began a long career with Eastman Kodak. He has five children and many, many grandkids. Now eighty-four years old, Gundlach flew a Cessna 172 in 2006. "Very different," he said, "from a Grumman Avenger."

Carl Webber made it into submarine service in time for one wartime run.

Carl Webber

The Last Run

*After eighteen months crisscrossing the Atlantic Ocean
on a battered World War I-era destroyer, Carl Webber
realized he liked the radios aboard but not the food. That
motivated him to join the submarine service.*

The destroyer, the USS Greene, was at State Pier in New London, Connecticut. There were submarines tied up there, and we asked to go aboard. Down in the mess hall you had a cup of coffee. You had toast and jam and butter. All this was available at most any time. On the Greene we used to have guys come around with tureens and that was your supper.

I said, "Holy smoke. This is living. I'm switching to submarines." And I did.

In sub school, we trained on World War I submarines. My first time down, I was on an "O" boat. We went out early in the morning, submerged in an assigned area, and took our stations to control the boat. The ship's crew watched over us. Submerging was no big deal—just cramped quarters.

From San Diego, I went to Australia on a relief crew. When the submarines came in after war patrol, we'd go in and check them out.

SOVIET
UNION

MONGOLIA

MANCHURIA

CHINA

KOREA

JAPAN

FRENCH
INDOCHINA
(VIETNAM)

OKINAWA

FORMOSA

MARIANA
ISLANDS

HONG KONG

GULF OF SIAM

LUZON

THAILAND

PHILIPPINES

GUAM

PACIFIC OCEAN

SUMATRA

DUTCH
BORNEO

NETHERLANDS EAST INDIES

NEW GUINEA

0   300   600   900

MILES

AUSTRALIA

Map source: United States Military Academy

One of the fellows in the radio room on the USS Bergall broke his arm, and I made the last run on the sub as his replacement.

We were out for about twenty-five days. We probably sank a thousand tons of small Japanese ships, anything that wasn't American. That was our mission. We used to come up the coast of Australia, go around the islands, and get over toward Vietnam and into the gulf. You had to look all over because it was very difficult to find any Japanese ships. This was April of 1945. The Japanese were pretty well beat up then.

The boat was three hundred and eighteen feet long, with maybe eighty guys on board. The Old Man was Johnny Hyde. He was a good skipper, one of the best, and a pretty savvy guy. He knew how to take care of the boat and the people.

Submarine duty was mostly sleep and eat. We stood four hours on, eight hours off. There was cleaning to be done and work in the radio room. You didn't do much for fun. There was always something going on. We had swim call in the middle of the ocean. You could jump in the water. They had to have a guy with a rifle out there for sharks.

The Navy decreed that submarine crews would get better food because of everything that could happen. You'd get two crates of steak and beef and one box of hamburger. The surface craft would get one box of steak and two of hamburger. The best meal we had was a bunch of lamb chops the commissary guy got in Fremantle, Australia. We probably ate three-quarters of the lamb chops, if not more, in one meal. He thought they'd be good for maybe three or four meals. We had a lot of garbage that night. It was all thrown over the side.

I was a third-class radio man. I used to do what they called copying FOX. The Navy would broadcast messages to all the ships, mostly from Hawaii. You had to copy numbered messages and make sure you had every number. On the submarines you'd have a tougher time because you'd have to dive and you couldn't receive under water. So you'd have to listen for the repeats. All this was coded. You had to copy it fairly well. Otherwise, you wouldn't break the code.

I was copying FOX the day the mine went off. We were in the

*Webber had no fear of submerging. He
stayed in the service after the war.*

Gulf of Siam. I was sitting there and all of sudden—*whooom*! My
chair went up. The transmitter behind me went off. I didn't know
what the hell was going on, so I just kept copying FOX. I didn't know
what else to do. The explosion knocked the boat a little bit out of the
water and messed everything up. The after-engine room took most of
the damage.

They have the torpedoes strapped down in racks. It bounced
them right onto the deck. To break those straps, it had to be a little
bit of a push. There were people back there, but luckily no one got
hurt.

In a few minutes, people started saying they thought it was a
radio-controlled mine that someone set off from shore. We tried

to get out of there as fast as we could. We ended up going to the Philippines, where there was a sub tender. They did a minor repair job because we were going back to the States, to the Portsmouth Naval Shipyard, for repairs.

Portsmouth had a bunch of bars. It's nothing like it is now for the tourists. It wasn't about tourists; it was about sailors. I don't know how many sailors there were because I wasn't counting. I was looking for girls. I'm not at liberty to say if I found any.

When the war ended, I think I was down in Salisbury Beach, drunk. We found out when we went on liberty. We were going to have a good time, and we did.

Carl Webber, who is eighty-three years old, remained in the Navy for twenty-six years, almost all of it served on submarines. He retired in 1965 and moved to Nashua, New Hampshire, where he worked on nuclear submarine development for the company that became BAE Systems. Webber and his wife still live in Nashua and have two children and four grandchildren.

Webber (center front) on the deck of his World War II submarine.

*Bill Snow was an expert marksman, but the
Army had other plans for him.*

Bill Snow

Sleeping with Rats

Bill Snow grew up in Concord. In 1944, after two years of
stateside duty, he was sent with the 374th Air Service Squadron
to the island of Biak, where he served for eighteen months.

Biak is a very small island, maybe twenty miles long and ten miles wide, off the tip of New Guinea near the Equator. It was almost all jungle, and there was just one native village on it. The infantry had cleaned out the Japanese pretty good where we were, though some were still living on the other side of the island.

I knew guns from A to Z. I was an expert in firing every rifle there ever was. I was a drill instructor before I went into the Air Force, but on Biak I never had a gun.

When we got there, there was still an awful stench from a cave full of dead Japanese. Our infantry had thrown in gas and burned them and just left them there. They were probably two hundred feet from our tent.

We were stationed at the end of the airstrip. We had a graveyard of B-24's there. They'd bring the bombers in to be fixed, and then off they'd go. I had worked in mechanical arts in high school in Concord, so I got a pretty good job. Whenever they needed a part, I could fix it or make it on the lathe.

The island was desolate, and the living conditions were rough.

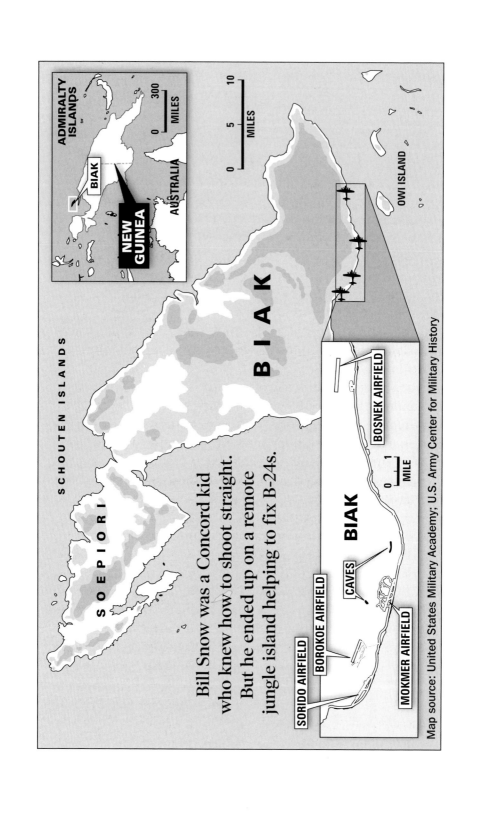

SCHOUTEN ISLANDS

SOEPIORI

BIAK

Bill Snow was a Concord kid
who knew how to shoot straight.
But he ended up on a remote
jungle island helping to fix B-24s.

BIAK

SORIDO AIRFIELD

BOROKOE AIRFIELD

CAVES

MOKMER AIRFIELD

BOSNEK AIRFIELD

0   1
MILE

0   5   10
MILES

OWI ISLAND

ADMIRALTY ISLANDS

BIAK

NEW GUINEA

AUSTRALIA

0   300
MILES

Map source: United States Military Academy; U.S. Army Center for Military History

Our squadron had about ten tents with five men in each of them. It rained all the time, and we had a lot of rats. The only time you got rid of them was when it rained really hard and there'd be six inches of water flowing right through the tent. It'd wash them right out of there. That's when you'd see a lot of drowned rats.

I never got bit by a rat. I made my bed way up high. Our captain had a P-51 (fighter plane), and he wanted some wing tanks for it. When they came, they had a frame around them. I cut the frame in half and put a half on each end of my bed. I took a tire and cut it into strips and made myself a nice bed about three feet off the ground. I didn't have much trouble, but the rest of the men in the tent did. They'd have rats running over their faces at night. It wasn't much fun.

We were so tired we didn't really pay much attention to the rats. We were soaking wet all the time. You'd take Atabrine tablets and two salt tablets, and by noon your uniform would be white from sweat. That didn't bother me.

We never got to know any of the men in the other tents. It was the funniest thing. We had our own little thing. We'd get on the flatbed in the morning, go to work, and that was it. It was such a desolate place. There was this one Scotsman from North Dakota in our tent, and he didn't say a word to anyone. But if you approached the tent and he was alone in there, he'd be giving somebody hell. He'd talk to himself all the time, but the minute you came in, he'd clam right up. The other three were great guys.

We didn't get any news—no papers, no radios. The only thing we had to eat was dried eggs, dried potatoes, anything dried. We never had canned goods, no meat, nothing. And that didn't bother me. I went from about a hundred and seventy to a hundred and thirty pounds.

The work was mainly machine work. Sometimes you'd have to go inside the plane and tear something apart. Or after they fixed an engine, you'd have to clean up. They had to be shining before they went out.

The Aussies flew in all the time to refuel. They were bringing the Japanese prisoners back from the Philippines and the other island battles to prison camps in Australia. At least they brought a few

*Snow heard hard things about how the
Australians disposed of Japanese prisoners.*

of them back. Most of them they threw out halfway across. It was awful. I saw one Aussie plane come in with no Japs at all. I never saw it done, but it was a known fact. Everybody knew it, everybody talked about it. The Aussies hated the Japs.

After the war, we saw the natives for the first time. They put on a show for us. They had bolos, and it was a dance, and they would chop at your head and you had to duck at the right time. This wasn't fooling around. What a show!

We also got hold of a battery and dynamite caps with wires on them, and we'd throw them out in the water and let 'em off, and boy you'd get more tuna—beautiful fish. They were stunned, and we'd grab them by the tail. The cooks cooked them for us.

We came home at Christmastime in 1945. I went to see my wife and—for the first time—my daughter. I don't think I'd had a shower in two years. I got in the tub and slipped and fell and broke three ribs.

Bill Snow and his family lived in Webster, New Hampshire, after the war. He worked as a surveyor, including ten years for the New Hampshire Fish & Game Department. Eighty-eight years old and living in Alton at the time of this interview, Snow died August 15, 2008.

Dr. Howard Lightfoot treated hundreds of cases of VD.

Dr. Howard Lightfoot

The Doctor Is In

Dr. Howard Lightfoot joined the Army while still a medical student at Boston University. By the time he started active duty in June 1943, he and his wife, Dorothy, had a baby daughter, Ann. After stateside training and a long voyage across the Atlantic, Lightfoot arrived in Scotland.

We were met by a bagpipe band. They piped us over to the train, and we went down to the Midlands of England.

I was there from September of '43 until June of '44. It was a gigantic camp, about ten thousand men. There was a railway battalion, ordnance, and so on. I was a family doctor to the battalion. I held sick call every morning, and the men came in with whatever ailed them. Then I had the rest of the day off. I read *Wuthering Heights, Return of the Native*, books that had to do with England.

I treated sore throats, colds, cut fingers, infections, and, maybe number one, venereal disease. It was before penicillin. The treatment for syphilis was neoarsphenamine, a purified form of arsenic. When the draft was established, if you had a venereal disease, they wouldn't take you. But as the demand for soldiers increased, the Army started taking people with venereal disease. At one point when I was in England, they dropped a company on us where every man had syphilis.

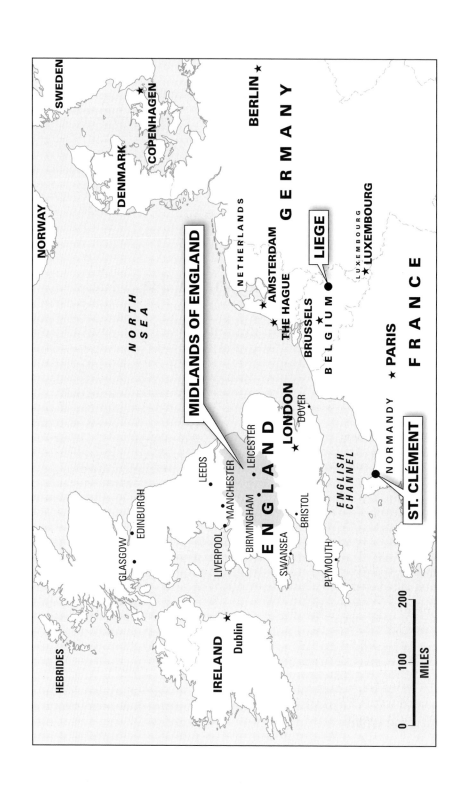

When our men went to town on pass for the night, they had to demonstrate two things to us: that they had a condom and that they had a prophylactic kit, a little tube of soap that a man would wash himself with after intercourse and a little tube of antiseptic jelly that he would inject. A "pro kit" they called it. He could be going to the movies, but he had to prove to us that he had a condom and a pro kit.

Once a month, I had to do a "short-arm inspection." I examined every man in the battalion. A thousand men walk by and show me their penises to make sure no pus was coming out. I'd find about a dozen each time.

A week or two after D-Day, we were shipped to the south of England. When we arrived off the coast of Normandy, a little landing craft came alongside our boat. The Navy man who ran it was a good sailor. We didn't even get our feet wet.

The towns along the beach were destroyed, just rubble. I saw thousands of men coming ashore in hundreds of boats—troops, troops, troops. No one on the beach had any idea where we were supposed to go. We hiked inland and spent the night lying on the side of the road.

The next day, we went to the little town of Saint Clement. My office was a tent with a big red cross on it in an orchard. Our job was to screen quartermaster troops coming into France and tell them where they were assigned. I took care of anybody who came in.

Late one day, a truck company came into an adjacent field. They had been given orders to dig slit trenches, but the captain of the company said, "It's too late at night to bother. Just crawl under your trucks and we'll dig in the morning." A bomb landed in that field and killed every man in the company. The captain was not killed. He just lost it. He jumped in his jeep and took off. I don't know what happened to him.

It was my first experience with violent death. I'd seen a lot of dead people, but never anything on a scale like this or the destruction of the bodies.

The Germans were only a few miles away. We were waiting for a breakthrough, and when it came, it was like pulling a plug. Nor-

When a V-1 rocket's motor stopped, Lightfoot knew, it was time to seek cover.

mandy, which had been filled with thousands and thousands of soldiers, just drained out.

Later they moved us by train to Liege, Belgium, where I spent the rest of the war. We lived in a schoolhouse. They gave me a dress shop in the middle of town as my dispensary. It was a nice city. Even during the war, they had movies and operas, which we went to see.

The Germans started sending what we called buzz bombs, V-1's.

The motor sounded like a truck going uphill. It would shut off when it ran out of fuel. Then it would crash. I saw the V-1's fly overhead. We knew when the noise of the motor stopped, get out of the way. Duck and cover! One landed on the building next-door. I walked out, and there were bodies in the rubble.

I wrote to (my wife) every day. I numbered the letters because they often arrived out of sequence. I wrote every single day for twenty-seven months, and so did she. I couldn't tell her where I was. I would just tell her what had gone on, if I'd gone to a movie or on a hike. She'd tell me what she was doing and how Ann was getting along. She was growing up without me.

I was among the first to come home. They had a big turkey dinner for us at Fort Devens. My wife was living in an apartment in Manchester. I called and said, "You can come down and get me tomorrow morning." She said, "Are you crazy?" She was there in an hour and a half. Heaven.

After the war, Howard Lightfoot moved his family to Contoocook, where he worked for decades as the local doctor. He has four children, five grandchildren, and six great-grandchildren.

Lightfoot poses with children somewhere in France.

Don Lumsden helped prepare Pacific beaches for Allied landings.

Don Lumsden

The Frogman

Don Lumsden, who summers in Newbury, New Hampshire, was
a hockey star with two years in at Northeastern University when
he joined the Navy in 1943. The wave of Allied beach invasions
was just beginning, and the Navy needed officers for the invasion
fleets. After attending Dartmouth College on a Navy program
and training at various sites, Lumsden decided on another course.
A superb swimmer, he volunteered to become a frogman.

At Tarawa, the Marines had gone in fully packed in daylight. They hit what they thought was shallow water. They had some fire support but no prior knowledge of what was there, no idea of obstacles, mines, water depth. They jumped out and found themselves in a twenty-foot lagoon. Many drowned before they got to shore.

The ones who didn't drown were sitting pigeons out there—they couldn't protect themselves or use their weapons. Their boats had already gone back, so they had only one way to go. The Japanese shot them as they struggled toward the shore. The casualties were tremendous.

Marines are tough, and some made it up and did what they could. But the higher-ups in the Marine Corps decided they needed to be

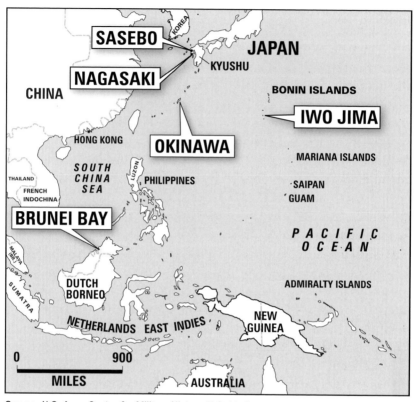

Source: U.S. Army Center for Military History, U.S. Marines

better prepared in the future. And they found us—the frogmen. We were already being trained, and after Tarawa no major invasion in the Pacific ever proceeded without underwater demolition teams going in first.

I became a member of UDT 11. For training, we went to Maui, where the advanced base was under Commander Draper Kauffman, who later became an admiral and head of the Naval Academy. We were top secret. My mother and father never knew what I did, and I wouldn't have told them anyway because it was just too dangerous.

In training we learned about underwater work from native Hawaiians who had been pearl divers. One of them could go down and hold his breath for more than five minutes. I timed him once. We had what was called a Jack Brown, a gas mask with the canister in the back, but we never used them in combat because they were too cumbersome.

We had fins and a dive mask and swam using underwater recovery strokes—breast stroke, a frog kick. We came up when we had to and continued with the same strokes. When your head is above water, it's easy to see. To make ourselves less visible from the beach, we first tried a black cap, but that was like standing up in the water saying, "Here we are!" Silver worked better because the sun reflected off it like it did off the water.

Our job was to reconnoiter and bring back information about potential landing areas and to blow up the obstacles on the beaches. The Japanese did the exact same thing on all the beaches I knew about—Iwo Jima, Okinawa, Borneo. To slow down a landing force, they put in three rows of posts about four feet high. They pounded them into the sand and coral—really pounded them in. The Navy tried to destroy them with torpedoes, but the result was nothing—just a hole in the ground.

For Iwo Jima, they sent three of our four teams—about two hundred and seventy men in all. The plan was for us to go in with tetratol, a powerful explosive which was much safer to handle than TNT. Our job was to lay a trunk line along the three rows of posts, attach a stick of tetratol to each post, and tie the primer cord from the tetratol stick to the trunk line.

The trunk line people were maybe fifty yards out to sea. We would signal them that everything was set and then swim out as quickly as we could. When we were gone, they would pull the fuse-lighters. The explosive travels through primer cord at more than five thousand feet per second, which meant if you pull the fuse-lighter here, a mile away, within a second, everything went. So that beach went up all at once. It was amazing stuff.

I never made it to Iwo Jima. Our commander initially decided we would have a night operation. Since all our training had been done in daytime, we went to an island near Iwo for a mock operation three days before the invasion.

We swam up, put charges on the obstacles, and headed just off-shore. We were in rubber boats. I had six enlisted men, and a hundred yards down the beach, Bill Lindsay, the other officer on our team, had six men. For the exercise, we had fuse-lighters, blasting caps, and primer cord right in our rubber boats.

Before we pulled the fuses, we were supposed to put the primer cord and blasting caps on flotation devices and paddle away from the shore. At one o'clock, a white flare would go up on the flagship. At 1:05, a green flare would go up, and you'd pull your fuse lighters.

We were sitting on our rubber boat just offshore. At one o'clock, the white flare didn't go. After a couple of minutes, I began to get suspicious. I called back to the flagship on my walkie-talkie, but I couldn't reach anyone.

At about 1:06, when the green flares didn't go up, I figured something was wrong and decided to get the explosives off the boat. I attached them to the end of a paddle, stretched out my arm, and held the paddle as far as I could reach off the back of the boat.

At 1:10 the beach went. We were thrown up in the air, and the rubber boat blew up. I was hurt and so were others, but if the explosives had been in the boat, it would have been much worse.

The flagship could see what was going on, and they sent people to bring us back. I lay in that litter on the deck looking up at Commander Kauffman, who was apologizing, and I was screaming at him about not being informed of any change in the fire signal. He kept saying, "Don, I sent the change, I sent the change." The medics were busy taking care of me.

The other officer, Bill Lindsay, was a former Texas Ranger—a tough guy and a super person. He hadn't taken any precaution. He lost his right leg from his ankle down, part of his left leg, and part of his arm, and his face was marred. All his enlisted men were wounded. None were killed, but several were maimed—some so badly they would rather have died.

I still have shrapnel in me from that night. My family doctor took it out of me for years.

Our team had to be replaced for the Iwo Jima invasion. They did that operation in daylight. You could see the enemy better, and they could see you better, but you could also have a lot of firepower behind you as you swam in and out.

My first actual work came at Okinawa. As we went into the beaches, we had fire support from boats less than a mile from shore all the way out to the cruisers and battleships. The Air Force knew when we were going in, and they dropped bombs along the shore.

We could see kamikazes circling above us searching for targets. The Navy didn't have the firepower to get them at five thousand feet, and they knew it. What saved us was that the kamikazes wanted battleships or cruisers, not our little ships. But one did come down and missed us by maybe fifteen feet. And we were loaded with tetratol.

The rubber boats dropped us a mile from shore. We were carrying all the explosives strapped on our back—two haversacks of twenty-four pounds each, although they weren't as heavy in the water as they were on land. I was also carrying a .45-caliber pistol and a knife. We did underwater strokes with as little splash as possible, and we swam fast. From when the boat dropped us off until we came back was probably two hours.

When we started toward Okinawa, we could see the obstacles on the beach, Japanese fire coming out, and the jungle beyond the beach. Of course, our fire was coming in, too, so the Japanese were keeping their noodles down as much as possible.

My platoon did a good job on the beach, but one of the teams had a misfire. That was a no-no. You risk your men's lives going in, and then you have a misfire. Part of the beach still had obstacles.

Commander Kauffman had confidence in my platoon, and he

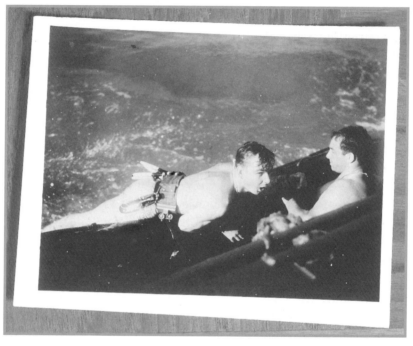

After a communication failure, Lumsden's quick thinking saved his team.

sent us back in. We went in early the next morning, at low tide. We put in a new trunk line and used many of the charges that were already on the obstacles. We also detonated a lot of mines along the beach. We took fire, and there were grenades dropping around us, but there was also a lot of fire directed on the Japanese.

Next we went to Borneo, which the Japanese controlled. The invasion there was to be with all Australian troops. Apparently because the Australians had helped General MacArthur get safely to Australia early in the Pacific war, he decided to take part in this invasion.

We swam in to reconnoiter Brunei Bay. We had a Plexiglas plate, and we made drawings of the terrain. British Bettys were bombing that day, and one of them dropped some bombs in the water. A bomb hit a boy I was swimming with—a direct hit. The concussion that killed him blew me eight or ten feet out of the water.

After the mission, we gave our information—water depth, natural obstacles, where the best approaches were for the invasion force—to one of our officers, Al Voorhees. He compiled a report for MacArthur, who would decide which beaches the troops would land on. We cleared more beaches than we were going to land on, of course, because we didn't want the Japanese to know exactly where we were coming in.

The next day, we went back in and destroyed the obstacles. That evening, I was invited with Al Voorhees and others to go aboard the cruiser Boise, where MacArthur had his headquarters. They wanted someone who had actually been in there.

After they presented everything to MacArthur, he said to me, "Sir, you swam into the beaches today, did you not?" I said, "Yes, I did, sir." He showed me the proposed plan and said, "Do you agree that these are the beaches we should go into tomorrow?" I said, "Sir, if you don't mind, I think we should go into these two beaches and avoid these two because we did a much better job of blowing the obstacles here. Your soldiers would find it easier getting in, the water depth is better there—" and so on.

He turned to another officer and said, "Do you know this gentleman well?" He said, "I do." MacArthur said, "Would you trust his judgment?" He said, "I certainly would." MacArthur turned to Al Voorhees and said, "You change your drawing."

MacArthur was formal when we were first there. He was smoking his corncob pipe, but he didn't sit back and look down on us at all. He was extremely polite. The longer we were there, the more it became a comfortable conversation. He told us that without our work, many of these operations would not have been successful. He needed our information, and he showed it.

Commander Kauffman wasn't there because he had been called to Washington to prep for the invasion of Japan. The first landing was going to be at Sasebo on the island of Kyushu—Operation Downfall. On our way there, we talked about it in the ward room and figured we would probably have fifty percent casualties. It was a Japanese home island, and they were fighting for everything they had.

After the atom bombs dropped and the Japanese surrendered, we went to Sasebo anyway. Other than POWs in Japan, we were among the first Americans there under peacetime conditions. We reconnoitered Sasebo because the Army or Marines wanted to occupy it in the takeover of Japan. They sent us in first because we knew about explosives. Our job was to make sure it was safe.

We had the same mission soon afterward in Nagasaki. We went in on September 20, seven weeks after the bomb. They wanted us to draw maps of the streets or whatever was there—right in the city, right where the atomic bomb had dropped.

We didn't know how the people would treat us. We didn't know if there would be any trees or buildings, or if somebody would be behind something with a machinegun or whatever. We had very little firepower.

We saw only a few people. When we approached them, they got down on their knees with their hands together in front of them, as if they were praying. They'd stay there kneeling until we walked by. They were in such a state of shock that even if they had wanted to, there was no way for them to resist.

I just couldn't believe what I saw. An atomic bomb—my God, that's almost like something supernatural. I knew nothing about the nature of the atomic bomb. Ashes covered everything, and we kicked them away—just kicked the ashes. We didn't know about radiation fallout. I'm not sure anyone did. And every so often, I do something stupid, and my wife, Brenda, says, "I knew it would catch up to you." [Laughs.]

Seeing Nagasaki was like seeing a city dump in New York. It was just leveled. I almost had tears in my eyes, knowing how many people had died. The people who bowed to us when we walked by had hated us three weeks before. And now they were treating us like gods because we had done something unimaginable to them.

Don Lumsden left the Navy in 1946. He and Brenda, who served in the Coast Guard during the war, were married on December 7, 1946. "I wanted a date I could remember," Lumsden said. For more than thirty-five years he ran a textile business in Needham, Massachusetts. Among other items, the company produced anti-embolism stockings used after surgeries and protective pads for athletes, including the New England Patriots and several other National Football League teams. Lumsden sold the business twenty-five years ago. He and Brenda had a ski chalet in New Hampshire's North Country for twenty years. They now spend summers in Newbury and winters on Florida's West Coast.

On a trip to Hitler's aerie, Lincoln Shedd encountered Ike.

Lincoln Shedd

A GI's General

Lincoln Shedd was an artillery communication chief with the
26th Infantry Division. He landed at Utah Beach after D-Day and
entered combat east of Paris with General George Patton's Third
Army. As part of the occupying army shortly after the war, he
visited Adolf Hitler's aerie at Bertchesgaden in Bavaria and had a
chance encounter with another leading figure of World War II.

We ended up in Czechoslovakia, where we met the Russians and became an army of occupation. They allowed us to travel in jeeps to visit Italy. I wasn't too interested in that, but I said to the motor sergeant, "Why don't you see if you can find a bus?" So we found a bus, and one of the trips we took was to Bertschesgaden.

In the lower parking lot, we got in a jeep and went around the spiral highway to the Eagle's Nest, Hitler's mountain house. There was a second parking lot a few hundred feet below the Eagle's Nest.

A jeep came in behind us, and two or three generals were riding in it. One of the generals got out and pointed to a sign that said, "Field-grade officers and higher only." It was next to an elevator, and only majors and up could ride this thing. The guy who pointed to the sign was General Eisenhower. One of the other generals there,

Source: U.S. Army Center for Military History

*Shortly after the war, Shedd took this
picture of Hitler's Bavarian aerie.*

Mark Clark, went over and took the sign and threw it over the side of the mountain. Now anybody could go up that elevator.

I was so impressed with that. I said, "Eisenhower's a GI's general."

I didn't go up the elevator. I walked up and went through the building. It was pretty much empty, but you could get the view, and that's what Hitler wanted. I had somebody take a picture of me outside the Eagle's Nest.

We drove down the mountain to the lower parking lot. And gee whiz if Eisenhower didn't show up down there, too, right behind us. We went over and asked if we could take a picture. He stood up, folded his hands, grinned, and said, "I feel like a movie actor." This guy was so darned humble.

That's where I took this picture, and I've never forgotten it.

After the war Lincoln Shedd went to work for the Air Force at Hanscom Field in Massachusetts. He retired after thirty years as a physical science research administrator in the Air Force Aerospace Program. With his wife, Ruth, he retired to Hopkinton, New Hampshire, in 1978.

Eisenhower was modest about posing.
Here's Shedd's snapshot.

*In his eloquent diary, Herb Church
chronicled the end of the war in Europe.*

Herbert Church Jr.

"Dear Mum"

Herbert Church Jr. was a Pennsylvanian who graduated from Saint Paul's School in Concord before World War II and went to Harvard. He enlisted at age twenty-one in late 1943 and became an officer with the 373rd Field Artillery Battalion. After arriving in France in October 1944, he served as a forward observer, posted with troops of the 100th Infantry Division to advise his battery on the effects of its firing during the advance toward and into Germany. In civilian life after the war, Church taught at Saint Paul's School and later Rundlett Middle School in Concord, heading the English department at each school for part of his tenure. With interruptions for further military service during the Korean Conflict and further education, he taught for forty-two years before retiring in 1988. He died in 2004. His widow, Gail, donated his letters and diaries to Saint Paul's School. Below are excerpts from the letters, which Herb Church wrote to his "Mum."

Somewhere in France, October 21, 1944

It's a sad France, with bomb damage everywhere, currency inflation (we exchange 50 francs for a dollar, which is giving the franc the benefit of a big doubt), and bad sanitary conditions. There is no

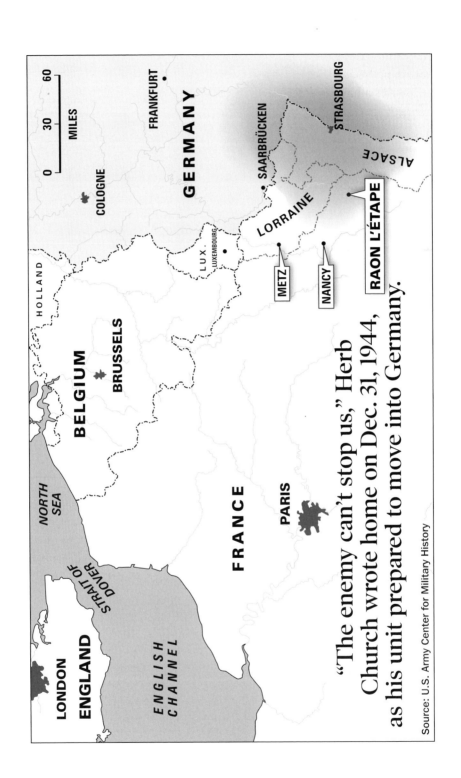

"The enemy can't stop us," Herb Church wrote home on Dec. 31, 1944, as his unit prepared to move into Germany.

Source: U.S. Army Center for Military History

starvation that I have seen, but people look hungry, and kids are always pathetically grateful for a little chocolate.

But it's a happy France, too, where every American is really and honestly loved as a liberator. If you get lost anywhere, and start haltingly to explain yourself, about forty people appear from nowhere anxious to help in any possible way. American, British, and French flags are everywhere. I just can't get over the happiness our appearance brings to these people. It is most moving.

And how they hate the Boche [derisive term for Germans]! I gathered that from an old gardener I was talking to this afternoon. He said he was "trois fois blessé" [three times wounded] in the last war, and showed me in detail where. His chief objection to them in this war was that they held "toujours le fusil" [a rifle at all times].

I looked around and saw a bunch of GI's talking to the local yokels, and horsing around. Not being in the front lines, but among friends, they were of course unarmed. Then I thought of a lot of "supermen," not so many months ago, stalking around, everywhere armed, among enemies, and I thought, with feeling, how lucky we were to have the people of France with us.

Somewhere in France, November 25, 1944

Now that we are in the scrap, frequently we are the first or second Allied occupants of French villages, and the fervor of deliverance still runs high. Nothing is too good for us. Precious bottles of Cognac are pulled out of underground hiding places, and handmade American, British, and French flags are pulled from behind cellar walls, and proudly displayed. Anything we ask, that is in their power to give, is ours.

I think they are actually glad to have American soldiers in their homes, being a little scared to live alone after over five years of occupation. There never was a better good-will ambassador than the GI. People can't understand a word he says, but they love him.

Somewhere in France, November 29, 1944

We are in Alsace-Lorraine . . . and the majority of the people, except in the larger towns, speak a curious dialect, which they call Alsatian, which sounds like Swedish, and which they say is almost the same as Flemish, spoken in Belgium.

The Nazis did a curious thing in this province—they treated it not as occupied France, but as a part of Germany. There are frontier posts on the French "border," and all signs and announcements to the east are in German. The people were better, though by no means well, treated, having considerably more and better food than the rest of the French. The kids, after four years of German schooling, all speak German. The older people usually talk this hybrid dialect. Result: I am out of luck!

France, December 31, 1944

It is now just a few hours from 1945. . . . We won't do much celebrating of the new year over here. But deep within me I am glad that it is coming, for I honestly feel, for the first time, that next year we can do it. I don't have any inside dope. . . . This is a feeling, not a thought.

I get that feeling when I see our planes, headed for Germany, in inconceivable numbers, just little silver specks against the blue, accompanied by a roar that continues over a long period of time. I get it when I go to the rear a bit, and see the mountains of supplies ever moving up to keep us going; but above all I get it when I hear our big guns hammering day and night, and see the doughs [from doughboys, World War I slang for American soldiers in Europe] trudging up to the line—tired, dirty, slovenly, by standards of the States, but combat-wise and never stopping.

The enemy can't stop us, because right is always stronger than might. I believed that in the darkest days of '40 and '41. Now we have the might as well as the right.

Somewhere in Germany, March 25, 1945

I was certainly sorry to hear that Ev Brown had been killed. He was a good Joe, and to get it while still in training is so darn pointless. If you are killed in action, at least you make a contribution to the future world. . . .

You will note that we are in Krautland. It is not nearly as much fun as being in France. We see no more streets gay with flags, get no more royal welcome. Indeed, when we do see evidences of friendship here, we are quick to turn them aside. We know that they are not genuine—some people are just trying to butter their bread on the other side. Most often, from the civilians, particularly the young ones, we just get looks full of smouldering hate. But they don't bother us—our force has them cowed.

The little part of Germany I have seen at first glance seems an improvement on France. The roads are better, the public utilities more in evidence, the houses bigger, more modern, and neater. The people are largely well-fed and fairly handsome, a sharp contrast from poor, looted, starving France. It is not hard to see how the Germans have been living off the rest of Europe for the last four years. No wonder they like war—they are only just now beginning to pay for their many sins.

One thing, though—we have sowed the seeds of doubt in the minds of many of them. I will long remember the scene in one village. The American army in all its roaring glory was rolling through. There were thousands of tanks, trucks, and guns rolling through the dust. The GI was everywhere in evidence—dirty, cussing, sweating, and powerful—the picture of the New World. Overhead were planes—more planes than you people in the States can conceive of. This scene of overwhelming power was too much for the Jerries. They stood by the road and gaped. Hitler had said it couldn't be done, yet they were watching it happen. Some of them were too overwhelmed to glower. They just let their jaws hang!

I wish I could adequately picture to you the scene of might that is our army on the march. Obstacles on the road? Up come the bulldozers, and out go the obstacles. When we roll, we roll. It's the most wonderful teamwork that I have ever seen.

We are not a pretty army. We don't march in neat uniforms and carry shiny equipment. We tackle war like we tackled the wilderness, and win out just as we did over the frontier. We are an army the likes of which the Krauts have never seen. And when we're through, I don't think they'll risk seeing us again!

Somewhere in Germany, March 31, 1945

Here we are, in just one little sector of a big front, and yet the roads are forever filled with trucks and armor. . . . When you think that this same picture is duplicated all along the Western front, and on dozens of islands in the Pacific; that the Red Army rolls largely on American equipment; and that, in addition, we have the world's largest Navy and largest Air Force—it makes you wonder how we ever let a little thing like a depression stop us. . . .

If we can do such a job as this, surely we can do anything, in war or peace.

Somewhere in Germany, April 15, 1945

The news of the President's death [Franklin D. Roosevelt died in Warm Springs, Georgia on April 12] was an awful sock in the jaw to most of us. It came to most of us on the morning of Friday the 13th—a dreary gray morning with a steady drizzle. Nature certainly played her part to perfection. . . .

History will judge the man, and, for all his faults, I am sure she will judge him great. But I refuse to believe all is lost. . . . (President Truman's) heart is in the right place, and if we all back him up I do not think he will let the world down.

Germany, April 20, 1945

Still these darn fool Krauts don't quit. They must be crazy. Insane bloodletters, they cannot win, and will not cease the slaughter. Actually, crazy though they are, the Germans are playing into our hands. Every village which they defend, till we destroy it, every soldier who fights and gets killed instead of surviving, will prolong the period before Germany can become dangerous again. And I'm in favor of making that period as long as eternity. The only problem is that it takes good guys, Russians, Tommies, Frogs, and our own doughs, to do it. . . .

The President seems to have gone so far without making a mistake. . . . I think democracy, working in its curious way, has found itself a good man for the crisis—steady, able to compromise, and the kind of personality who will keep the confidence of America after the war, when the idealistic, dramatic, Wilson-Roosevelt type so frequently goes into disfavor.

Cannes, France, May 9, 1945

My last day of vacation! This evening I start back to the outfit. I thought you might like to know how V-E Day looked in Cannes. We got the news from Winnie [Winston Churchill] at 1500 yesterday afternoon, after several days of rumors.

The town at once went crazy. A French battery poured shells out into the sea, a French cruiser anchored off shore fired a few guns, and civilians just went screaming around. A few hours later the "Stars and Stripes" appeared, with a huge headline in red type, "It's Over, Over Here." And last night there were fire-works outside, and fire-water inside every Frenchman.

Strangely enough, the end meant little to myself and the other soldiers here, because for us it is not the end. Whether we occupy, or go to fight the Japs, our job is unfinished. So we let the French celebrate by themselves. And I certainly don't blame them. This is the moment they had been praying for for nearly six years. The war is not ended, but much else is: there will be no more Robot bombs, no more concentration camps in Europe. The lights are on again all over the continent. . . . And now we are free to turn everything we have on those yellow #&-//&#-! in the Pacific, and make them regret they were ever born.

Somewhere in Germany, May 14, 1945

Do you want to know what really won the war in Europe? First of all, of course, the dirty, hard-hitting ground forces of the Allied countries. Without their guts, nothing could be done. But I must admit that German fighting men were physically brave, too, though they have no moral guts. . . .

We did have something the Germans did not have, and that is, American technological wizardry. . . . Though wrecked by the Germans, European ports are handling more tonnage than ever in peacetime. The Germans blew up every Rhine bridge except the historic one at Remagen, so our first crossing had to be on pontoon bridges. But not now. Coming home [back to his unit from leave in Cannes], I passed over between two big German cities. The bridge is three lanes wide, a wooden trestle similar to those across Barnegat Bay in Jersey. You don't even have to slow down crossing it. Just upstream is a brand new railroad bridge (called "Ernie Pyle Memorial Bridge"—every soldier really loved that little guy), over which traffic moves. Most locomotives "made in the USA"—a large part of the box cars, likewise.

The railroad now runs deep into Germany, but where it stops, the trucks take over: huge things, hauling more stuff faster than it ever was hauled in the States. The roads are beautifully maintained and marked—by the Army. It's hard to get lost. And the rear areas are all connected by Army telephone systems: not the field telephones we use, but a regular American style net-work, with American poles and crossbars (very different from the European).

Alone of the world's armies, ours handles war like our country handled the Frontier, or Grand Coulee Dam—as a big job. And no people in the world can excel us in getting a job done.

APPENDIXES

Appendix 1:
More Stories from the War Years

More than one hundred people responded to our request for stories from the World War II era. We heard from family members, hairdressers, neighbors, nursing home employees, and the veterans themselves. We are grateful to them all. Many of these stories are reprinted in this book, but even here we did not have room for some of the oral histories that appeared in the Monitor's My War *project. Those stories do appear in full in the project's website, concordmonitor.com/mywar. Here are brief summaries:*

LEO FRASER, CONCORD: The war was nearly over by the time Fraser, a Marine, arrived in the South Pacific. Although his official job was field telephone operator, he spent most of his tour playing baseball to boost morale. The league was impromptu, the competition fierce. Fraser's ball-field skills eventually brought him to the attention of the general in charge of the North China Theater.

JOHN GRADY, CONCORD: When the United States entered the war, Grady had already served eight years in the Army, but the government didn't want him on the front lines. Instead, he became a professor of military science at the University of Tennessee. He sent hundreds of young men off to war and a few to nearby Oak Ridge, where they worked on the project that eventually ended the war.

JON HUTCHINSON, CONCORD: Two weeks after D-Day, Hutchinson landed on Utah Beach and took command of two hundred men. He had excelled in officers' training at the University of Connecticut, but as his platoon marched west, he learned that school can teach a person only so much about war. By the time the war ended, not a single man who had landed on D-Day remained in his platoon.

HAROLD JAQUES, CONCORD: Boats were not standard equipment for combat engineers in Europe, so Jacques was puzzled when his unit began practicing river crossings in small skiffs. Soon, they were testing their skills under live fire when the Allies crossed the Rhine. Jaques died on September 7, 2008.

BILL KUHLMAN, CONCORD: Kuhlman served as a gunner on a naval patrol bomber in the Pacific. He and his shipmates sailed through Pearl Harbor soon after the Japanese attack. He wrote many letters home to his family and shared some with us.

BERNARD ROBINSON, EPSOM: As a young man, Robinson ran a machine shop in Massachusetts. When war broke out, the Navy needed his mechanical expertise on a repair ship called the USS Oahu. At a hundred and two years old, Robinson was the oldest person to participate in the My War project. During the interview he told us he'd gladly join the Navy again.

EUGENE SCHMIDT, BRADFORD: "Easy" doesn't describe any of the eighteen missions Schmidt flew as a B-17 tail gunner, but one was particularly harrowing. Two engines went out, and the only way to stay airborne was to lighten their load. The men tossed out anything they could reach: radios, guns, even their shoes.

JACK SHERBURNE, DEERFIELD: As a P-51 Mustang pilot stationed in Italy, Sherburne flew missions over Germany and other Axis-controlled countries, working to cripple the enemy's ability strike back at American forces.

RAY UNGER, CONCORD: At seventeen, Unger quit Enfield High School and joined the Navy. As a signalman aboard the USS Wasatch, he witnessed the largest naval battle in history at Leyte Gulf. He also shared details about the worst date of his life.

The following men and women were interviewed by students from John Stark Regional High School. As part of the assignment the students prepared mini-documentaries about each subject. You'll find their videos online at concordmonitor.com/mywar.

DAVID ARNOLD, ARMY; ARMANDO BONANNO, NAVY; ED CRABTREE, ARMY; LARRY DRAPER, NAVY; EDWIN DWYER, ARMY; FOREST FOLEY, ARMY; WARREN GEISSINGER, ARMY AIR CORPS; ALAN HALL, NAVY; LIZ LAZICH, CIVILIAN IN DENMARK; ANTHONY MAIOLA, MARINES; TOM PILLSBURY, ARMY; PAUL RANKIN, ARMY; PAUL RUBNER, MARINES; LOU RULE, ARMY; LINCOLN SHEDD, ARMY; GERALD TURNER, NAVY; JOE WAGNER, ARMY; ORIN WATSON, NAVY.

Appendix 2:
An Interview Primer

We hope this book has inspired you to help someone tell a story. It might be about World War II, some more recent conflict, or maybe even a key event in your family or your community. Whatever the subject, here are some tips for conducting an effective interview:

Do your homework. Before visiting with veterans, we researched the guns they carried, the airplanes they flew, and the battles in which they fought. Many units and ships maintain websites. They're a great place to start. So are history books. For more local matters, visit your public library or historical society.

Keep it simple. Complex questions bog down interviews. Start with short, broad questions or this simple request: "Please tell me about Event X." Afterward, walk your subject through the story again, asking for details along the way.

Avoid yes-or-no questions. Start your questions with "how," "what," and "why." You'll get longer, more personal answers. Use "where," "when," and "who" to clarify. Be careful when asking for specific dates. We found many subjects grew frustrated when they couldn't remember. Circle back later or look it up after the interview.

Focus on the firsthand. You want to live for a moment behind your subject's eyes, not hear a summary of the history he's read. Ask questions that evoke visceral, personal memories. What did the food taste like? How did the jungle smell?

Double back. Sometimes, even when you're listening actively during an interview, it takes a few moments to realize that a subject has just hit upon a particularly interesting point. Don't be afraid to go back and ask the question again in search of more detail.

Surprise your subject. Especially when a person has told a story many times, he or she can get in a rut and leave out the details. If you sense this is happening, break in and ask for elaboration on a particular point. One of our most successful questions during these interviews was: What were you carrying when you went out on patrol or when you made that beach landing? In most cases, the subject will stop and reflect, and this can reopen passages in memory.

Don't be afraid to challenge your subject. As sharp as memories of intense youthful events can be, memory is also a faulty vessel. If, upon transcribing the interview and checking the facts, you have questions about whether the subject misremembered, bring them up. In every case we found that our subjects were happy to have the record set straight. They wanted their stories to be as accurate as possible.

Props and primary documents. Ask for scrapbooks, letters, journals, and photos. It's fascinating to compare immediate impressions with the perspective of decades. Historical maps or diagrams of aircraft and ships can help clarify details. One caveat here: Ask about these papers *after* the interview. You want to hear the person's story as he or she remembers it, and looking for facts in printed matter during the interview will sometimes cause a subject to lose his or her train of thought.

Tools to record. In collecting stories for this book, we used a pair of Olympus digital voice recorders with stereo microphones, transferred the files to a PC, and, when necessary, edited the sound on a free program called Audacity. If you're into Macs, try editing through GarageBand.

As for video, we're still learning. Our advice thus far: Position the subject against a clean backdrop. Check your lighting. Copy the data before trying to edit. When all else fails, do what we did: Find some smart teenagers and ask them for help.

Regardless of the tools you choose, set up in a quiet, comfortable room. Test everything. And don't forget extra batteries.

INDEX

Index

Index

ABOUT THE AUTHORS

MEG HECKMAN is a journalist and New Hampshire native. A reporter for the *Concord Monitor*, she has been named both New Hampshire Writer of the Year and New England Community Reporter of the Year. She graduated from the University of New Hampshire and has completed fellowships with the Poynter Institute for Media Studies and the New York Times Foundation. In her spare time, she teaches writing and alpine skiing. She lives in Concord.

MIKE PRIDE is a journalist and historian. He was the editor of the *Concord Monitor* for twenty-five years and managing editor for five years before that. A former Nieman Fellow, he served nine years on the Pulitzer Prize board, including 2007–08 as co-chair. Pride is co-author of *My Brave Boys*, a history of a New Hampshire Civil War regiment, and *Too Dead to Die*, the memoir of a Bataan Death March survivor, and co-editor of *The New Hampshire Century*. He lives in Concord with his wife, Monique.